Walk in the Light Series

The Scriptures

An Examination of How the Creator Communicates with Creation

D1604049

Todd D. Bennett

Shema Yisrael Publications

The Scriptures
An Examination of How the Creator Communicates with
Creation
First printing 2013

Copyright © 2013 by Shema Yisrael Publications. All rights reserved. No part of this book may be used or reproduced in any manner whatsoever without written permission of the publisher, except in the case of brief quotations in articles and reviews. For information write:
Shema Yisrael Publications
123 Court Street
Herkimer, New York 13350.

ISBN 10: 0985000406
ISBN 13: 978-0-9850004-0-0
Library of Congress Number: 2013900070

Printed in the United States of America.

Please visit our website for other titles:
www.shemayisrael.net

For information regarding publicity for author interviews call
(866) 866-2211

The Scriptures

An Examination of How the Creator Communicates with Creation

"This Scroll of the Torah
shall not depart from your mouth; but you shall meditate
therein day and night, that you may observe to do according to
all that is written therein: for then you shall make your way
prosperous, and then you shall have good success."
Joshua (Yahushua) 1:8

Table of Contents

Acknowledgments

I must first and foremost acknowledge my Creator, Redeemer and Savior who opened my eyes and showed me the Light. He never gave up on me even when, at times, it seemed that I gave up on Him. He is ever patient and truly awesome. His blessings, mercies and love endure forever and my gratitude and thanksgiving cannot be fully expressed in words.

Were it not for the patience, prayers, love and support of my beautiful wife Janet, and my extraordinary children Morgan and Shemuel, I would never have been able to accomplish this work. They gave me the freedom to pursue the vision and dreams that my Heavenly Father placed within me, and for that I am so very grateful. I love them all more than they will ever know.

Loving thanks to my father for his faithfulness along with his helpful comments and editing. He tirelessly watched and held things together at the office while I was away traveling, researching, speaking and writing.

Introduction

This book is part of a larger body of educational work called the "Walk in the Light" series. In fact, it is a compilation of various content found throughout the rest of the series, which was written as a result of my search for the truth. Having grown up in a major protestant denomination since I was a small child, I had been steeped in doctrine that often times seemed to contradict the very words contained within the Scriptures. I always considered myself to be a Christian although I never took the time to research the origins of Christianity or to understand exactly what the term Christian meant. I simply grew up believing that Christianity was right and every other religion was wrong or deficient.

Now my beliefs were founded on more than simply blind faith. I had experienced a "living God," my life had been transformed by a loving Redeemer and I had been filled with a powerful Spirit. I knew that I was on the right track, regrettably I always felt something was lacking. I was certain that there was something more to this religion called Christianity; not in terms of a different God, but what composed this belief system that I subscribed to, and this label that I wore like a badge.

Throughout my Christian walk I experienced many highs and some lows, but along the way I never felt like I fully understood what my faith was all about. Sure, I knew that "Jesus died on the cross for my sins" and that I needed to believe in my heart and confess with my mouth in order

to "be saved." I "asked Jesus into my heart" when I was a child and sincerely believed in what I had done, but something always felt like it was missing. As I grew older, I found myself progressing through different denominations, each time learning and growing, always adding some pieces to the puzzle, but never seeing the entire picture.

College ministry brought me into contact with the baptism of the Holy Spirit and more charismatic assemblies yet, while these people seemed to practice a more complete faith than those in my previous denominations, many of my original questions remained unanswered and even more questions arose. It seemed that at each new step in my faith I added a new adjective to the already ambiguous label "Christian". I went from being a mere Christian to a Full Gospel, New Testament, Charismatic, Spirit Filled, Born Again Christian; although I could never get away from the lingering uneasiness that something was still missing.

For instance, when I read Matthew 7:21-23 I always felt uncomfortable. In that Scripture most English Bibles indicate that Jesus says: *"Not everyone who says to Me, Lord, Lord, will enter the kingdom of heaven, but he who does the will of My Father Who is in heaven. Many will say to Me on that day, Lord, Lord, have we not prophesied in Your name and driven out demons in Your name and done many mighty works in Your name? And then I will say to them openly (publicly), I never knew you; depart from Me, you who act wickedly [disregarding My commands]."* The Amplified Bible.

This passage of Scripture always bothered me because it sounded an awful lot like the modern day Christian Church, in particular, the charismatic churches which I had been attending where the gifts of the Spirit

were operating. According to the Scripture passage it was not the people who *believed* in the spiritual manifestations that were being rejected, it was those who were *actually doing* them. I would think that this would give every Christian pause for concern.

First of all "in that day" there are *many* people who will be calling Him "Lord." They will also be performing incredible spiritual acts in His Name. Ultimately though, the Messiah will openly and publicly tell them to depart from Him. He will tell them that He never knew them and specifically He defines them by their actions, which is the reason for their rejection; they acted wickedly or lawlessly. In short, they disobeyed His commandments. Also, it seems very possible that while they thought they were doing these things in His Name, they were not, because they may have never known His Name. In essence, they did not know Him and He did not know them.

I think that many Christians are haunted by this Scripture because they do not understand who it applies to or what it means and if they were truly honest they must admit that there is no other group on the face of the planet that it can refer to except for the "Christian Church." This series provides the answer to that question and should provide resolution for any who have suffered anxiety over this verse.

Ultimately, my search for answers brought me right back to the starting point of my faith. I was left with the question: "What is the origin and substance of this religion called Christianity?" I was forced to examine the very foundations of my faith and to examine many of the beliefs which I subscribed to and test them against the truth of the Scriptures.

What I found out was nothing short of earth

shattering. I experienced a parapettio, which is a moment in Greek tragedies where the hero realizes that everything he knew was wrong. I discovered that many of the foundations of my faith were not rocks of truth, but rather the sands of lies, deception, corruption and paganism. I saw the Scripture in Jeremiah come true right before my eyes. In many translations, this passage reads: "*O LORD, my strength and my fortress, My refuge in the day of affliction, The Gentiles shall come to You from the ends of the earth and say, "Surely our fathers have inherited lies, worthlessness and unprofitable things. Will a man make gods for himself, which are not gods?"* Jeremiah 16:19-20 NKJV

I discovered that I had inherited lies and false doctrines from the fathers of my faith. I discovered that the faith which I had been steeped in had made gods which were not gods and I saw very clearly how many could say "Lord, Lord" and not really know the Messiah. I discovered that these lies were not just minor discrepancies but critical errors which could possibly have the effect of keeping me out of the New Jerusalem if I continued to practice them. (Revelation 21:27; 22:15).

While part of the problem stemmed from false doctrines which have crept into the Christian religion, it also had to do with anti-Semitism imbedded throughout the centuries and even translation errors in the very Scriptures that I was basing may beliefs upon. A good example is the next verse from the Prophet Jeremiah (Yirmeyahu) where most translations provide: "*Therefore behold, I will this once cause them to know, I will cause them to know My hand and My might; and they shall know that My Name is the LORD.*" Yirmeyahu 16:21 NKJV.

Could our Heavenly Father really be telling us that His Name is "The LORD"? This is a title, not a name and

by the way, won't many people be crying out "Lord, Lord" and be told that He never knew them? It is obvious that you should know someone's name in order to have a relationship with them. How could you possibly say that you know someone if you do not even know their name. So then we must ask: "What is the Name of our Heavenly Father?" The answer to this seeming mystery lies just beneath the surface of the translated text. In fact, if most people took the time to read the translators notes in the front of their "Bible" they would easily discover the problem.

You see the Name of our Creator is found in the Hebrew Scriptures almost 7,000 times. Long ago a false doctrine was perpetrated regarding speaking the Name. It was determined that the Name either could not, or should not, be pronounced and therefore it was replaced. Thus, over the centuries the Name of the Creator which was given to us so that we could know Him and be, not only His children, but also His friends, was suppressed and altered. You will now find people using descriptions, titles and variations to replace the Name. Some examples are: God, Lord, Adonai, Jehovah and Ha Shem ("The Name"). These titles, particularly The LORD, are inserted in place of the actual Name that was revealed in the Hebrew text. What a tragedy and what a mistake!

One of the Ten Commandments, also known as the Ten Words, specifically instructs us not to take the Name of the Creator "in vain" and *"He will not hold him guiltless who takes His Name in vain."* (Exodus 20:7). Most Christians have been taught that this simply warns of using the Name lightly or in the context of swearing or in some other disrespectful manner. This certainly is one aspect of the commandment, but if we look further into the Hebrew word for vain - שׁוא (pronounced shav) we find that it has a deeper meaning in the sense of "desolating, uselessness or naught."

Therefore, we have been warned not only to avoid using the Name lightly or disrespectfully, but also not to bring it to naught, which is exactly what has been done over the centuries. The Name of our Creator, which we have the privilege of calling on and praising, has been suppressed to the point where most people do not even know the Name, let alone use it.

This sounds like a conspiracy of cosmic proportions, and it is. Anyone who believes the Scriptures must understand that there is a battle between good and evil. There is an enemy, ha shatan (the adversary), who understands very well the battle which has been raging since the beginning. He will do anything to distract or destroy those searching for the truth, and he is very good at what he does. As you read this book I hope that you will see how people have been confused and deceived regarding the content and meaning of the Scriptures.

My hope is that every reader has an eye opening experience and is forever changed. I sincerely believe that the truths contained in this book, and the "Walk in the Light Series," are essential to avoid the great deception that is being perpetrated upon those who profess to believe in, and follow the Holy One of Yisrael.

This book, and the entire series, is intended to be read by anyone who is searching for the truth. Depending upon your particular religion, customs and traditions, you may find some of the information offensive, difficult to believe or contrary to the doctrines and teachings which you have read or heard throughout your life. This is to be expected and is perfectly understandable, but please realize

that none of the information is meant to criticize anyone or any faith, but merely to reveal truth.

The information contained in this book had better stir up some things or else there would be no reason to write it in the first place. The ultimate question is whether the contents align with the Scriptures and the will of the Creator. My goal is to strip away the layers of tradition that many of us have inherited, and get to the core of the faith that is described in the Scriptures.

This book should challenge your thinking and your beliefs and hopefully aid you on your search for truth. May you be blessed in your journey of faith as you endeavor to Walk in the Light.

I

In the Beginning

Communication is at the center of any relationship. If and how we communicate is a significant factor in the quantity and quality of our personal relationships. Indeed, the ability to effectively communicate is the glue that binds successful personal, familial and cultural relationships. In this modern age, thanks to technology, it is very easy to speak to someone on the other side of the planet or even while flying through the sky in an airplane, something unheard of merely decades ago.

We can now telephone, text, tweet, email along with numerous other forms of communication – all thanks to our gadgets and modern innovations. Interestingly, even with all of this technology we still have problems communicating with one another. We still argue about facts and truth. Even with this enormous trail of data and documentation, recordings and transcripts, it is very difficult to discern truth from lies. If this is true in the technologically advanced present, what about the past. If we have trouble with relationships and fact finding now, with all of this communication technology, how can we reliably trust a communication from 50, 100 or 1,000 years in the past.

This will be the focus of our discussion – finding

truth amidst all of the information swirling about the universe. In order to do this, we must travel back into the past, back to the beginning. There is a book in existence that purports to explain the origins of the world as we know it. Commonly known as "The Bible" this compilation of writings was produced over a period of centuries and contains ancient manuscripts written primarily in Hebrew and Greek.

We will examine the compilation process further in the discussion, but for now the focus will be on the first writing, commonly called Genesis. Genesis is a Greek word which means: "origin, creation, generation." It derives from the root word "genos" which means: "race, birth, descent."

Now it is important to understand that the text of Genesis was not written in the Greek Language. In fact, the Greek language did not exist at the time that the text was written, or the events described in the text occurred. Actually, the "beginnings" described in the text occurred approximately 6,000 years prior to the writing of this book.[1] According to many popular translations of the text, there was no one around except "God."

Now this is the point when we should probably start correcting some common errors promulgated in popular religious speech. The text never refers to the Creator as "God." God is a word of Teutonic origin which refers to a pagan deity.[2] Just as the text was not written in Greek, it also was not written in English, a language which is only about 500 years old. The text of Genesis was written in Ancient Hebrew, a language rarely seen in this era where Modern Hebrew has dominated those who speak the Hebrew tongue. As a result, we will be investigating the "original" Hebrew

throughout this discussion in the hope of gaining a greater understanding of our beginnings, as well as our end.

The title used in the Hebrew text to describe the Creator is Elohim. It is the plural form of El, which means "Mighty One" or "Power." Therefore it was Elohim Who was present during Creation and therefore Elohim Who can provide a witness to Creation. Interestingly, there is a powerful Scriptural precedent which requires at least 2 witnesses to establish a fact.[3] As noted, Elohim is plural, and therefore Elohim fulfills that requirement. This will become clearer as the discussion continues. In fact, we can see an amazing truth from the first sentence of the text.

The first sentence contains seven Hebrew words, six of which are commonly translated into English as: *"In the beginning God created the heavens and the earth."* In Modern Hebrew it appears as follows: "הַשָּׁמַיִם וְאֵת הָאָרֶץ בְּרֵאשִׁית בָּרָא אֱלֹהִים אֵת". Notice all of the dots, dashes and other markings above and below each Hebrew character. These are known as vowel points, called "neqqudot," in Hebrew. They were added by the Masorites to assist people in pronouncing the language. These markings are man-made additions, and are not found in original Hebrew texts.

In fact, it is important to understand that the so-called "Modern Hebrew" language does not represent the original Hebrew language. Modern Hebrew was brought back from Babylon after the exile of the House of Judah (Yahudah).[4] It was not the language written by the very ancient patriarchs. Therefore, throughout our investigation for truth, we will be examining the Ancient Script, which was the original language spoken and written by mankind, and which actually tells a story through pictographs.[5]

If we look at the first five English words quoted above, we see only three Hebrew words – "Beresheet bara Elohim." Now if this were written in Ancient Hebrew it would read from right to left as follows:[6]

𐤁𐤓𐤀𐤔𐤉𐤕 𐤁𐤓𐤀 𐤀𐤋𐤄𐤉𐤌

There are many mysteries contained within the Hebrew script, which cannot be readily discerned from simply reading a translation. In fact, if we look at the first word, we see a great mystery.

𐤁𐤓𐤀𐤔𐤉𐤕

The first Hebrew word in the Scriptures, translated as "in the beginning," is "beresheet." As seen above, it begins with the letter "bet" (𐤁) which means: "house." The character actually represents the floor plan for a tent or a house. This particular bet (𐤁) is quite unique, because it is the second letter in the Hebrew alphabet, and the first letter in the Scriptures. Many question why the Scriptures did not begin with the aleph (𐤀), which is the first letter in the Hebrew alphabet. This is a mystery only understood in the timing of the creation of the spiritual universe before the physical universe.[7]

The Aleph (𐤀) actually first appears as the third letter in the Hebrew text and completes the word "bara" (𐤁𐤓𐤀) contained within beresheet (𐤁𐤓𐤀𐤔𐤉𐤕). "Bara" actually means: "create." It was not only the first

three letters in the Hebrew text, but also the second word in the text. So we see "create" two times in the first two words of the Hebrew text indicating that there were two creations, the creation of a spiritual universe followed by the physical universe.

After the two creations we see the third word, which begins with the aleph (𐤀). This first primary usage reveals the significance of the letter throughout the text, and that third word is Elohim (𐤉𐤆𐤄𐤋𐤀). Elohim literally means: "Mighty Ones" or "Powers." So the Aleph (𐤀) represents the "Powers" which interestingly is plural and signifies Elohim transcending both the spiritual and physical existence.

So the Aleph (𐤀) is hidden "in the beginning" and the first letter in the text is the bet (𐤁). The first bet (𐤁) is also unique because it is larger than the other letters. While some might think that this is simply a decorative touch, or illuminated letter, added by a scribe, they would be missing a tremendous truth. You see, throughout the Hebrew text there are instances of these "jots and tittles" which are intended to emphasize a point or send a message.[8]

From the beginning of the Scriptures we can see that there is an emphasis on "the house." As it turns out, all of creation is intended as a House, and through the process of time, Elohim is building a "family" to fill that House. Indeed, from this "first" word we can discern many things. For instance, if we remove the House, the bet (𐤁), we are left with "resheet" (𐤕𐤉𐤔𐤀𐤓). Resheet means: "first – choicest." It is sometimes translated as "firstfruits." So we can see a message in the first word that the House is for the firstfruits of Elohim.

We also see the word "brit" (𐤕𐤉𐤓𐤁)

surrounding the word "esh" (W𐤟). Brit means: "cutting or covenant" and esh means: "fire." So we should be looking for a covenant involving fire as a means of gathering the Firstfruits into the House. We also see the Aleph (𐤟) and the Taw (X) surrounding the mysterious word "shi" (ʒW), which means: "gift or present."[9] So we see the gift or offering couched within the Aleph Taw (X𐤟), a subject of great importance that will be examined throughout this book.

So there are important messages built into the language, although this is only one way of studying the Scriptures. Another is through the study of the numerical values of the letters and words. This form of examination is commonly called Gematria. It is important to understand that each Hebrew character has a numerical value. There is no separate set of numbers in the Hebrew language, so every word has multiple dimensions of meaning as well as a numerical value. The values for each character can be seen in the Hebrew Language Study Chart in the Appendix.[10]

Throughout this text we will, at times, examine the numerical values of the words, which can expand our understanding, and reinforce certain ideas. For instance, the numerical value of "beresheet" is 913. The word for house is "beit" (Xʒ𐤟), and it has a numerical value of 412. The word for head is "rosh" (W𐤟ꝗ), and it has a numerical value of 501. When combined, their values equal 913 – the same as beresheet.[11] So we can see that the beginning is all about the house.

Now each of these words, "beit" (Xʒ𐤟) and "rosh" (W𐤟ꝗ), have Hebrew characters associated with them. As we already discussed, the Hebrew character bet (𐤟), means "house." The Hebrew character "resh" (ꝗ)

means: "head." When we combine bet ($\mathit{9}$) and resh ($\mathit{4}$) we have "bar" ($\mathit{49}$). The Hebrew word "bar" ($\mathit{49}$) is not only the first two letters of "beresheet," but also the word for "son."[12] The possibilities and avenues of discovery are endless, and they reveal the beauty and spirituality of the Language of the Creator. Indeed, it is the very language of Creation.

Aside from the first word, which is a study in and of itsself, the rest of the first sentence has more profound information about how this house will be filled. It even provides a framework for time. Here is the entire sentence.

$$ \text{ᛗᚴᚨ ᚷᛈᛘ ᛘᛁᛘᚩᚨ ᚷᛈ ᛘᛁᚨᛁᛈ ᛈᚴᚷ ᛘᛁᚹᛈᚴᚷ} $$

| 7 | 6 | 5 | 4 | 3 | 2 | 1 ← |

Now remember that Hebrew reads from right to left. That is why you see the first word Beresheet, all the way to the right. Phonetically the sentence reads as follows:

Beresheet bara Elohim et ha'shamayim w'et ha'eretz

→ 1   2   3   4   5   6   7

If you read it out loud, you just spoke Hebrew. There are seven words, although only six are translated into English. In a basic English translation you will read "In the beginning Elohim created the heavens and the earth." There is something critical that never gets translated out of the Hebrew, and it is essential to understanding how the Covenant House would be built.

This verse actually contains two instances of the mysterious Aleph Taw ($\mathit{X}\mathit{K}$).[13] While the Aleph Taw

($X\langle$) is spoken in Hebrew, pronounced "et," it goes untranslated and unnoticed in the English. The aleph ($\langle$) is the first letter in the Hebrew alphabet. It symbolizes a "bull or ox" and means: "strength." The taw (X) is the last letter in the Hebrew alphabet. It represents a "mark or covenant." So this "strength of the covenant" is present 2 times in the first seven Hebrew words of the Scriptures.

In the first instance we see the Aleph Taw ($X\langle$) stand alone in position 4, untranslated but spoken. In the second instance it is in position 6, attached to a "vav," or rather "waw" (Y), which represents a "peg" or a "nail." Again, in the second instance the Aleph Taw ($X\langle$) is untranslated but spoken.

Some interpret this untranslated but spoken Aleph Taw ($X\langle$) as representing the Messiah, revealed as the Word, sometimes referred to as the Memra.[14] The reason is because the Aleph Taw ($X\langle$) contains within it all the characters of the Hebrew language. Therefore, it is believed that the Messiah is the manifestation of Elohim within creation, all of which was accomplished through the language – the spoken word.[15]

If that is true, then there are two instances of the Messiah, one being hidden and the other attached to a "nail" which literally stands between the heavens ($Y\langle YW\rangle$) and the earth ($\triangleright\langle\langle\rangle$). That fits in perfectly with the notion that Creation is all about a House for the first son, the Messiah, Who will be the head of the House filled with the firstfruits of His harvest. This will become clearer as we continue the discussion.

It is commonly believed that this verse begins a pattern of sevens that will be repeated throughout the

Scriptures, and providing seven millennium as the framework for the ages of time that we are currently within. As we continue to examine the text, we read about how Elohim actually created everything in six days and rested on the seventh. So these seven words reveal the pattern of sevens.

The phrase "in the beginning" is essentially describing the beginning of the physical existence that we presently know and observe. It also describes the very beginning of time as we know it. It has been proven that time is a physical dimension, and as with other matters in this physical creation, it can be measured.[16]

So far, these two simple examples of the enlarged bet (𝘠) and the Aleph Taw (𝗫𝘅) should demonstrate the importance of examining the text in the original language. It is through the letters of this particular language that the Creator chose to express His purpose and plan. While translations into another language are an attempt to transmit this ancient message to more modern cultures and peoples, they will always fall short. A translation will never be able to relate all of the hidden messages and nuances that are contained in the ancient text. After all, every translation out of the original language is actually an interpretation.

Now some may find that statement offensive and repulsive, especially those who have decided to idolize a particular translation of the Bible. I know that while I was growing up, I was surrounded by "King James only" adherents. They are people who believe that the King James English translation was the only true "inspired" version of the Bible.

It is my hope that through this discussion the reader will see how such a position is really missing the point. While the King James Version of the Bible may have been a valiant attempt to translate ancient texts into a modern language, it certainly has its shortcomings, which will be explored to some degree in this book.

The purpose of this book is not to pick on any particular version of the Bible, but hopefully excite the reader into moving beyond a translation to the actual source of truth. That having been said, let us look a bit further into the beginning, or rather "the first." It must be stated that this author completely and unequivocally rejects the notion of evolution as it attempts to explain creation.

The notion that this incredible finite universe in which we live out our existence was the result of some random explosive event is beyond absurdity – it is sheer lunacy. The possibility of such an occurrence is beyond statistical possibility and defies reality.[7]

Those who propound such a notion typically do so to support their disbelief in a Creator. They propound their religion, or rather anti-religion, with more faith than someone who believes in a Creator. This is so because they utterly fail to explain where the matter and energy came from that were the ingredients of the explosion. They also fail to explain how the space that the event occurred within came into existence.

There clearly was a creation event, but instead of being chaotic, which could only result in perpetual chaos, we see incredible order coming out of chaos. That order derives, in part, from the unseen and also unexplained force that has been labeled gravity. There have been recent discoveries concerning dark matter, which reveal that there is much hidden in this marvelous and complex universe.

The cosmos are actually held together and kept in order by invisible forces, which should be a constant reminder that there is a Creator keeping Creation in check. We see in this order certain predictable and constant "laws" which can actually be distilled down to mathematical equations. Indeed, at the heart of this ordered, albeit sometimes tumultuous universe, is mathematics.[18]

Like software running a universal supercomputer, math, combined with the fuel of the Creator, keeps everything running. There are "laws of physics" which are predictable, known and calculated. Due to the existence of these known determinants we can be assured that this Creation was indeed, intelligently designed. Mathematics, as it turns out, is one of the ways that we know there is a Creator. Indeed, many great minds unwittingly communicate with the Creator when they search for truth through formulas and equations.

Essentially, they are seeking constants and truths within the framework of our physical existence. If they were merely evolutionists, this would, of course, be absurd since life, to the evolutionist, is a result of chaos, chance and time. To seek out constants in a universe of chaos would be an exercise of futility. Thus every mathematician must have, at a minimum, a spark of faith to seek truth in numbers. As we shall soon see, mathematics is actually the language of the Creator when we recognize that numbers and letters are really one and the same.[19]

With that understanding, we can then look directly to the handiwork of the Creator to learn more about Him and His plan.

2

Creation

Let us now explore the creative process further. The second verse of Beresheet reads as follows: "*The earth was without form, and void; and darkness was on the face of the deep. And the Spirit of God was hovering over the face of the waters.*" Beresheet 1:2

This is actually describing the creation, or recreation, of the physical universe although it is quite a mysterious text. I find it helpful to examine the text using a more mechanical translation as follows: "*and the land had existed in confusion and was unfilled and darkness was upon the face of the deep sea and the wind of "Elohiym [Powers]" was much fluttering upon the face of the water*"[20]

An interesting part of this event is the Spirit, which is ruach (𐤇𐤅𐤓) in the Hebrew. The head is the point of the body were we breath and "ruach" means: "breath." Interestingly, when we look at the word for "spirit" we can see the head that emits the breath which "connects" (𐤅) the fence (𐤇). So we can see how the "ruach" brought order to Creation. The Creator, the unseen Aleph (𐤀), actually emitted or exhaled all of the matter into existence through the Aleph Bet. He then bound it together through the vav (𐤅), and then set a fence around the cosmos, essentially placing it into a

container. The universe, after all, is finite.

The first word of the text actually gives some further insight into creation. Again, if we look at the first three letters of the word beresheet, "in beginning," we see "bara" (𐤊𐤘𐤁) which means "created." This word literally means: "son (𐤘𐤁) aleph (𐤊)." So we see the "son of Aleph" creating at the beginning.[21] This may be why the text begins with a bet (𐤁), instead of an aleph (𐤊). It appears that the mysterious Aleph Taw (𐤕𐤊) is a hint to the Son, the Word or Memra of Elohim in the physical creation, being instrumental in the Creation process. Once we understand that Elohim, through Aleph Taw (𐤕𐤊) created the Heavens and Earth, we are then told how everything was created – through speaking the Aleph Taw (𐤕𐤊).

The "ruach" was "hovering" or "fluttering" over the deep. The word in Hebrew is "merachefet" (𐤕𐤐𐤇𐤓𐤌). The root of this word is "rachaf" which is likened to "shaking or vibrating." This gives an indication of how things were created. Up to this point we are not specifically told how the earth and the waters were created. After we are told of the Spirit "vibrating" we then understand that Elohim created through speech.

Speech involves sound, which is actually vibration. "Sound is a mechanical wave that is an oscillation of pressure transmitted through a solid, liquid, or gas, composed of frequencies within the range of hearing."[22]

Therefore, creation involved frequencies and while sound is often thought to be separate from light, it must be understood that the major difference from mankind's perspective of these frequencies is the result of our different and unique organs that help us detect sound and light. We have eyes to detect light and ears to detect sound, but there is evidence to suggest that our brain can actually "see sound."[23]

These frequencies that went forth from the Creator created or set straight the chaos that already existed.[24] From those frequencies emitted by the Creator we exist and we too receive and transmit frequencies. Many fail to recognize this very fundamental form of communication and the power that is contained therein.

Every aspect of Creation involves frequencies, and we all act and react according to the frequencies that surround us. A kind word or a beautiful song can uplift your mood, while an insult or noise can bring you down. These particular frequencies can result in what is known as wave phenomena, the ability of sound to organize and repattern matter. They essentially have power to create and power to destroy. That was what was happening when the Spirit was hovering over the waters.

So we can see that there is a power in the spoken word, and thus there is a great degree of importance that attaches to the spoken word. This brings us back to the Hebrew language, specifically the Ancient Hebrew language. No one knows for sure what the earliest script looked like, since we only have archaeological finds that were written by different individuals, there are obviously variations.

If you had ten different individuals write out Beresheet 1:1 in English in their own handwriting, you would very likely have ten different looking sets of characters. While they would all be in English, and while they would all be representing the same letters and words, they would all look a bit different. Likewise, when we look at ancient renderings of the Hebrew

language, we have variations.

Thankfully, the different characters of the ancient language have known meanings, which helps us discern their likely rendering. For the purpose of this discussion, the author has developed a character set of the ancient language using examples from archaeology. This character set should aid the reader in their understanding of the language.

Interestingly, there are 22 characters in the Ancient Hebrew language. Each tells a story and has a message. The fact that there are 22 characters is by design, as we shall see. Everything was created by and through the Hebrew alphabet (alephbet), spoken, well before anything was written. Since we were not there we must read what happened. The Psalms record: *"By the Word of the LORD the heavens were made, and all the host of them by the breath (ruach) of His mouth."* Psalms 33:6.

Now we read this text in English, but it was originally spoken and written in Hebrew. Not in Modern Hebrew, but Ancient Hebrew. So this text has various levels of translation, and it is describing how the physical universe was created by The LORD. So far we have seen that Elohim created, and Elohim is a title. In this text we are actually provided the Name of Elohim in Hebrew, but the English translators have hidden the Name by using yet another title – The LORD.

If we look at the Hebrew text we see an actual Name spelled yud (𐤆) hey (𐤄) vav (𐤅) hey (𐤄) – 𐤄𐤅𐤄𐤆. The Name of the Creator is represented by 4 Ancient pictographs. In more ancient levels of antiquity it may have been represented as this: 𐤔𐤏𐤔𐤋. In the Modern Hebrew it would look like this: יהוה.[25] While each character is a pictograph with meaning, for pronunciation purposes, each character is treated as a consonant.

There are no written vowels in the Hebrew language, thus the invention of the "neqqudot" that were previously mentioned. The added vowel points would guide people in the verbalization of the text although the ancient texts did not contain any vowel points. Therefore, throughout this book, to aid the reader in pronouncing the Name, we will use the English equivalent of those consonants written from left to right – YHWH.

Here again, we have another simple yet powerful example of issues that must be recognized and addressed in our quest for truth concerning Creation and the Creator. It is important to understand that the letters and characters spoken by the breath, or spirit, of YHWH and found in Modern Hebrew texts are not the same as the most Ancient Language. If we desire to truly understand the original meaning it is best to view the original language.

While we now have a compilation of Hebrew texts known as the Torah, the Prophets and the Writings where we find accounts of the past, it is important to recognize that these texts were not available for thousands of years. The alephbet itself contained the truth of Creation and a message for all of the world. That truth can be seen in the pictographs. Each character represented a picture that cannot necessarily be recognized in the more modern scripts.

Those pictures told a story, as we have already seen. For instance the Aleph (𐤀) appeared as an "ox." It had two horns that signified strength, and it was the first of all the letters. It is followed by the bet (𐤁), which signifies the "house." When we combine these two letters together we have "ab" (𐤉𐤊), which represents the "strength of the house." The word "ab" (𐤉𐤊) actually means: "father." The third letter is gimel (𐤂), which represents a camel. It means to "lift up" or "transport." The gimel (𐤂) is followed by the dalet (𐤃), which means: "door." So we can see from the first 4 letters that the strength of the house, the father, will raise us up to the door of the house."

The story continues on multiple levels as we trace the alephbet in its order and examine the meanings of, not only the characters, but the relationships of the meanings. There is even deep meaning in the numerical values of the characters and the combination of letters. As the Aleph (𐤊) proceeds to the Taw (X), the entire covenant is revealed. Indeed the Taw (X) is a mark, which represents a "covenant." So the entire alephbet leads us to a covenant.

The ancient alephbet contains the entire plan of Elohim for His Creation. The blueprint is essentially encrypted within the characters in their specific order seen here from right to left.

X W 𐤒 𐤘 𐤓 𐤉 ⊙ 𐤅 𐤔 𐤌 𐤋 Y 𐤆 ⊗ 𐤇 𐤆 Y 𐤄 𐤃 𐤂 𐤉 𐤊

As we already saw, the Bet (𐤉) was actually the first letter in the written Scriptures and the Bet (𐤉) actually represented the "house" of creation. When we examine these 22 letters with the understanding that the Aleph (𐤊) preceded and was outside of that created "house" we are left with 21 letters in the created "house."

This explains the patterns of seven that are so interlaced throughout creation as we can see with light and time. In fact, the characters of the alephbet are actually the building blocks of creation when empowered by the Creator.

It is the original representation of the sound frequencies emitted by the Creator. It is actually the physical, visual representation of the sound of creation. So essentially, the pictographs unify the frequencies of sound and light.[26]

When we combine those characters, especially into groupings of three, we are provided with concepts and roots that develop into words. It has been said that: "the letters of the Hebrew alphabet are like stones, and each whole word is like a house. Just as a house is built of stones, so is a word built of letters."[27]

This book is written in English, which is a western language. Western languages are very different from eastern languages. These language distinctions (east v. west) are important because they determine the way people communicate, and how they think. Believe it or not, people in the East actually think differently from people in the West. Eastern thought tends to be cyclical, while Western thought is linear.

Western languages tend to be very abstract, while Eastern Languages tend to be very concrete. Western languages tend to be static while Eastern languages are active. In fact, an example of how opposite they are is demonstrated by the fact that Eastern languages typically flow from right to left, while Western languages tend to flow from the left to the right.

This is significant and explains why there are often so many differences between Eastern and Western religions. Language actually influences the way we think and the way we perceive the world that we live in. This

is the source of many of the tensions that exist in the world today – the disconnect between Eastern and Western cultures.

This is what occurred when Christianity and Judaism originally both strayed from the Covenant made with Israel (Yisrael), and developed into two religions. Christianity became heavily influenced by the west, and Judaism remained an eastern religion.[28] Now both have a mixture of Eastern and Western influences, but the original separation remains.

Therefore, to properly understand the Creator and His Creation, it is helpful and even necessary to examine the language of Creation. The original alephbet, as we shall see, tells a story through the pictures that they represent. At the very heart of the alephbet, we see the kaph lamed ($\mathcal{C}$ Y). The kaph represents a "hand" (Y), and the lamed ($\mathcal{C}$) represents a "shepherd's staff."

So amidst and centered between the Aleph ($\mathcal{K}$) and the Taw (X) is kaph lamed ($\mathcal{C}$ Y). We can see then that the Aleph Taw (X$\mathcal{K}$) is there to lead as a shepherd – the Great Shepherd. That is at the heart of the story, and through this discussion we will be examining that story which has been told both through language and creation – a story lived by mankind.

3

Mankind

After the creation of the physical universe described in the first five days, mankind was created on day six followed by the seventh day, which was set apart. The set apart seventh day was the only day given a name. It was called the Sabbath, essentially the crescendo of creation.[29]

We are not told of an eighth day so the assumption is that a seven day cycle continues from that time forward. Indeed, there is every reason to believe that the day count that exists today constitutes an unbroken cycle of sevens that began the first week of creation.

During the creation process we see the formation of the physical universe, including time itself. The sun and the moon were actually provided to mark time, and we know that time flowed in cycles. We saw that the bet (ב) was the first letter in the written Torah, and it was enlarged to draw our attention to it. While the bet (ב) was the first letter in the written Scriptures, it was not the first letter spoken.

Indeed, the first word spoken by Elohim is found further on at Beresheet 1:3. In English we read "Let there be" which is "yehi" (יהי) in Hebrew. It comes from

the root "hayah" (ﬡﬡﬡ) which means: "be or exist." In each case the emphasis is on the arm (ﬡ) and the spirit or breath (ﬡ). We are shown to "behold" (ﬡ) "the arm" (ﬡ). This was none other than the Arm of the Creator bringing forth His will in the physical creation. The first creative words spoken involved two Hebrew words, consisting of 6 characters - ﬡﬡﬡ ﬡﬡﬡ.

In English we read: "let there be light" or "exist light." So the first thing that was brought forth into the creation was "light" – "owr" (ﬡﬡﬡ). The Hebrew script reveals "strength" or "first" represented by the aleph (ﬡ), connected by the vav (ﬡ) to a head (ﬡ). So this "light" is preeminent in creation. Remembering that each Hebrew character has a numerical equivalent we can discern that the gematria for the word light is 207 (ﬡ = 1, ﬡ = 6, ﬡ = 200).

Interestingly, the word for "light" has the same numerical value as "adabar" (ﬡﬡﬡﬡ) when YHWH was talking about obeying all "the words" that He would speak.[30] It also has the same value as the word "ra'ah" (ﬡﬡﬡ), which means: "see." In fact, that word actually has the same characters as "light" (ﬡﬡﬡ). The concept of "seeing" and "light" are therefore very intimately connected.

So this owr (ﬡﬡﬡ) is related to the spoken word of YHWH, and it is something to be seen. We will be exploring this further as we continue with the discussion. At this point, it is important to note that this light was not the sun or the stars, as we often think of as sources of light. The heavenly bodies that emit light were not created until the 4th day. So the light of the first day was different from the light of the fourth day.

After all of creation was spoken we read about a

special place known as the Garden of Eden more accurately the Garden in Eden. Eden (𐤏𐤃𐤍) is often interpreted to mean "paradise" and this Garden was located within Eden. Interestingly, when we examine this word in Hebrew it is more revealing. It actually proclaims: "see" (𐤏) "the door" (𐤃) "to life" (𐤍). So in this special place we are to see the door to life. That door leads to the Garden.

The word for Garden is gan (𐤍𐤂), which means an "enclosed space." So this would have been the place with the door. The gimel (𐤂) represents a "camel" and means to "lift up" or "transport." Once again, the nun (𐤍) which represents "life." Amazingly, it looks like a sperm cell, which is the method that YHWH chose to plant the life of man.

So there was a special enclosed place in Paradise that was separated from the rest of creation. It was meant as a place to lift up and carry life – the life of mankind. One could say that it was like a womb. In fact, this is where ✗𐤊-the man (𐤍𐤃𐤊𐤀-✗𐤊) was placed. In the English you cannot see the Aleph Taw (✗𐤊), but the Hebrew plainly reveals a mystery with this man.

The gematria value of Eden is 124. This is the same value as the word "moadi" (𐤆𐤃𐤏𐤍), found in Vayiqra 23:44, which means: "appointed time." Interestingly, in that passage we see ✗𐤊-moadi (𐤆𐤃𐤏𐤍-✗𐤊). So the Aleph Taw (✗𐤊) is connected with the Appointed Times. These refer to specific times when the Creator decides to meet with His people at the place that He resides. In other words, He invites us to His House, and we can see from this connection that His House is Paradise.

The gematria value for gan (𐤍𐤂) is 53. This is

interesting because there are some very important concepts in the Scriptures that carry the same value. For instance, the word "aben" ($4\,\mathcal{I}\mathbf{\mathcal{K}}$), which means "stone," has the value of 53. The stone is something with much Messianic meaning, particularly when we examine an event where Jacob actually "lifts up" a stone and anoints it with oil. That stone was called the et-ha'aben ($4\,\mathcal{I}\mathbf{\mathcal{K}}\,\mathcal{A}$-$\mathbf{X}\mathbf{\mathcal{K}}$). Notice the Aleph Taw ($\mathbf{X}\mathbf{\mathcal{K}}$) attached to this anointed stone. To anoint something is "moshiach" in Hebrew – the source of the word "messiah."[31]

The aben is also very intriguing because it constitutes the unity of two words – father ($\mathcal{I}\mathbf{\mathcal{K}}$) and son ($4\,\mathcal{I}$). The father is the "strength" ($\mathbf{\mathcal{K}}$) of the house ($\mathcal{I}$) while the son fills the house ($\mathcal{I}$) with life or seed (4). Both of these words are united at the bet ($\mathcal{I}$) - the House.

The gematria value for father ($\mathcal{I}\mathbf{\mathcal{K}}$) is 3, and the value of son ($4\,\mathcal{I}$) is 52. When added together we have 55 which is the same value as the land – ha'adamah ($\mathcal{A}\,\mathcal{Y}\mathbf{\triangleleft}\mathbf{\mathcal{K}}\,\mathcal{A}$). This is the word used to describe the planet in Beresheet 1:25. The earth is the house that we saw being built from the first letter of the Hebrew Scriptures – the enlarged bet ($\mathcal{I}$).

Since the father ($\mathcal{I}\mathbf{\mathcal{K}}$) and the son ($4\,\mathcal{I}$) each have a bet ($\mathcal{I}$), when they are combined into one word they are connected by one house. As a result the gematria value for aben ($4\,\mathcal{I}\mathbf{\mathcal{K}}$) is 53. Another word with incredible significance that equals 53 is "ha'yovel" ($\mathcal{L}\,\mathcal{I}\,\mathbf{Y}\,\mathbf{7}\,\mathcal{A}$), also known as the Jubilee.

The Jubilee is a year that occurs every 50 years on the Calendar of YHWH.[32] This is an important time when Land and inheritance rights are restored. The

Jubilee is all about being restored to our homes, which we have lost. We should all anticipate the future Jubilee when mankind is permitted back in the Garden.

The principles of life were found in the Garden. It was there that we find the source of life – the Tree of Life. We also saw that YHWH used the seed to propagate and multiply life. In the Garden there was food to eat, only that which was seed bearing and was green.[33] Man was placed within the garden and commanded to "be fruitful multiply." His residency came with certain conditions. It was the very House of YHWH, and this of course was where YHWH would communicate with man – face to face. So we can see through the creation process, the many levels that YHWH chose to communicate by and through His Creation.

Now let us examine the creation of man. As man was brought into existence we see something very interesting. In the Hebrew text it describes the man as "et-haAdam" (𝕐𝝙𝕂𝕒-𝝬𝕂).[34] Only in the Hebrew do we see the Aleph Taw (𝝬𝕂) attached to haAdam (𝕐𝝙𝕂𝕒) which literally means: "the man." Therefore, we see man made in the image of Elohim, because this was a pattern. The Image of Elohim in creation was the Aleph Taw (𝝬𝕂).

Elohim placed man in the House and gave him a job. This was the place where man was given purpose: "to work and to guard." (Beresheet 2:15). Elohim was revealing through this man the purpose of His Creation. Once man was placed in a House, represented by the Garden, it was time to fill the House. A mate would come from "the adam" made in the image of YHWH. This revealed that YHWH would bring forth a mate for Himself, from

Himself.

We read about the "birthing" process by which this was accomplished in Beresheet 2:21-22. *"²¹ And YHWH Elohim caused a deep sleep to fall on Adam, and he slept; and He took one of his ribs, and closed up the flesh in its place. ²² Then the rib which YHWH Elohim had taken from man He made into a woman, and He brought her to the man."*

Notice that Adam was placed in a "deep sleep." The word to describe this "deep sleep" in Hebrew is "tardemah" (𐤀𐤀𐤀𐤀𐤀), which is like "a trance, coma or death." So we are given a picture of Adam dying and giving birth to the woman. After the "birth" he is resurrected. This is a pattern that would be repeated again in the future.[35] Ultimately, the Messiah would come as a "Last Adam," and He too would give birth to a family to fill the House of Elohim – Beit El.

This leads to a very important detail regarding the "birthing" process from Adam. In the text, we read how a "rib" was taken from the man to form the woman. Some believe that it was not actually a rib that was taken from Adam, but rather something even more profound. The word for "the rib" in the passage is: "et-hatzelah" (𐤀𐤀𐤀-𐤀𐤀). The first thing that should grab your attention is the fact that there is the Aleph Taw (𐤀𐤀) actually attached to the word: "hatzelah" (𐤀𐤀𐤀𐤀).

This reveals that something special is going on in this "birthing" process. It could be that the Aleph Taw (𐤀𐤀) is actually participating in the creation of woman. The hey (𐤀) is translated as "the" but it also means: "behold." So we should really focus on the root word "tzelah" (𐤀𐤀𐤀). This word is simply translated to mean: "curve," "slope" or "side." This leads many to think of a rib, which is curved.

When we look at the word we see something even more incredible. The tsade (ᵍ) actually represents a "hook" and means: "righteous." The lamed (ℓ) represents a staff or a goad and means: "control, instruct." The ayin (◉) represents an eye and means: "to see or know." Notice that all three characters are curved and when combined they mean: "righteous instruction seen."

The gematria for "tzelah" is 190 and it shares the same value as "qetz" (ᵍ ᵠ), which means: "end" as in "end of a cycle" or "end of an age." It also shares the same value with the Hebrew word "tzeetz" (ᵍ Ζ ᵍ), which means: "flower, bloom or wings." It is the root of "tzitzit" (Χ ᵍ Ζ ᵍ), which are the "wings" or "tassels" that we are to wear on the four corners of our garments. Containing a thread of blue, the tzitzit are intended to remind us of the commandments. (Bemidbar 15:38).

So we see through this process the righteous instructions brought forth from the man, which would bloom or take flight through the woman.

There is something in our bodies where the righteous instructions of the Creator are located – our DNA. Therefore "the curve," that is referred to could very likely be the DNA double helix. In other words, the Aleph Taw (Χ ᚴ) took the genetic code from the man, and from that same coding He made the woman. Of course, a rib would clearly contain DNA so that is a very plausible situation, but it is amazing how many levels of understanding can be found in the Hebrew language.

When we look at the ordinal values in the alephbet we see that the tsade (ᵍ) is number 18, the lamed (ℓ) is number 12 and the ayin (◉) is number 16. When these values are added together they amount to 46,

which amazingly is the number of chromosomes per cell in the DNA of mankind.

This gets interesting when we realize that the Aleph (𐤀) is the first letter in the Aleph Bet, which has an ordinal value of 1. The Taw (X) is the last letter in the alephbet, which has an ordinal value of 22. Therefore, the Aleph Taw (X𐤀) has a value of 23, the number of chromosomes in a sperm and an egg. This is also the gematria value for "live" which is rendered as 𐤀𐤆𐤇 in Beresheet 1:20, and 𐤆𐤇𐤀 in Beresheet 6:19. In both instances their gematria value for "live" is 23.

It is intriguing when we examine the union between man and woman. The text records: 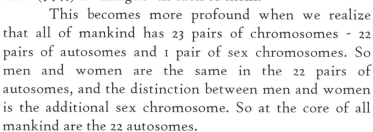 *"Therefore a man shall leave his X𐤀-father and X𐤀-mother and be joined to his wife, and they shall become one flesh."* Beresheet 2:24. When the text mentions father and mother there is an Aleph Taw (X𐤀) attached to each, revealing that both man and woman are made in the image of Elohim, and the Aleph Taw (X𐤀) is "imaged" in each of them.

This becomes more profound when we realize that all of mankind has 23 pairs of chromosomes - 22 pairs of autosomes and 1 pair of sex chromosomes. So men and women are the same in the 22 pairs of autosomes, and the distinction between men and women is the additional sex chromosome. So at the core of all mankind are the 22 autosomes.

Remember that there are 22 letters in the alephbet. If the Aleph Taw (X𐤀) consists of all the letters in the alephbet, then we can see that the image of the Aleph Taw (X𐤀) would look like a man. We can also discern that those letters were meant to create and procreate.

There are a number of related words that all share the same gematria value as 22, such as "sacrifice," "sprinkle" and "hyssop."[36]

When the 23 chromosomes of a man are added to the 23 chromosomes of a woman, they become united as one, which is "echad" (◁Ħ𐤊) in Hebrew. This union results in total of 46. Amazingly, the word "elohi" (𐤆𐤀𐤋𐤊), equals 46, as was used to describe YHWH the Elohi of Shem, Noah's son. (Beresheet 9:26).

Each DNA molecule holds an incredible amount of information, placed there by none other than the Creator. DNA carries our genetic information, and is found within the nucleus of every living cell. Therefore, the righteous instructions from the Creator are within each of us - in every living cell of every living organism.

DNA is the familiar double helix shape connected with the four base letters - Adenine, Cytosine, Guanine, Thymine or ACGT. The 4 Base letters ACGT with each combination of 3 make Codons, the 64 Codons which in turn deliver specific instruction to cellular chemistry. Codons manufacture protein. It is the various sequencing of amino acids within the proteins that give rise to specific shapes and functions of the proteins.

Thus, there is a language built into this process and scientists have even assigned alphabetical letters to amino acids. This process is empowered, instructed and controlled by DNA. It is known as "The Language of Life" and evolutionists are plagued with the question "What is the source of the biological messages encoded within the DNA?" Without DNA there is no replication, and evolution cannot explain life without the existence of DNA.

The manner in which that DNA transmits the

"righteous instructions" is nothing short of a miracle. The DNA strand actually unravels during a process known as "transcription." A messenger RNA strand reads the instructions. This RNA is processed and exported from the nucleus into the cytoplasm, where it is translated by ribosomes, and then constructed into protein chains as per the transmitted instructions.

Those chains are then folded into a protein and transported to the needed location. This entire process is life, and it is powered by an invisible force that no evolutionist could possibly explain through mere electrochemical reactions. It is the very power of the word "EXIST" spoken at the beginning by the Creator.

This process played out by the DNA is the very essence of creation. Through "the Word" Elohim created all that is in existence. In fact, it has been said that the Hebrew language is actually the DNA of creation.[37]

As the DNA opens, transmits and closes, we see how YHWH creates. Adam was opened, his information was transmitted to the woman, and then he was closed. The man and the woman were then intended to be unified to become one flesh – echad. Through that union the woman is opened, the man plants his seed into the womb of the woman, and she bears fruit.

Unification is known as "echad," and it is how the Creator creates. We see this through all of creation, it is the trademark of YHWH. We even saw this with a day, as YHWH unified day and night to make a unified day on Day 1. He divided the light from the dark, and then unified. YHWH also describes Himself as Echad. So He too has been divided and unified so that He can create.[38] This is why He uses the descriptor "Elohim" which is the plural form of El.

Echad (◁Ħ𐤊) has a gematria value of 13, which shares the same value as love – ahabah (𐤉𐤉𐤉𐤊). Now anyone familiar with the Name of YHWH should see the similarity. YHWH (𐤉Y𐤉𐤆) has a gematria value of 26, which is essentially "love unified." The only difference between these two words is the "ab" (𐤉𐤊) which means "father," and the "yaw" (Y𐤆), which means: "arm unites."

So we can see great truths hidden within the Name of YHWH, and through the DNA we can see YHWH actually communicating on a cellular level. One could say that DNA is the cellular language of life. It is the fingerprint of YHWH - it is His Image. So Adam being made in the image of YHWH involved YHWH placing His DNA within the man.

In fact, the life of the man is the blood, which pumps through his veins.[39] His name actually refers to that blood, which is "dam" (𐤘◁) in Hebrew. The gematria value of blood is 44. Again, we can see the 22 letters of the alephbet intimately connected with the blood by a factor of 2. Remember that the Hebrew letter with the gematria value of 2 is bet (𐤘), and the bet (𐤘), literally represents a "house."

The blood is very interesting because YHWH chose it as the means to maintain life in "the adam." Some have speculated that blood is, in fact, congealed light.[40] This notion makes for interesting thought as we consider the speeding up of the blood into light. This would make sense as those who follow the Ways of YHWH are often referred to as Children of Light.[41]

This is particularly interesting when we consider the fact that blood, which sustains our life, contains somatids. Somatids are "ultramicrosopic subcellular

living and reproducing entities, which many scientists believe are the precursor of DNA, and which may be the building block of all terrestrial life."[42]

So man and woman were created by the voice of YHWH. They were filled with His Spirit of Life – the light of life imparted into His Creation. They were given instructions, and they were actually designed and built specifically to obey His instructions.

Sadly, the man and the woman disobeyed by partaking of the "forbidden fruit" from the Tree of Knowledge of Good and Evil. This event involved more than eating a piece of fruit. It was a perversion of the creative process previously described through the union of the man and the woman. It was so bad that the man and woman felt compelled to sew fig leaves together and cover their sexual organs.

It is interesting that they chose the fig leaf for a covering. The word "fig" in Hebrew is "te'en" (𐤉𐤊𐤕). It has a gematria value of 451. The first word in the Scriptures with a value of 451 is "deep" or "tehom" (𐤉𐤉𐤀𐤕) in Hebrew. This was the chaotic state of the planet prior to the creation account following Beresheet 1:2, which likely resulted from a previous judgment. They were essentially wearing that judgment as they attempted to cover themselves from their physical nakedness. Since they were both naked and "cunning", it would take more than fig leaves to cover their transgression.

When they heard the voice of YHWH in the Garden they hid themselves. Interesting the Hebrew text inserts the Aleph Taw (𐤕𐤊) between "hear" (shema) and "the voice of YHWH Elohim." (Beresheet 3:8). Indeed the Aleph Taw (𐤕𐤊) is literally connected to the "voice" - ℓ𝕐ϙ-X𝕏.

So YHWH called out to the man and the woman. He communicated through speech, and His voice is connected with the Aleph Taw (X𝕏). They could not hide for long, they were eventually found and needed to come clean. Their conduct had repercussions. Their disobedience upset the equilibrium of creation and shook the cosmos. It infected a holy, set apart, creation and spread like a disease.

YHWH had to protect His creation and quarantine man before he partook of the Tree of Life. This would have upset all of creation and likely led to his demise. By quarantining man, it allowed an opportunity to salvage, or "save" him. He could not remain in the house, but YHWH revealed His plan of restoration through the punishments rendered upon the perpetrators.

When rendering judgment on the nachash (W𝐻𝕐), often referred to as the serpent, YHWH Elohim made the following proclamation: "*And I will put enmity between you and the woman, and between your seed and her seed; it shall bruise your head, and you shall* ⅄X𝕏 *bruise his heel.*" Beresheet 3:15.

What is really interesting in this passage is the inclusion of the word "beyn" (𝕐ℤ𝕐) four times in the Hebrew text. It can mean "between" but also means "perceive or understand." You will not see this in an English translation, but it would seem that the text is crying out for us to understand a mystery hidden within the passage - a mystery connected with the Aleph Taw (X𝕏). Remember that the hey (⅄) means: "behold." So the solution to the problem seems to be provided – "*Behold the* X𝕏 *Who will be bruised.*"

Thereafter, YHWH shed the blood of innocent

animals to reveal that innocent blood would provide an atonement, or covering, for the sin of man. YHWH clothed the man and the woman in the skins of the slaughtered animals. They were like costumes or disguises, which hid their sin from the face of YHWH.

The sin was still there, just covered. As a result, the inner sin began to work death in both the man and the woman. Beings which were created in the image of an eternal Elohim, intended to live forever, were now infected with sin and were dying. Death is very repulsive to the Creator as it is the antithesis of His essence, which is life.

So disobedience resulted in expulsion from the source of life in the garden, and it introduced the process of death into creation. Creation and the events surrounding the Garden communicate the truth of YHWH. We are not provided much information regarding life outside the Garden, but it was surely not paradise.

We know this from the punishments meted out to the participants of the sin in the Garden. (Beresheet 3:14-19). In the midst of the punishment, there was a promise given which gave hope to mankind, the Promise of a deliverer.[43] There were patterns built into Creation and the cycles of time intended to reveal how this deliverer would accomplish the task.

4

Signs

We know from the first week of Creation that time was reckoned by the passage of days. Each day is controlled by the circuit of the sun and progresses from evening to night to morning and back to evening. A day actually begins at evening and ends the following evening.[44] There would be six days followed by the seventh day, called the Sabbath, and then the count would reset.

This seven day count is a remembrance of Creation and constitutes a week, known as a "shabua" (⊙𐤔W) in Hebrew. The seven day week count has continued since the very first week. The passage of weeks was therefore marked by the sun.

Interestingly, this count began before there was a sun. Recall that the sun, the moon, the planets and the stars were not created until day four. So the sun actually marked a passage of time that could be calculated prior to its creation. Here is an account of what occurred on Day 4 of creation week:

"*[14] Then Elohim said, 'Let there be lights in the firmament of the heavens to divide the day from the night; and let them be for signs and seasons (moadim), and for days and years; [15] and let them be for lights in the firmament of*

the heavens to give light on the earth' and it
was so. [16] Then Elohim made two great lights:
the greater light to rule the day, and the lesser
light to rule the night. He made the stars also.
[17] Elohim set them in the firmament of the
heavens to give light on the earth, [18] and to rule
over the day and over the night, and to divide
the light from the darkness. And Elohim saw
that it was good. [19] So the evening and the
morning were the fourth day." Beresheet 1:14-
19.

We see that there were specific lights placed in
the firmament of the heavens. These were to help divide
and distinguish the day from the night. The sun is the
greater light – "gadol" (ᗉᐊ1) in Hebrew. This means it
is greater in rank, power and magnitude. Indeed, the
moon emanates no light from itself, but rather reflects
the light of the sun.

The moon is known as the lesser light, but it still
has a very specific and important purpose. It actually
rules the sky by night along with the stars. Indeed, the
moon is considered to be a faithful witness.[45] The moon
is actually made for what are commonly translated as
"seasons." "*He appointed the moon for seasons (moadim); the
sun knows its going down.*" Psalm 104:19.

Up to this point we have quoted some common
English translations where the moon has been associated
with "seasons." That is a serious translation error, and
you should have noticed the word "moadim" in
parenthesis. The word often translated as "seasons" is
"moadim" (Ꭹᘔᐊ⊙ᏔᎩ) in Hebrew. It is another form
of the word "moadi" (ᘔᐊ⊙Ꭹ) that we already
mentioned is an Appointed Time.

The reason this is a translation error is because "moadim" does not refer to seasons, but rather specific "Appointed Times." Again, these Appointed Times are special times that occur each year as a pattern to reveal the plan of YHWH to His people. They are a way that YHWH communicates to His people through Creation and time. As people observe these Appointed Times, they learn about YHWH, His righteous path and His plan to redeem His people. We will be discussing the significance of the Appointed Times throughout this book. The important thing, for now, is to realize that they are not seasons as some believe - i.e. spring, summer, fall and winter.[46]

So from the beginning YHWH built these Appointed Times into creation and used the sun and the moon as virtual "hands on the clock" to tell time. The sun marks the passage of days. The passage of solar day cycles also marks the passage of weeks. The progression of the moon, from one new moon to another, marks the passage of months.

Now through the passage of months we obviously see the progression of the seasons, but the Appointed Times are not the seasons themselves. The seasons are actually determined by times known generally as tequfahs or tequfot. These tequfot are essentially "turns," commonly known as the solstices and equinoxes.

The word for return, "shuwb" (𐤔𐤅𐤁), also has great significance as the seasons "return" to their beginnings. Just as Creation turns and returns, we are also to remember to turn from wickedness and return to YHWH. Therefore, as we live our lives through these visual cycles of Creation we are reminded of our relationship with the Creator. This, of course, is the

meaning of the Appointed Times. They are intended to draw us back to YHWH, and keep us on His path. The Appointed Times are a rehearsal revealing how we "teshuwbah" (𐤕𐤔𐤅𐤁𐤄).

So aside from telling time and marking the Appointed Times, we learn from Beresheet 1:14 that the sun, the moon and the stars are also made to be "signs." Now in our modern English we usually think of a sign as something two dimensional with words written on it which provides information. The sun, the moon and the stars were the first signs, and the word in Hebrew for sign is "owt" (𐤀𐤅𐤕). Notice that the word is very similar to light - owr (𐤀𐤅𐤓). That is because they share the same root (𐤀𐤅), which literally means - "strength or power connects."

Interestingly, the aleph (𐤀) with a value of 1, is often attributed to YHWH. The vav (𐤅), with a value of 6, is often attributed to man. As YHWH "connects" to man we are left with the value of 7, and we can see why the number 7 is so predominate in Creation.

Because of this shared root with light, we discern that the sign is illuminated and something to be seen. Accordingly, those heavenly bodies designated for signs emit and/or reflect light. Very interestingly, the first time that a "sign" is mentioned in the text is Beresheet 1:14 and it is not spelled 𐤀𐤅𐤕, but rather 𐤀𐤕. You will find 𐤀𐤕𐤕 in the text, but the final 𐤕 is to pluralize the word from "sign" to "signs." So the "first" sign is clearly the Aleph Taw (𐤀𐤕), and one could conclude that all signs point and lead to the Aleph Taw (𐤀𐤕) - the Messiah.

Now on the subject of signs we include the stars which have heretofore been excluded from the subject of time and Appointed Times. Stars are unique from the greater light and the lesser light. To begin, they are much further away than the sun and the moon. The sun heats and lights our planet. While earth revolves around the sun, the moon revolves around the earth. Scientists believe that the moon actually came from the earth as both orbs share many of the same components. Of course the spiritual implications of the moon being "birthed" from the earth are quite interesting.[47]

The sun and the moon are both specifically and intimately associated with our planet. The stars, on the other hand, vary in distance and intensity, and all have their center in some other planetary system. One could say that their center of attention is focused elsewhere, and their interest in our solar system is ancillary. Despite their remote nature, it is clear that they have a purpose which is relevant to us. Each one even has a name that is known in our universe.

"[2] YHWH, builds up Jerusalem! He gathers together the exiles of Yisrael, [3] healing the broken-hearted and binding up their wounds; [4] He counts out the number of the stars, and gives each one of them a name.[5] O great is our Master, mighty in power, His wisdom is beyond all telling." Psalm 147:2-5.[48]

So we know that YHWH counts out the numbers of the stars, and gives each one of them a name. This is actually an incredible statement since there are billions of galaxies, each containing billions of stars. That is a lot of counting, and a lot of names. Clearly we cannot see all of these stars with our naked eyes or even the most powerful telescope. We therefore do not know all of the names, but we do know some.

We can find some of them in what is believed to be the oldest book in existence – the Book of Job. "[9] He

has made the Bear and Orion, the Pleiades and the Mansions of the South.[10] The works he does are great and unfathomable, and his marvels cannot be counted." Job 9:9-10. "[31] Can you tie up the cords of the Pleiades or loosen the belt of Orion? [32] Can you lead out the constellations of the mazzaroth (zodiac) in their season or guide the Arcturus and his sons (Great Bear and its cubs)? [33] O you know the ordinances of the sky? Can you determine how they affect the earth?" Job 38:31-33.

"Distinct and unmistakable references are contained in it to the constellations as we still have them. We there read of 'Arcturus with his sons,' 'the sweet influences of Pleiades,' ' the bands of Orion,' and 'the fleeing serpent.' We there likewise read of 'Mazzaroth,' with its 'seasons' - stopping-places - which, according to the margin of our English Bible, the Jewish Targum, and the ablest Christian interpreters, is nothing more nor less than the Solar Zodiac."[49]

Notice that the word commonly understood as "zodiac" is actually "mazzaroth" (XY92ש) in Hebrew. The mazzaroth are referring to the constellations that are seen from our planet. These constellations only have their unique shapes and sizes from the perspective of our planet. When viewed from a different perspective in the universe they would, of course be unrecognizable.

So from these different passages we can deduce that there is an order and purpose to the mazzaroth. Viewed from earth, specific groupings of stars combine to depict characters and beings. These stars actually act as signs in the skies, which must therefore transmit information or messages. Those signs, as it turns out, were a way that the Creator chose to communicate with His Creation.

Indeed, we read: *"The heavens declare his righteousness, and all the peoples have seen His glory."* Psalms 97:6. The word "declare" is "messapherim"  (ᵞᏃᏋᏋᏋᎮ) and means: "to speak, to show forth." So then how did the heavens speak? Well we understand better by looking at the root "sepher" (ᏋᏋᎮ) which means: "to inscribe." It also means: "scroll." So then it would appear that the heavens are unrolled like a scroll, and the "glory" (kabod) of Elohim is written thereon.

This is reinforced by the following passage. *"[1] The heavens declare the glory (kabod) of Elohim; and the firmament shows His handiwork. [2] Day unto day utters speech, and night unto night shows knowledge. [3] There is no speech nor words; their voice is not heard. [4] Their line is gone out through all the earth, and their words to the end of the world. In them hath He set a tabernacle for the sun, [5] Which is as a bridegroom coming out of his chamber, and rejoiceth as a strong man to run his course. [6] His going forth is from the end of the heavens, and his circuit unto the ends of it; and there is nothing hid from the heat thereof."* Psalms 19:1-6.

So we can see that from the beginning all of creation actually testified to the plan and purposes of YHWH. It was written in the stars and those who understood taught and transmitted the truth orally. The mazzaroth speak in a visible language that can be understood by all. In fact, we know that these constellations share the same meanings throughout the various languages and cultures of the world. This attests to a very ancient and singular source.

The mazzaroth not only had meaning in the beginning, but they reveal truth through to the end. Only when the "Day of YHWH" arrives will their light pass, and at that point they will no longer provide signs. "*For the stars of the heaven and their constellations will not give light, the sun will be darkened in its going forth and the moon will not cause its light to shine.*" Isaiah 13:10

Interestingly, the Hebrew root for "constellations" in this passage is "kisel" (𐤊𐤎𐤉𐤋). Some translate this word as "Orion" while others translate it as "constellations." Since the word found in Isaiah is actually plural, the context seems to be referencing all of the lights in the heavens. Of particular note is the gematria value of "kisel" (𐤊𐤎𐤉𐤋), which is 120.

We will see further on in the discussion that the number 120 is actually linked to a time limit given to

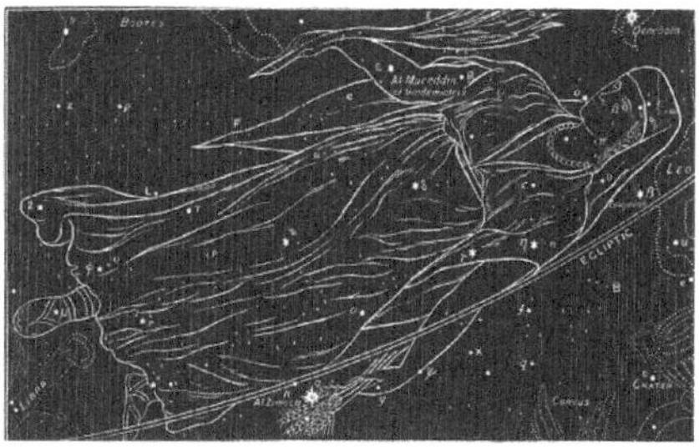

mankind on Earth. So the constellations actually tell a story from the beginning to the end. There are 12 constellations and each constellation has 3 associated "decans." Therefore, we actually have 48 signs in the sky associated with the mazzaroth. A very significant word that has a gematria value of 48 is "yobel" (𐤉𐤅𐤁𐤋), which is translated as "jubilee." We already mentioned that "ha'yobel" (ל 𐤉 Y ך 𐤄) - the Jubilee - is intimately connected with time and the Land. We now can see that it is also connected with the signs, and the allotted time given to creation.

It is clear that there is incredible significance in each of the constellations along with their three associated decans. If, for instance, we look at the constellation "Virgo," or "Bethulah" in Hebrew, we see a virgin holding a sheaf of grain or branch, associated with the star "spica." Spica is the brightest star in Bethulah, known as "tsemech" (𐤄 𐤼 𐤂) in Hebrew.

The word "tsemech" (𐤄 𐤼 𐤂) means "branch" and we know from later prophecies that the Messiah would be known as "the Branch" (Psalm 80:15; Isaiah 4:2, 11:1; Jeremiah 23:5, 33:15; Zechariah 3:8). We also know that the Messiah would come from a "virgin." (Isaiah 7:14). Actually, the first prophecy given in the Garden of Eden involved the Seed of a woman. (Beresheet 3:15). So we can see the culmination of various prophecies concerning the Messiah, given throughout time, depicted in this one constellation that existed from the beginning.

As with every constellation, Bethulah is accompanied by three decans. The first is known as "Coma" which means: "the desired son." This revealed that a Son would come through a virgin birth. The second decan is often called a "centaur." It is "bezeh" in Hebrew and means "the despised or the vile one." The decan depicts a half man, half beast carrying a spear – piercing a victim. So it appears that this "mixed seed" will pierce the Son. The third decan associated with Bethulah is called "Bootes," and it means: "the coming one." Bootes is commonly depicted as a shepherd and a harvester, carrying a shepherds crook and a sickle. So

there are two roles associated with the Son – a shepherd caring for flocks and a reaper reaping a harvest.

Anyone with even a basic knowledge of the Scriptures can see the Messianic and prophetic implications of this one constellation and its associated decans. As we examine all of the twelve constellations we see them culminating with Leo the Lion, otherwise known as Ariel – the Lion of the Tribe of Judah. There 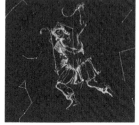 was, of course, no coincidence that there are twelve tribes of Israel, and each has a banner related to a constellation. Some actually believe that the Tribes camped in formation associated with their related mazzaroth.

Now we have the benefit of examining these messages in the light of written prophecies, but imagine having this information in the heavens from the 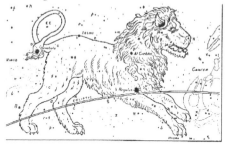 beginning. The mazzaroth have been described as prophecy "written in the heavens in order that the messengers may read and know" things to befall men.[50] Apparently, these prophecies were known in ancient days. Much of the message has been lost or forgotten, obscured or distorted through time. In days past, it was likely a visual story that was explained by those with knowledge.

In fact, creation scientists have suggested that prior to the

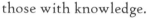

flood, there was a translucent shell that surrounded the earth. It was the firmament above, frozen and compacted water that appeared like translucent beaten metal, called the "riqiya" (ⵔⵣⵯⵠ). This dome would have acted as a negative meniscus lens, and provided the largest viewing screen in the universe. This was a free transmission from the Creator displaying the story of the cosmos provided nightly for all of the inhabitants of the planet.

Surely children would ask their parents what they were watching each night, and the meaning of the story would be transmitted orally throughout the generations. There were always learned men, Melchizedek priests such as Adam and Enoch who could teach the people. While this is my personal opinion, it appears to be a valid understanding, supported by scientific evidence.

We now do not have the benefit of the riqiya, which was destroyed during the judgment involving Noah's flood. The massive amounts of water that came from above were from the shattered riqiya raining down upon the earth. As a result, the mazzaroth likely appeared different, and that is why we cannot always easily discern the shapes they are supposed to represent. We still know their meanings and it is possible to piece together the story that was once clearly displayed for all to see.

The understanding that the mazzaroth displayed a story is confirmed through history and writings. "Cassini refers to Philo for the assertion that 'Terah, the father of Abraham, who lived more that 100 years with Noah, had much studied astronomy, and taught it to Abraham,' who according to Josephus and others, taught it to the Egyptians during his sojourn in that country.

It is well known that the religion of the ancient

Babylonians and contiguous peoples, which consist of the worship of the heavenly bodies, was based on astronomy, astrology, and the starry configurations – so much so that one was an essential part of the other, and the two were really one. But it is now demonstrated, from the recovered remains of these ancient peoples, that the Chaldean religion and mythology were already wrought out in a complete and finished system as early as two thousand years before the beginning of our era, so that a settled astronomical science must necessarily have existed a considerable period prior to that date."[51]

So from the beginning there were signs in the sky for all of mankind to see. This was likely the primary method that YHWH used to communicate His Plan to all of Creation. Some of those declarations are mysteries lost in time and translation, although they were very likely understood by Adam and the generations that followed.

5

Generations

During the early days following creation there was a righteous line of individuals who descended from Adam. We know that a mate was brought forth out of Adam. The first woman was named Hawah, although she is commonly called Eve. She had two sons, the first was named Qayin, commonly called Cain. She had another son Hebel, commonly called Abel. Interestingly, the names of all of these individuals have been altered through translations, tradition and common usage.

Names are extremely important in the Scriptures, because they actually tell a story. For instance, the name Hawah (ᗋᎩᗋ) means: "life giver." The name Qayin (ᎩᏃᎧ) means: "spear" and the name Hebel (ᗱᎩᗋ) means: "emptiness or vanity."

The first time that we see these three names together in the Hebrew text something very interesting occurs. Here is a translation with the names in Hebrew.

"*¹ And Adam knew ᗋᎩᗋ-Ⅹᛕ his wife; and she conceived, and bare ᎩᏃᎧ-Ⅹᛕ, and said, I have gotten a man from ᗋᎩᗋᏃ-Ⅹᛕ. ² And she again bare Ꮓᗋᛕ-Ⅹᛕ (his brother) ᗱᎩᗋ-Ⅹᛕ. And ᗱᎩᗋ-ᏃᗋᏃ was a keeper of sheep, but ᎩᏃᎧ ᗋᏃᗋ was a tiller of the ground.*" Beresheet 4:1-2.

There is a wealth of information found in this passage, but you will glean very little from a translation.

When viewed in the Hebrew, this passage is filled with mysteries. The account begins with Adam having relations with his wife. It only states that Adam "knew" Hawah once – yet she bore two sons. There is a distinct possibility that these sons were twins. We then see the Aleph Taw (𐤗𐤗) associated with the names Hawah, Qayin, Hebel, YHWH and the word "brother." All of these are connected by the Aleph Taw (𐤗𐤗) in the Hebrew text.

We then see 𐤆𐤇𐤆 associated with Hebel, and 𐤇𐤆𐤇 associated with Qayin. Remember that 𐤆𐤇𐤆 was the first word spoken by YHWH when He declared "exist (𐤆𐤇𐤆) light." So Hebel was directly connected with this light that was brought forth from darkness at the beginning. Indeed, it is used repeatedly and continuously as creation is brought forth by the spoken Word of Elohim.

Interestingly, the order of the brothers is reversed when it describes their professions. Essentially, Hebel "creates" through the propagation of living animals, while Qayin "creates" through the propagation of living plants. The seed of life that Hebel was propagating involved blood. The seed of life that Qayin was propagating needed to be planted in the ground. This is a very profound distinction between the two brothers. Another distinction involved their relationship with the Creator.

As we proceed further in the English text we are told of a time when they both appeared to present offerings to YHWH. "³ *And in the process of time it came to pass that Qayin brought an offering of the fruit of the ground to YHWH.* ⁴ *Hebel also brought of the firstborn of his flock and of their fat. And YHWH respected Hebel and his offering, ⁵ but He did not respect Qayin and his offering. And Qayin was very angry, and his countenance fell.*" Beresheet 4:3-5.

We are told how "in the process of time" Qayin brought an offering to YHWH of the fruit of the ground. Hebel also brought the "firstlings" (bikkurim) of his flocks, and the fat thereof. YHWH had "respect" for Hebel and his offering, but YHWH did not have respect for Qayin and his offering. The word for "respect" is "sha'ah" (𐤔𐤏𐤄), and it has to do with "looking or gazing upon." Indeed, we can see the ayin (𐤏) gazing from the midst of the word.

So we can glean from this text that there is a right way to approach YHWH and a wrong way. Interestingly, neither Adam or Hawah are mentioned, but they must have relayed this information to the two brothers who knew to appear at a particular time. In fact, the time was actually known as the "m'qetz yomim" (𐤉𐤅𐤌𐤉𐤌 𐤒𐤑), which literally means the "end of days."

We should all desire to properly bring our offerings before YHWH so that He will look upon us. When He looks upon us He accepts us. Interestingly, when the man and the woman transgressed in the Garden they covered themselves and hid so that YHWH could not look upon them. They disobeyed and were ashamed. The objective then should be to do right.

Qayin surely knew what to do. He appeared at the right time, but it does not record him bringing his "bikkurim" (first fruits). The bikkurim are the best. He also did not offer blood, which seems to be at the heart of the matter.

Remember the lesson of atonement provided in

the Garden as the sins of man and woman were atoned, and they thereafter wore the skin of the animal that shed the blood. They were covered, so YHWH could once again look upon them. Their sin was no longer directly in His face, it was covered by the blood. Sadly, the atonement in the Garden was only temporary. The skins of those animals would eventually wear out and expose the sin that remained beneath them. A permanent atonement was needed to wash away the sin that corrupted mankind, and it could not be accomplished by an animal.

Qayin's failure to bring a blood sacrifice meant that his sins were not atoned. He was wroth after the event, and YHWH told him that if he did well he would be accepted. If he did not do well – offense and punishment would overtake him.

Qayin did not heed the warning. He succumbed to his emotions, and let murder enter into his heart. He thereafter "spoke" to Hebel "his brother." We do not know exactly what he said, and the substance of his conversation will be explored later. For now we know that they both ended up in the field where Qayin then murdered his brother. Throughout the text, Hebel is repeatedly referred to as Qayin's brother. So the emphasis of this story is on the relationship between these two individuals.

In Beresheet 4:8 we read that Qayin talked with his brother and then killed him in the field. In between the account of speaking and killing we read in the Hebrew "exist," "exist," and "arise." This is profound, as it appears to hint of creation and resurrection in the middle of the account of the first murder.

In fact, after Qayin killed his brother, YHWH

indicates to Qayin that He heard the "voice" of his brother's blood. Remember how the Aleph Taw (✗✗) was connected with the "voice" of YHWH Elohim in the Garden.

Here we read that the blood of Hebel had a "voice." There was life in the blood, and the blood cried out - even after Hebel was killed. That blood is also connected with the Aleph Taw (✗✗). In the Hebrew we read "et-dami" (𐤆𐤉𐤃-✗✗). Indeed, the Aleph Taw (✗✗) is filled through the text in this account. (Beresheet 4:11) We are provided with this information because it is a very important pattern for the future.

As with all sin, it has consequences. Qayin's conduct resulted in punishment. "*And now art thou cursed* ✗✗ *from the earth, which hath opened* ✗✗ *her mouth to receive thy brother's blood from thy hand.*" Beresheet 4:11. So Qayin was cursed and Hebel was dead. There did not seem to be much hope for the family of Adam and Hawah. Interestingly, Hebel was later replaced by another son named Seth.

We read about a time when Adam knew Hawah again. "*And Adam knew his* ✗✗-*wife again; and she bare a son, and called his* ✗✗-*name Seth: For Elohim, said she, hath appointed me another seed instead of Hebel, whom Qayin slew.*" Beresheet 4:25. So by his very name we understand that Seth was a substitute for Hebel, and through Seth the righteous line from Adam would continue.

While Adam and Hawah had many children, we are told of a righteous line that descended from Adam through Seth. Tradition holds that these men knew how to discern the signs in the Heavens, and knew their meanings. We do not know exactly when this information was revealed to men. The Book of Enoch

(Henoch) recounts that the Messenger Uriel instructed Henoch in all matters of the stars and the heavenly bodies. So while mankind clearly maintained an oral tradition concerning their history, including the murder of Hebel by Qayin, it is very likely that they could look up in the sky and recount the events and their meaning through the constellation Bethula and the related decans.

That particular constellation tells of a desired son coming forth from a virgin, which could have represented Hawah. The son was then killed by the spear of the half man, half beast, represented by Qayin – the spear. We then see from the decan Bootes that the son would come again through Seth with a sickle and a shepherd's staff.

There are many more levels of interpretation for that constellation including prophetic patterns concerning the promised Messiah. It is important to understand that Adam was alive for 930 years. This would have allowed him to pass on the truths that he had learned in the Garden, and he was alive long enough to ensure that those truths were properly understood for nearly 1,000 years.

We know that oral traditions can often become distorted and changed, but in the case of Adam, the normal rules do not apply due to his longevity. He was around to insure that the truth was retold accurately and anyone could verify history directly from him. Accordingly, we can trace the righteous line from Adam and be confident that they all accurately knew and understood the ways of YHWH.

These men are listed as follows: Adam, Seth, Enosh, Qenan, Mahalaleel, Jered, Henoch, Methuselah, Lamech and Noah. These are all Hebrew names and they each have specific meaning. We already saw the importance of getting names straight. In the Hebrew, this list of names actually provides a prophetic glimpse into the future. As men passed on their lineage, they also passed on truth through the names of their progeny.

The meaning of the names in this lineage is as follows:

1) Adam (𐤌𐤃𐤀) is the combination of the Aleph (𐤀) and blood (𐤌𐤃). The word is literally strength or first blood. The name means: "man."

2) Seth (𐤕𐤔) was the third son of Adam and Hawah. His name literally means "appointed or substituted." He was in place of Hebel.

3) Enosh (𐤔𐤅𐤍𐤀) means: "feeble, frail, mortality." It derives from Hebrew word "anash" (𐤔𐤍𐤀).

4) Qenan (𐤍𐤍𐤉𐤒) means: "a fixed dwelling place."

5) Mahalaleel (𐤋𐤀𐤋𐤋𐤄𐤌) means: "the praised Elohim."

6) Yared (𐤃𐤓𐤉) means "to descend, go down."

7) Henoch (𐤇𐤅𐤍𐤇) comes from the Hebrew word chanak (𐤇𐤍𐤇) which means "to train up or to teach." This man, commonly called Enoch, was taken up by Elohim. So this seventh son is closely associated with Elohim. His name is surrounded by a fence, represented by the het (𐤇).

8) Methuselach (𐤇𐤋𐤔𐤅𐤕𐤌) is a

combination of two roots "muth" which means "his death," and "shelach" which means "send forth." Therefore the name means "his death shall bring forth".

9)   Lamech (ᚺᛦᛚ) means: "brought low or humble." Some also believe that it might derive from the Hebrew word "makah," which means: "a blow, by implication, a wound; figuratively, carnage, also beaten, slaughter, smote, stripe, stroke, wound, wounded."

10)   Noach (ᚺᛦ) means: "to bring rest." Noach obeyed and was protected from judgment. Because of his obedience, and his family's subsequent obedience, they were all delivered through the waters of judgment. Those 8 people in the ark represented the Covenant people dwelling in safety through judgment.

If we translate those names, and the message that they are relating, we are left with an incredible message: "Man is appointed mortality. In a fixed dwelling place (body of flesh) the blessed Elohim comes down to instruct. His death shall bring to the humble rest, (and deliverance through judgment for those in the Covenant family)."

So it appears that there was a truth revealed through creation, which was distorted and confused by certain men. The story was declared in the heavens from the beginning. It was later prophesied in the Garden, and even declared through the righteous genealogy that descended from Adam. The truth was plain for all to see and know. Creation needed to be restored, and YHWH had a plan imbedded within creation.

     As the generations progressing up to Noah would ultimately lead to judgment by a flood, the names of this righteous line provided a plan for restoration. That truth would ultimately become lost after the flood by men who created a false religious system directed away from the Creator, and focused instead on creation. Despite mankind's rebellion, YHWH continued to communicate with those who chose to follow His prescribed path. That path was made clear through covenants.

6

Covenants

Despite the fact that Adam and Hawah were expelled from the Garden, we have seen the truth of Elohim was known by mankind. It was found in the language, and it was declared in the heavens for all to see. The righteous line from Adam described the Plan of YHWH as the generations progressed through time. Further, Adam himself would have acted as a High Priest to his offspring. He was, after all, the head of his tribe - the clan of man.

Adam would have told his children about his time in the Garden, his talks with YHWH as well as the mistakes made, punishments rendered and the solution offered by YHWH. Obviously, man's troubles began with disobedience, so it was important for man to obey and follow the instructions of YHWH. Those instructions would have been transmitted by Adam to his descendants. In fact, it was their failure to obey which led to the flood.

Sadly, the sin of the garden was like a virus that spread throughout the world. Adam was taken from the ground and mankind was intimately tied to the rest of creation. As the sin of man continued, it corrupted all of creation.

It appears that things spiraled when "the sons of

Elohim" began mating with "the daughters of men."

"¹ Now it came to pass, when men began to multiply on the face of the earth, and daughters were born to them, ² that the sons of Elohim saw the ✕✦-daughters of men, that they were beautiful; and they took wives for themselves of all whom they chose. ³ And YHWH said, My Spirit shall not strive with man forever, for he is indeed flesh; yet his days shall be one hundred and twenty years. ⁴ There were giants on the earth in those days, and also afterward, when the sons of Elohim came in to the daughters of men and they bore children to them. Those were the mighty men who were of old, men of renown. ⁵ Then YHWH saw that the wickedness of man was great in the earth, and that every intent of the thoughts of his heart was only evil continually. ⁶ And YHWH was sorry that He had made man on the earth, and He was grieved in His heart. ⁷ So YHWH said, 'I will destroy man whom I have created from the face of the earth, both man and beast, creeping thing and birds of the air, for I am sorry that I have made them.' ⁸ But Noah found grace in the eyes of YHWH."
Beresheet 6:1-8.

There are many who speculate what exactly was happening with the "sons of Elohim." To qualify as a son of Elohim, one must be a directly related to Elohim. The beings known as "angels," or "melachim" (✦ℨ✶✦ℓℓℨ✶) in Hebrew, were direct creations of Elohim. They were the "messengers" of Elohim, and throughout the Scriptures they were often referred to as "sons of

Elohim." The term "sons of Elohim" is "beni ha'Elohim" (𐤁𐤍𐤉-𐤄𐤀𐤋𐤄𐤉𐤌) in Hebrew.

We will look at this in more detail later, but for now it appears that there was cross breeding occurring. The sons of Elohim mating with women resulted in a mutant race of giants, sometimes referred to as Nephilim. These giants were a corruption of YHWH's creation. They were an abomination, and this is why we often read about YHWH instructing His people to completely destroy certain people groups – their DNA was corrupted. Somehow, this abomination transcended past the flood. We can expect to see a resurgence of such genetic issues as we proceed toward the end of the age. (Matthew 24:37, Luke 17:26).

So there is no doubt that mankind was in a fallen state. They no longer dwelled in the House of Elohim, and their actions reflected that fact. The hope was to get mankind reunited and restored, but men could no longer be classified with the sons of Elohim. While Adam was originally created in the image of Elohim, after the fall men were born in the image of Adam. (Beresheet 5:3). So the fallen messengers, called the Watchers or "the fallen ones," were breeding with the "daughters of men" or rather "the daughters of the man" (𐤀𐤕-𐤁𐤍𐤅𐤕 𐤄𐤀𐤃𐤌). Notice the Aleph Taw (𐤀𐤕) affixed to the word translated as "daughters" (𐤁𐤍𐤅𐤕) in Beresheet 6:2. There is a great mystery in this text seen only in the Hebrew.

The perfect order of creation was being polluted, down to the level of genetics. In fact, it appears that there was corruption of the pure genetic coding within creation. This resulted in not only the race of giants, but also other genetic aberrations. (Beresheet 6:4).

Archaeologists routinely discover giant remains throughout the earth, and they attempt to explain this "phenomenon" as related to some disease or defect, such as the pituitary gland.[52]

The appearance of giants was not an isolated phenomenon, and as their numbers increased matters only got worse. Creation was corrupted to such an extent that YHWH was determined to destroy the physical world. Now it is important to realize that man was highly advanced. Indeed there were specialties attached to certain individuals very early on after the creation account. (Beresheet 4:19-22). Adam, himself had been "plugged in" to the Creator while in the Garden. In fact, man was at his pinnacle in the Garden, and has been in a state of decline ever since. That is diametrically opposed to the evolutionary model that portrays man on a path of ascension, rather than decline.

Remember how the message of YHWH was imbedded in the very blood and genetic makeup of man. The cross breeding and resulting abominations were a direct affront to YHWH. It appears though, that not everything was corrupted. There was still an unblemished bloodline in Noah. While some of the preflood myths seem to indicate that there was cross breeding throughout creation, There were also pure bloodlines in certain animals.[53]

We understand that Noah found "grace." This word is "hen" (𐤇𐤍) which is "favor or kindness." Interestingly, from the ancient language we see the het (𐤇) which looks like a fence, and the nun (𐤍) which looks like a "seed." So we can discern that Noah was genetically pure. His seed was protected and untainted. In fact, Noah was described as *"a just man, perfect in his*

generations. Noah walked with Elohim." Beresheet 6:9.

Noah walked with Elohim, which means he obeyed the commandments. The word for "just" is "tsedeek" (𐤒𐤃𐤑) which means: "righteous." The word for "perfect" is "tamayim" (𐤌𐤉𐤌𐤕) which actually means: "without spot or undefiled"

Because of his undefiled condition, Noah was chosen by YHWH to enter into a Covenant relationship. He was told about a covenant that YHWH would establish with him. *"¹⁷ I am going to bring floodwaters on the earth to destroy all life under the heavens, every creature that has the breath of life in it. Everything on earth will perish. ¹⁸ But I will establish* X𐤀 *My Covenant with you, and you will enter the Ark - you and your sons and your wife and your sons' wives with you. ¹⁹ You are to bring into the ark two of all living creatures, male and female, to keep them alive with you. ²⁰ Two of every kind of bird, of every kind of animal and of every kind of creature that moves along the ground will come to you to be kept alive. ²¹ You are to take every kind of food that is to be eaten and store it away as food for you and for them. ²² Noah did everything just as Elohim commanded him."* Beresheet 6:17-22.

Elohim informed Noah that He was going to wipe out life on the planet, but would "establish" His Covenant with Noah. The word "establish" derives from the Hebrew word "quwm" (𐤌𐤒) which means "to stand" or "raise up." In the Hebrew text we see that the Aleph Taw (X𐤀) is an integral element of "establishing" the Covenant which specifically belonged to YHWH. He chose Noah to enter into His Covenant relationship.

As a result, Noah would be saved along with his family and every creature sent to him by YHWH. The rest of existence would be destroyed. At this time certain corrupted species likely became extinct, as can be seen from the fossil record. While this deliverance from destruction was good news for Noah and his family, it was only the beginning of the Covenant process. At that point, it was simply a promise that came with conditions. Noah was required to perform his part - he had to build the vessel of his deliverance, which would protect him from the judgment of YHWH. It was also incumbent upon him to store all of the food required for the Ark's passengers. This was a lot of hard work.

If Noah did not build the Ark, he would have been killed along with the rest of creation. Instead, Noah believed the promise, and his actions were consistent with his belief. Because of the obedience of Noah we see the continuation of man and animals. Noah was, in essence, like Adam. He was the father of all of mankind, and because of his obedience man would continue their physical existence.

When Adam disobeyed, mankind experienced a separation from YHWH and separation from the Tree of Life. The Tree of Life, known as the "etz ha'chaim" (𐤇𐤉𐤉𐤄𐤅 𐤏𐤑), was the life giving source of YHWH on planet Earth. It was located in the Garden, which represented the House of YHWH. As long as man had access to the House, he also had access to the Tree.

The expulsion from the Garden exposed mankind to both physical death and spiritual death. Due to the deterioration of the inhabitants of the planet, YHWH was prepared to wipe them out. Because of the obedience of Noah, mankind would be spared annihilation and all subsequent generations owe their existence to the mercy of YHWH, and the obedience of Noah.

This flies in the face of many in modern Christianity who believe that man bears no responsibility to act in the Covenant relationship. On the contrary, man has often been required to obey. While it was always YHWH Who did the saving, man had to follow instructions to be in the right place at the right time to be saved. This misunderstanding is largely the result of bad translations and doctrines developed from Scriptural texts. As we continue this discussion we will see the enormous role that a proper understanding of texts has on our perception of YHWH and His relationship with mankind. This is why we are evaluating the communication that occurred before the Bible actually came into existence.

Regardless of how you perceive Noah and the flood, there is no way around the fact that it was his conduct – his obedience – which set him apart. Because of his walk, he found favor in the eyes of YHWH, and he and his family would be spared from the flood. Noah was not an arbitrary choice, he was chosen because of his walk. He was chosen to build an Ark – a vessel that would save a portion of creation.

The word "ark" in the Hebrew text is "tebah" (𐤀𐤏𐤕). It is a very curious and unique word, and if you look at most Hebrew dictionaries you will find that the origin of the word is at question. Some actually believe that it is borrowed from Egyptian or Arabic where similar sounding words refer to a "chest" or a "coffin." Essentially the word has been given its meaning from the context of the passage, not necessarily because of the root meaning.

Once again, it is helpful to look at the ancient language, and in the case of "tebah" (𐤀𐤏𐤕) we see the taw (X), the bet (𝟋) and the hey (𝟃). The taw (X) is a mark which means: "covenant." The bet (𝟋) means: "house," and the hey (𝟃) represents a "window."

This word tebah (𝟃𝟋X) seems to be describing much more than a boat, it is pointing us to something deeply significant. A literal definition from the ancient script could mean: "behold the covenant house." It is demonstrating that if we follow the instructions of YHWH, and remain in Covenant with Him, we can enter into His House, where there is protection from the waters of judgment.

There was a window, so this was not a coffin, as many liken the word. In this protected place man could see and be seen – it was a place of safety meant for the living. It was not a place for the dead, it was a place separated and apart from judgment and death. Death was on the outside, and life was on the inside.

After YHWH gave the promise there came a time when He commanded Noah to actually build the Ark. According to the Dead Sea Scrolls Noah was told by a messenger that a flood would occur after a certain number of Shemitah cycles. Most people are unfamiliar with the concept of Shemitah cycles, but it is a most important pattern established on the first week of creation – the pattern of sevens. In the case of the Shemitah cycle, it is a pattern of seven years.

Every seventh year in the count is a Shemitah year which, essentially is a Sabbath year – a year of rest. These Shemitah years are then counted seven times and after the seventh Shemitah year is a Jubilee year. This is how the Creator gauges time, and it is this calculation of time that is imbedded within the Covenant relationship with YHWH.

Therefore, every Jubilee cycle contains seven Shemitah Cycles each consisting of seven years. The seven Shemitah cycles, totaling 49 years, are followed by one Jubilee Year. These 50 years form a Jubilee cycle. You might be wondering why this is important when talking about the story of the flood. The reason why it is mentioned here is because, according to the Dead Sea Scrolls 1 QapGen Col. 6, the flood was to occur in the year that followed a Shemitah cycle.[54]

This would have either been Year 1 of a new Shemitah cycle or a Jubilee Year. The point is that YHWH had Noah counting Shemitah cycles. The importance of the Shemitah count is extremely significant when examining time and creation.[55]

In fact, through this system of reckoning time it was actually revealed how much time man would be given on Earth. The Scriptures record that when YHWH saw the condition of things He declared: *"My Spirit shall not strive with man forever, for he is indeed flesh; yet his days shall be one hundred and twenty (120) years."* Beresheet 6:3.

Many believe that YHWH was giving a limit to the number of years that individual men would be allowed to live, but that is clearly not the context nor is it true since men were recorded as living far longer than 120 years after that declaration. YHWH was speaking of mankind and indicated that he was not going to allow their existence to continue forever.

Clearly men were rebellious, and YHWH was not going to contend with them forever. He was establishing a limit, and it would be within that period of time He would gather His chosen into His Kingdom through His Covenant. The 120 "years" that YHWH was referring to are actually 120 "cycles" – more specifically – Jubilee Cycles. Since a Jubilee Cycle is 50 years we can discern that YHWH was giving mankind 6,000 years. So this finite universe was given an expiration date when man's reign on earth would end. According to the pattern of the week, YHWH was giving man six "days" that would be followed by a Sabbath "day" or rather millennium.

This pattern was, of course, established during the first week of creation. As a result, many understand that YHWH would allow men 6,000 years until He would establish His Sabbath reign – the millennial Kingdom. For the time being, He was going to allow them to continue, but He would start over with a righteous man and his seed.

The Scriptures record that: "*Noah did everything just as Elohim commanded him.*" Beresheet 6:22. As a result, the Ark was ready to deliver him and his family when the flood waters came. "*¹ YHWH then said to Noah, 'Go into the Ark, you and your whole family, because I have found you righteous in this generation. ² Take with you seven (7) of every kind of clean animal, a male and its mate, and two (2) of every kind of unclean animal, a male and its mate, ³ and also seven (7) of every kind of bird, male and female, to keep their*

various kinds alive throughout the earth. ⁴ Seven (7) days from now I will send rain on the earth for forty (40) days and forty (40) nights, and I will wipe from the face of the earth every living creature I have made." Beresheet 7:1-4.

The Scriptures then specifically report the fact that: "*Noah did all that YHWH commanded him.*" Beresheet

7:5. The point is quite clear, Noah obeyed the instructions of YHWH. Notice that Noah was commanded to take seven (7) pairs of clean animals. Previously we read about two (2) of each animal and now we read about seven (7) clean animals. It is important to understand that there is, and always was, a distinction between clean and unclean, righteousness and sin. We currently find those distinctions written as instructions within the Torah, but they were always present in creation.[56]

Clearly, Noah knew those distinctions, and we already discussed that he was literally described as "righteous" and "clean." The instructions of YHWH were no doubt handed down by Adam although, by this time, very few were actually following them.

Aside from these distinctions, it is also interesting to look at the significance of numbers in the text. Numbers are very prominent in the account of the flood. We know that Noah was six hundred (600) years old when the floodwaters came. The number six (6) is closely tied with man, since man was created on Day 6. Six thousand (6,000) is the number of years given to man.

The floodwaters did indeed come and wiped out all men, animals and mutant beings. All were destroyed except for those in the Covenant House – the Ark. When the floodwaters receded, it was time for a new beginning.

Interestingly, YHWH protected those in the Ark, and He also replanted plants and trees. In fact, the olive tree was the first tree mentioned in this renewed creation. As a result, the olive tree actually represents the "firsts" or "beginnings" (resheet) of YHWH, as we shall later see with Yisrael. When Noah exited the Ark, we read that he and his sons entered into a Covenant with YHWH. Blood was shed as Noah, acting as a mediator for all of mankind, made an altar and made sacrifice unto YHWH.

"*8 Then Elohim spoke to Noah and to his sons with him, saying: 9 And as for Me, behold, I establish My Covenant with you and with your descendants after you, 10 and with every living creature that is with you: the birds, the cattle, and every beast of the earth with you, of all that go out of the ark, every beast of the earth. 11 Thus I establish My Covenant with you: Never again shall all flesh be cut off by the waters of the flood; never again shall there be a flood to destroy the earth. 12 And Elohim said: This is the sign of the Covenant which I make between Me and you, and every living creature that is with you, for perpetual generations: 13 I set My rainbow in the cloud, and it shall be for the sign of the Covenant between Me and the earth. 14 It shall be, when I bring a cloud over the earth, that the rainbow shall be seen in the cloud; 15 and I will remember My Covenant which is between Me and you and every living creature of all flesh; the waters shall never again become a flood to destroy all flesh. 16 The rainbow shall be in the cloud, and I will look on it to remember the everlasting Covenant between Elohim and every living creature of all flesh that is on the earth. 17 And Elohim said to Noah, This is the sign of the Covenant which I have established between Me and all flesh that is on the earth." Beresheet 9:8-17.*

Notice that YHWH repeatedly refers to the Covenant as "My Covenant." In other words, it belongs to Him and no one else. This Covenant is an everlasting Covenant. The word "everlasting" is "olam" (𐤏𐤋𐤌) in Hebrew and actually refers to something hidden or

concealed. It is generally understood to mean "through the ages." It went beyond the life of Noah, or his immediate descendants for that matter. YHWH promised that He would never again cut off all flesh by a flood, and never again would He use a flood to destroy the whole earth.

There was no corresponding duty or obligation required from man or the animals. The Covenant was a promise accompanied by a sign – the bow. So the ultimate blessing associated with this Covenant was unconditional. There was no further obligation from mankind. Noah had done the work to get them to the point of the Covenant. He had paid the price, and now the rest of mankind and creation would reap the reward – the sakar. We see the pattern of a "clean" and "righteous" man working in collaboration with YHWH to save. Their work would benefit others who would follow in the Covenant.

The fact that there was a sign attached to the Covenant is significant. Remember that the Hebrew word for sign is owt (✗Υ𐤊). It can mean a "mark" or a

"token" and is intended to be a visible sign or reminder of the Covenant, just like the sun, the moon and the stars were meant for signs. We shall see that YHWH attaches these marks or signs to His Covenants. In the case of the Covenant with Noah and all creation, we see the bow as the sign of that particular Covenant. It was a sign placed in the sky visible to all creation.

The word for bow in Hebrew is qesheth (✗W𐤒).

One cannot help but see the relationship between the first sliver of a renewed moon, which marks the beginning of a month, and the rainbow, which is also a sliver of light. Instead of a new month, YHWH was revealing a new age.[57]

It is interesting that the light of the qesheth consists of seven colors. These seven colors correlate to the seven ages, or days, in the weekly plan of YHWH. They also correlate to the seven Spirits described by the Prophet Isaiah (Yeshayahu)[58] which are represented in the menorah.

In addition, from Elohim's perspective in the heavens, the bow was held backward, an ancient sign by which warriors often indicated that a battle was over.[59] We can still see the bow to this day. It is a reminder of His Covenant, which is essentially a demonstration of His mercy and restraint.

While we continue to see floods on the earth, we have never seen the entire planet judged by water since the time of Noah – a promise kept. The earth is full of sin that cries out for judgment. This cry is heard in the Throne Room of YHWH, which is colored by the sign of the promise as a continual reminder. As a result, YHWH remembers His Covenant and keeps His promise by not judging the earth by a flood.

There is a pattern established here. As YHWH makes Covenant with His creation, He uses a man as the mediator. In this instance, Noah represented mankind and creation. Part of this Covenant process also involved the shedding of blood.

The Scriptures record: *"[20] Noah built an altar to YHWH, and took of every clean animal and of every clean bird, and offered burnt offerings on the altar. [21] And smelled*

YHWH ✕𐤊 *a soothing aroma. Then YHWH said in His heart, 'I will never again curse* ✕𐤊 *the ground for man's sake, although the imagination of man's heart is evil from his youth; nor will I again destroy* ✕𐤊 *every living thing as I have done.'*" Beresheet 8:20-21.

Noah had already been saved, but the future promise was sealed by the shedding of the blood. So the Covenant with Noah was essentially two fold. First, Noah had to obey and act in faith in order to be in a place where he and his family, along with the animals, could be saved. Second, YHWH promised that He would never again destroy the planet by a flood.

This was an everlasting Covenant made for all of mankind as Elohim had done with Adam, except that this Covenant was unconditional. It is a unilateral Covenant made between YHWH and mankind. Only YHWH has to keep the Covenant, and He gave a continuing sign of this Covenant for all future generations to see.

Man could not save himself from judgment, and the only way to life was through obedience. Ultimately, it was YHWH Who provided the salvation. To emphasize this point, there are three instances of the untranslated Aleph Taw (✕𐤊) in Beresheet 8:21 when the burnt offerings were being made to YHWH. There are also three instances of the Aleph Taw (✕𐤊) when YHWH declares that He will make a Covenant. (Beresheet 9:9-10). So we can see that the Aleph Taw (✕𐤊) would be at the center of the salvation and restoration of Creation through a Covenant with YHWH.

YHWH did not have to enter into this Covenant with man. He could have easily stated "If you continue to sin I will flood the planet again until you learn your lesson." On the contrary, He unilaterally stated that He would never do such a thing again. This is very telling.

It must have grieved the Creator to destroy His creation through the flood. As bad as things had deteriorated, it was still His creation. It was a very difficult decision, and He waited a long time before He finally rendered judgment, which demonstrates His patience. The fact that He made this Covenant with man immediately after the judgment by water is a demonstration that YHWH is a merciful Elohim. He made this Covenant as part of His plan to restore His creation, which reveals His mercy and love.

When Adam and Hawah transgressed His commandments, YHWH could have just killed them and scrapped all of creation. Likewise when the planet was corrupted during the age of Noah, He could have simply destroyed everything and started over. Instead, He continued to work with certain men to bring about a restoration.

This is the repeating theme that we shall see as we examine the Scriptures - the Covenants are specifically designed to bring about the restoration of all things. YHWH always preserves a righteous line through which He operates His Covenant promises. Thanks to the mercy of the Almighty and the obedience of Noah we are alive today to participate in this process.

Sadly, it did not take long for corruption to infiltrate mankind, and men eventually rebelled against YHWH. Men began to worship creation and developed a form of worship in Babylon commonly called "sun worship." This was at the center of the Tower of Babel incident. (Beresheet 11). Men had developed a form of

worship that was contrary to the ways of YHWH. They distorted the meanings of the Mazzaroth

As a result of man's rebellion, the languages were confused. Man was no longer united, but now essentially the earth was divided into different nations and tongues. It is also speculated that this was when the seven continents were actually separated from one unified land mass.[60]

Prior to Babel, all of mankind spoke one language, and that language was Hebrew. As with the genealogy from Adam to Noah, there was a righteous line continuing from Noah that walked according to the ways of YHWH. That line descended through Shem for another ten (10) generations until the Covenant was developed and revealed through the life of a man named Abram.

As we read about Abram, the son of Terah, we see a man born into Babylon, the origin of rebellious and adulterous religions acting contrary to the ways of YHWH. Abram was called out of Babylon, out of his pagan surroundings, and promised land for his descendants. So from Noah we saw the Covenant providing deliverance and protection from judgment and death. Now through Abram we see a Covenant family being established. A family that would grow into nations.

We can read in the Scriptures that YHWH spoke to Abram, and Abram actually tithed to Melchizedek - the righteous king of Jerusalem. We do not know for certain whether there were written texts at the time of Abram describing the plan of YHWH. There were the signs in the heavens, which were built into creation. This is likely why, after Abram met with Melchizedek, the

Word of YHWH appeared to him in a vision. He brought Abram outside and told him to look at the heavens.

Here is what we read in English: *"Then He brought him outside and said, 'Look now toward heaven, and count the stars if you are able to number them.' And He said to him, 'So shall your descendants be.'"* Beresheet 15:5. Interestingly, in the Hebrew, Abram was told to "sepher" (ꭏꞁꚍ) the stars if he is able to "sepher" (ꭏꞁꚍ) them (ꚍꭓꚃ). The word "sepher" (ꭏꞁꚍ) means: "to mark, to record, to inscribe."

In fact, a scroll is referred to as a "sepher." It is the same word as used in the passage, and it implies something written down. The heavens are the scroll of YHWH, and He has written His Words in the sky. Abram was essentially being told that the story written on that heavenly scroll would be the story of his seed. Abram believed what he read and what he heard, and it was counted as righteousness. (Beresheet 15:6). But we are getting ahead of ourselves.

As YHWH entered into a Covenant relationship with Abram, we see that the life of this man is very instructive, and provided a prophetic pattern of the Covenant walk. So let us examine it from the beginning.

When Abram was in Babylon he was immersed in a pagan system. YHWH spoke to Abram and told him: *"Get out of your country, from your family and from your father's house."* (Beresheet 12:1). A person who desires to be in Covenant with YHWH must "come out of Babylon" and "cross over." The word for "cross over" is "eber" (ꭏꝪꙨ), and it is the source for the word "Hebrew." A Hebrew is one who comes out of Babylon and crosses over.

Once Abram fully obeyed and entered into the Land of Canaan at Shechem we read: *"Then YHWH appeared to Abram and said 'To your descendants I will give this land.' And there he built an altar to YHWH, Who appeared to him."* Beresheet 12:7.

The building of an altar is significant. Blood was shed and, as with Noah, the promise made by YHWH was sealed with blood. Abram then moved to the mountain east of Bethel and west of Ai. Bethel means "House of El" and Ai means: "ruinous heap." Actually, while the English text seems to refer to Ai as a city, the Hebrew refers to ha'Ai, "the heap."

So Abram had a promise of Land, but it was not immediate. He had left his fathers house in the east, and was headed to the House of El in the west. He was now residing between the heap, which represented the Babylon where he had come out of. He was on his way to the House of El, but the journey was not complete. He was at the place of the altar. He was still "east of Eden" so to speak. The symbolism of the geography is incredible. So it is clear that the physical locations where Abram pitched his tent had significance.

There was a famine in the land and Abram moved to Egypt. During his time in Egypt, his bride was taken captive by Pharaoh. A series of plagues upon the Pharaoh led to the release of his bride, and Abram was provided great wealth when he departed Egypt. He left Egypt very rich, and he also left with a woman named Hagar. Her name is literally ha'ger (אֵגֵר) in Hebrew which means: "the stranger."

So we see Abram depart Egypt with his freed bride and another woman. This stranger became part of his family, and would also become his bride. This event has profound prophetic symbolism relative to his Covenant seed who would later become enslaved in Egypt.

After exiting Egypt, something very interesting occurs. We read in English the following account: "*³ And he went on his journey from the South as far as ◁⊙-Bethel, to the place where his tent had been at the beginning, between Bethel and Ai, ⁴ to the place of the altar which he had made there at first. And there Abram called on the name of YHWH.*" Beresheet 13:3-4.

In the Hebrew text there is much more going on. For instance, Abram placed his tent where it had been "in the beginning." This was a return, which is "shuwb" (𐤔𐤅𐤁) in Hebrew. The cycle was complete, and Egypt was an important part of the cycle.

Abram returned to the place of the altar between Bethel and ha'Ai, between the House of El and "the heap." Only now something was different. In the Hebrew we see a very interesting distinction. We see an "ad" (◁⊙) attached to the House of El and "the place." The "ad" (◁⊙) was not present during the previous mention, but after the return from Egypt we see: 𐤌𐤅𐤐𐤌-◁⊙ 𐤋𐤊-𐤗𐤉𐤁-◁𐤊.

Now one might justify a grammatical reason why the ad (◁⊙) is attached to this word here, but the application would not be consistent with the previous portion. The "ad" (◁⊙) consists of an ayin (⊙) which is an "eye" and means "see." The dalet (◁) is a "door" So the Ayin Dalet (◁⊙) is telling us – "see the door." At this place, east of the House and west of the heap. At the place of the altar, the place of the beginning, at the completion of the cycle – see the door.

We also see the word shem (𐤔𐤌) four times in

the text. Now shem (**ᵞW**) commonly means: "name," but only once in the text is the word translated as "name" - when Abram called on the Name of YHWH. In all the other instances it is translated as "there," but when you read the Hebrew there is no doubt that there is an emphasis on the Name, and it was also emphasized to "see the door."

It was at this point in the journey that Abram had to separate from Lot. It appeared from the beginning that Abram was to completely separate from his family, but Lot had been with him thus far. Once the separation was completed YHWH was ready to continue the Covenant journey with Abram.

"*[14] And YHWH said to Abram, after Lot had separated from him: 'Lift your eyes now and look from the place where you are: northward, southward, eastward, and westward; [15] for* ✗𝄐*-all-the land which you see I give to you and your descendants forever. [16] And I will make your* ✗𝄐*-descendants (seed) as the dust of the earth; so that if a man could number* ✗𝄐*-the dust of the earth, then your descendants also could be numbered. [17] Arise, walk in the land through its length and its width, for I give it to you.' [18] Then Abram moved his tent, and went and dwelt by the terebinth trees of Mamre, which are in Hebron, and built an altar there to YHWH.*" Beresheet 13:14-18.

So we read that YHWH was starting to get more specific about the land that would be given. The descendants of Abram would be very numerous – like the dust of the earth. Abram then set out to walk the boundaries of the land and eventually settled in Hebron. Interestingly, the root of Hebron is eber (**ᴿ𝄐𝄐**). It means: "cross over, beyond, on the other side." It is the same root as the word for Hebrew, and Abram became known as a Hebrew because of how he lived and where he dwelled – Hebron. (see Beresheet 14:13). Specifically, he dwelled by the terebinth trees of Mamre, the Amorite.

There came a time, after Abram and Lot separated, that Lot was taken captive after certain local kings were defeated in the Valley of Sodom. Abram actually had an army consisting of 318 trained fighting men. These were not mercenaries, they were born in his house. As a result, he was able to hunt down the captors and retrieve Lot, along with the plunder taken from the local kings. So Abram was a travelling nation with a standing army, more powerful than the people he dwelled amongst.

After his return, we read about one of the most mysterious events in the Scriptures as Abram meets Melchizedek. *"18 Then Melchizedek king of Salem brought out bread and wine; he was the priest of Elohim Most High. 19 And he blessed him and said: 'Blessed be Abram of El Most High, Possessor of heaven and earth; 20 And blessed be El Most High, Who has delivered your enemies into your hand.' And he gave him a tithe of all."* Beresheet 14:18-20.

This is the only direct mention of the mysterious Melchizedek in the Hebrew Scriptures, except for Psalms 110:4. The word melchizedek means: "righteous king." This was a priest and a king and was a hint to a future righteous priestly king from Jerusalem – the Messiah.

"After these things the Word of YHWH came to Abram in a vision, saying, Do not be afraid, Abram. I am your shield, your exceedingly great reward." Beresheet 15:1. This is quite an interesting passage, because we assume the Word of YHWH, Debar-YHWH (𐤉𐤄𐤅𐤄-𐤓𐤁𐤃), was something audible. From the text we see that it is

connected to YHWH. We know that YHWH previously spoke to Abram, but now we have the Word of YHWH speaking "in a vision."

The word for "vision" is "machazah" (𐤀𐤆𐤇𐤌), and can mean "vision" or "light." It is something gazed at, seen and perceived. So this "Word" was something audible and visible. This has always been something of a mystery and as previously mentioned, the Aramaic Targums refer to the Memra of YHWH. So it has been understood that The Word, or the Memra, was a special and unique manifestation of YHWH. We will be exploring this further in the discussion.

After he was given this promise, Abram was concerned because he had no child. He did not understand how his heirs would inherit the land if he had no children. He thought that maybe his servant Eliezer would be his heir. Here is the response that he received:

"*⁴ And behold, the Word of YHWH came to him, saying, 'This one shall not be your heir, but one who will come from your own body shall be your heir.' ⁵ Then He brought him outside and said, 'Look now toward heaven, and sepher the stars if you are able to sepher them.' And He said to him, 'So shall your descendants be.' ⁶ And he believed in YHWH, and He accounted it to him for righteousness. ⁷ Then He said to him, 'I am YHWH, who brought you out of Ur of the Chaldeans, to give you this land to inherit it.' ⁸ And he said, 'Master YHWH, how shall I know that I will inherit it?' ⁹ So He said to him, 'Bring Me a three-year-old heifer, a three-year-old female goat, a three-year-old ram, a turtledove, and a* young pigeon.' *¹⁰ Then he brought all these to Him and cut them in two, down the middle, and placed each piece opposite the other; but he did not cut the birds in two. ¹¹ And when the vultures came down on the carcasses, Abram drove them away. ¹² Now when the sun was going down, a deep sleep fell upon Abram; and behold, horror and great darkness fell upon him. ¹³ Then He said to Abram: 'Know certainly that your descendants will be strangers in a land that is not theirs, and will serve them, and they will afflict them four hundred years. ¹⁴ And also the nation whom they serve I will judge; afterward they shall come out with great possessions. ¹⁵ Now as for you, you shall go to your fathers in peace; you shall be buried at a good old age. ¹⁶ But in the fourth generation they shall return here, for the iniquity of the Amorites is not yet complete.' ¹⁷ And it came to pass, when the sun went down and it was dark, that behold, there appeared a smoking oven and a fire (esh) torch that passed between those pieces. ¹⁸ On the same day YHWH made a Covenant with Abram, saying: 'To your descendants I have given this land, from the river of Egypt to the great river, the River Euphrates - ¹⁹ the Kenites, the Kenezzites, the Kadmonites, ²⁰ the Hittites, the Perizzites, the Rephaim, ²¹ the Amorites, the Canaanites, the Girgashites, and the Jebusites." Beresheet 15:4-21.*

One cannot help but recognize the emphasis placed on this passage. Here the Word of YHWH

(𐤉𐤅𐤄𐤆-𐤄𐤁𐤃) was speaking to Abram, but now we are instructed to "behold." There was a promise found in the stars in the heavens. Abram believed this promise and YHWH accounted it to him as righteousness. We also see a great promise of land with very specific and large boundaries - from the Nile River to the Euphrates River.

This promise was sealed in and through a Covenant. What makes this Covenant unique was that it was unconditional and unilateral. In other words, after expressing belief and making the preparations for the Covenant, Abram was not an active participant in the actual covenant ceremony. Just as with Noah, an active faith was required, while YHWH actually fulfilled the Promise of the Covenant.

Typically, in a blood covenant, both parties would walk through the blood of the slaughtered pieces, symbolizing the penalty associated with breaking the covenant. In this case there were three animals divided in two, and two birds that were not divided. So there was blood shed from five animals. These would be the clean animals used later in the Temple. Three of them were divided in half and the birds were set opposite each other, which amounted to eight pieces total.

The number eight is extremely significant in this covenant relationship. It is the equivalent of the het (𐤇) which again, looks like an untwisted DNA strand. This Covenant is all about repairing our DNA so we can get back into the family of YHWH and into His House.

When you combine five and eight you get thirteen. Thirteen is actually the gematria for the word "echad" (𐤃𐤇𐤀) - one. The first time we saw this word was when the night and the day were unified and became one (◁日⟨). This Covenant event was taking place at the exact time that the day and night were unified - often called "twilight" or "between the evenings." This is evident from the time described between Beresheet 15:12, when the sun was going down, to Beresheet 15:17 when the sun went down and it was dark. This has always been an important time in the Covenant process, as we will later see with the Passover. The other connecting point, known as "the dawning of the day" is also important.

This was a very traumatic event for Abram. He was in a "deep sleep" (tardemah), the same condition as Adam when Hawah was taken from him. He experienced "horror" and "great darkness." It sounds like he died and went to Sheol or Gehenom – Hell.

Of important note was the fact that Abram did not walk between the pieces and through the blood. This was, after all, a blood covenant. Instead, only the "smoking oven and fire torch" passed through. This is another mystery imbedded within the Covenant, revealed as YHWH led the Children of Yisrael by day with a pillar of smoke and at night with a pillar of fire. The smoke and the fire in the Covenant represented the One Who watches over and leads Yisrael, the children of the Covenant. Also, neither Abram nor his descendants were subject to any penalty for breaking this Covenant, only the One Who passed through the pieces.

When Abram was 86 years old he had a son named Yishmael through Hagar. While it appeared that the promise would flow through Yishmael, YHWH had chosen the womb of Sarai for the seed to be planted. The promised son would come through her, thirteen years later.

"*¹ When Abram was ninety-nine years old, YHWH appeared to Abram and said to him, 'I am Almighty Elohim; walk before Me and be blameless. ² And I will make My Covenant between Me and you, and will multiply you exceedingly.' ³ Then Abram fell on his face, and* ✕𐤊 *Elohim talked with him, saying: ⁴ 'As for Me, behold, My Covenant is with you, and you shall be a father of many nations. ⁵ No longer shall your* ✕𐤊-*name be called Abram, but* 𐤀𐤆𐤀 *your name shall be Abraham; for I have made you a* 𐤆𐤉 *father of many nations. ⁶ I will make you exceedingly fruitful; and I will make nations of you, and kings shall come from you. ⁷ And I will establish My* ✕𐤊-*Covenant between Me and you and your descendants after you in their generations, for an everlasting Covenant, to be Elohim to you and your descendants after you. ⁸ Also I give to you and your descendants after you* ✕𐤊 *the land in which you are a stranger* ✕𐤊 *all the land of Canaan, as an everlasting possession; and I will be their Elohim.' ⁹ And Elohim said to Abraham: 'As for you, you shall keep* ✕𐤊 *My Covenant, you and your descendants after you throughout their generations. ¹⁰ This is My Covenant which you shall keep, between Me and you and your descendants after you: Every male child among you shall be circumcised; ¹¹ and you shall be circumcised* ✕𐤊 *in the flesh of your foreskins, and it shall be a sign of the Covenant between Me and you. ¹² He who is eight days old among you shall be circumcised, every male*

child in your generations, he who is born in your house or bought with money from any foreigner who is not your descendant. *¹³ He who is born in your house and he who is bought with your money must be circumcised, and My Covenant shall be in your flesh for an everlasting Covenant. ¹⁴ And the uncircumcised male child, who is not circumcised in the flesh of his foreskin, that person shall be cut off from his people; he has broken My Covenant.' ¹⁵ Then Elohim said to Abraham, 'As for Sarai your wife, you shall not call her ✕✦-name Sarai, but Sarah shall be her name. ¹⁶ And I will bless her and also give you a son by her; then I will bless her, and she shall be a mother of nations; kings of peoples shall be from her.' ¹⁷ Then Abraham fell on his face and laughed, and said in his heart, 'Shall a child be born to a man who is one hundred years old? And shall Sarah, who is ninety years old, bear a child?' ¹⁸ And Abraham said to Elohim, 'Oh, that Yishmael might live before You!' ¹⁹ Then Elohim said: 'No, Sarah your wife shall bear you a son, and you shall call his name Isaac (Yitshaq); I will establish My Covenant with him for an everlasting covenant, and with his descendants after him. ²⁰ And as for Yishmael, I have heard you. Behold, I have blessed him, and will make him fruitful, and will multiply him exceedingly. He shall beget twelve princes, and I will make him a great nation. ²¹ But My ✕✦-Covenant I will establish with ✕✦-Isaac (Yitshaq), whom Sarah shall bear to you at the Appointed Time*

(moad) next year.' ²² Then He finished talking with him, and Elohim went up from Abraham. ²³ So Abraham took Yishmael his son, all who were born in his house and all who were bought with his money, every male among the men of Abraham's house, and circumcised the flesh of their foreskins that very same day, as Elohim had said to him. ²⁴ Abraham was ninety-nine years old when he was circumcised in the flesh of his foreskin. ²⁵ And Yishmael his son was thirteen years old when he was circumcised in the flesh of his foreskin. ²⁶ That very same day Abraham was circumcised, and his son Yishmael; ²⁷ and all the men of his house, born in the house or bought with money from a foreigner, were circumcised with him." Beresheet 17:1-27.

Notice that the names of both individuals were changed. Abram's name was changed to Abraham. Sarai's name was changed to Sarah. Each name had a "hey" (𐤄) added. The "hey" (𐤄) represents a person with their arms upstretched. It literally means: "behold." Notice also the presence of the Aleph Taw (𐤕𐤀) when referencing that they would receive these new names.

From this event we see something marvelous resulting from the union of Abraham and Sarah. The hey (𐤄) also represents "breath" or "spirit," and it is believed that this was similar to the creation of Adam and Hawah. Remember that Elohim breathed life into the man. Elohim made man in His image and called him "et-haAdam" (𐤅𐤃𐤀𐤄-𐤕𐤀). (Beresheet 1:27). When Elohim took the "rib" from the man to create the woman, he took "et-hatzela" (𐤏𐤋𐤑𐤄-𐤕𐤀).

So, Adam and Hawah both originally contained the Aleph Taw (𝗫𝗞). It was imprinted into their very beings – their DNA. When they fell, their DNA was corrupted. Through the Covenant process we see Abraham and Sarah becoming new creations for the purpose of bearing the promised son of the Covenant. That is why the passage clearly attaches the Aleph Taw (𝗫𝗞) to Yitshaq.

Through the Covenant man would be restored to the Image of Elohim. Through the Aleph Taw (𝗫𝗞) their DNA would be restored. That is why the Covenant was in the flesh and marked by the shedding of blood on the male organ – the conduit for the seed. The shedding of blood occurred on the eighth day, and we again see the het (𝗛), the DNA, being emphasized. So the plans and purposes of YHWH point to the union of two becoming one - echad. Through this physical and spiritual union the Covenant is established. The Covenant between Elohim and man is, after all, a Marriage Covenant.

This was a prophetic event, and it had as much to do with the spiritual as it did the physical. It was very much about his seed - the descendants of promise. As we saw the Aleph Taw (𝗫𝗞) repeatedly included in the text we recognize that this is not just about Yitshaq. In fact, only some of the instances of the Aleph Taw (𝗫𝗞) are displayed above, there are many others in the text. We see the Covenant of Circumcision wherein the seed of the man passes through the cutting of the Covenant on his body, just as the smoke and the fire torch passed through the cuttings.

Circumcision is a sign of the Covenant. Both the act of circumcising the male child on the eighth day, and the subsequent mark are the sign. It is a visible act, and a

visible mark. Both are meant to be seen. While many cultures circumcise their children, only those in Covenant with YHWH specifically circumcise on the eighth day. Again, the number eight is an important part of the Covenant and it is related to a special Appointed Time that occurs on the eighth day, known as Shemini Atzeret.[61]

The text literally reads that you will "*cut off* ✕𐤊 *the flesh of the foreskin.*" The Hebrew word for "circumcise" is "muyl" (𐤋𐤖), and it involves removing the covering of flesh from a male organ. The removed flesh forms a circle, and one cannot ignore the similarity with the crescent moon and rainbow. All of these signs are circular, and remember the connection between light and blood. So the sign of circumcision is made in the Children of Light, the children of the Covenant. Therefore, circumcision is a visible sign of light. It also speaks to another spiritual circumcision, the circumcision of the heart. The heart is the major organ that transmits the blood through the body. Again, the Covenant is intimately involved with the blood.

Abraham and all of the males in his household were immediately circumcised. They had to bear the sign of the Covenant if they were to dwell in the midst of a Covenant people.

We later read of a time when YHWH came to visit Abraham while he was residing in Hebron. "*¹ Then YHWH appeared to him by the terebinth trees of Mamre, as he was sitting in the tent door in the heat of the day. ² So he lifted his eyes and looked, and behold, three men were standing by him; and when he saw them, he ran from the tent door to meet them, and bowed himself to the ground . . .*" Beresheet 18:1-2.

Abraham entices YHWH and His companions to stop and rest. He offers "a little water" and "a morsel of bread." He ends up preparing a small feast. YHWH actually sits down and has a meal with Abraham. During the course of their time together YHWH informed Abraham ". . . *at the Appointed Time I will return to you, according to the time of life, and Sarah shall have a son.*" Beresheet 18:14. YHWH then allowed Abraham to negotiate regarding the impending punishment to be rendered upon Sodom.

After the destruction of the cities on the plain Abraham moved South to Gerar, between Kadesh and Shur. Here again we see him dwelling between two places, and one should expect to find special meaning. Typically, if you only read the text in English you will not see the underlying message contained in the passage. This is how the Hebrew Scriptures describe the two locations: "bein-qadesh v'bein shur" (ᕴYW 𐤉ᙆ𐤉Y Wᐊ𐤘-𐤉ᙆᕼ). Interestingly there is a "bein" (𐤉ᙆᕼ) at each location, which translates as "perceive." So we are directed in the Hebrew to perceive something.

The question is: What are we supposed to perceive? The circumcised Abraham moved in between Qadesh, which essentially means "holy, set apart" and Shur, which means "journey." The life of Abraham was a pattern for the Covenant path. His life, therefore, was a holy, or rather, set apart journey that all in the Covenant can follow.

In the midst of this "set apart journey" we are told that Abraham lived in a place called Gerar, which derives from the word "stranger" - ger (ᕴᐟ). Remember the name of his wife Hager – the ger. "Gerar" means: "to pull or drag away, as in fish in a net." The significance is

profound when we consider the journey of the Covenant, and perceive that the promises of Abraham and Sarah involved their offspring becoming kings and royalty.

The plan was to draw together the chosen people from around the world, like fish in a net, into the kingdom. These people would be apparent "strangers" engrafted and joined into the Covenant. This is clear when we read the prophets such as Jeremiah (Yirmeyahu)[62] who later proclaimed: "*Behold I will send for many fishermen, says YHWH, and they shall fish them . . .*" (Yirmeyahu 16:16). We also know that the Messiah sought out "fishers of men" in furtherance of this prophecy.

While in Gerar we read about another Egypt-like experience involving Abimelech, the King of Gerar. Abimelech means: "father of the King" and like Pharaoh, he took Sarah. Abimelech was told that Sarah was Abraham's sister, which was a half truth. YHWH protected Sarah and cursed Abimelech who eventually released her and blessed Abraham. He sarcastically rebuked Sarah by proclaiming "*Behold I have given your brother a thousand pieces of silver.*" Beresheet 20:16.

These stories are encouraging because they reveal the imperfections of the patriarchs and matriarchs of the faith. They reveal that YHWH remains faithful to his promises even when we make unwise decisions and lack the requisite faith.

We later read how YHWH appeared to Sarah. "*[1] And YHWH visited* ✗✗*-Sarah as He had said, and YHWH did for Sarah as He had spoken. [2] For Sarah conceived and bore Abraham a son in his old age, at the Appointed Time of which Elohim had spoken to him. [3] And Abraham called* ✗✗*-the name of his son who was born to him*

- *whom Sarah bore to him - Yitshaq.* ⁴ *Then Abraham circumcised his son* X𝋔-*Yitshaq when he was eight days old, as Elohim had commanded him.*" Beresheet 21:1-4.

In the Hebrew we see an emphasis on the Aleph Taw (X𝋔) and the Word (ЯУ◁) "spoken" by YHWH regarding the promised son Yitshaq. Yitshaq was born at an Appointed Time, and we continue to see the lives of these individuals as they become integragated with time itself. Creation begins to get realigned as the Covenant people come into synchronicity with YHWH and His cycles of time, known as the Appointed Times (moadim).⁶³

In what is likely the most mysterious and profound event of this Covenant family, YHWH told Abraham to take Yitshaq, the promised son, and sacrifice him. It appears at this time that Abraham was residing in Beersheba, which means: "well of seven." This was the place were Abraham dug a well, planted a tree and gave Abimelech seven lambs.

Abraham took his son to the mountains of Moriah, which was in the region of Jerusalem, where Melchizedek reigned. It was there that he took his son, built an altar and prepared to slaughter him. The thing that most people miss when reading this story is the fact that Abraham fully expected his son to be resurrected. That was the only way that the promises of the Covenant could be fulfilled. It was evident from the directives that he gave to the young men who accompanied him to the mountain. "*Stay here with the donkey; the lad and I will go yonder and worship, and <u>we will come back to you</u>.*" Beresheet 22:5.

When the father and son walked up the hill, Yitshaq prophetically carried the wood on his back.

When asked about the sacrifice Abraham prophetically stated: *"Elohim will provide Himself the Lamb."* Beresheet 22:8. Abraham erected the altar, placed the wood and bound his son. As he was about to slaughter Yitshaq, the Messenger of YHWH called out from heaven and told him not to harm his son. YHWH then provided a ram caught in a thicket by its horns.

So through the life of Abram, and later Abraham, we see how YHWH communicated His Covenant path through His chosen vessel. YHWH spoke to the man, the Word of YHWH appeared in a vision, YHWH appeared and even ate with him. This man's life revealed the Covenant path, and the Plan of YHWH to fill His House. We can see an interesting progression from sound to sight, when the Word (sound) appeared (sight). We see the encounters progress from a vision to personal appearances and then intimate fellowship. The life of Abraham carried a message and a pattern for future generations within the Covenant.

What is particularly interesting is that YHWH appeared as well as His Word. This begs the question; "What was the Word?" We already saw that it is connected with the Light. In the beginning Elohim brought forth this light into the physical realm. Indeed, it appears that the Word was actually a physical manifestation of sound – the spoken words of Elohim. So the utterance of the Creator entered Creation as and through the Word.

This journey continued through the Covenant children of Abraham. We learn important lessons from the life of Yitshaq and his bride Rivkah (Rebecca). They then had twins named Esau and Yaakob. Yaakob was actually born grabbing the heel of his twin brother. So

Esau was technically the first to be born, he was entitled to all the rights and privileges of the firstborn.

Yaakob ultimately obtained that birthright from both his brother and his father through questionable means and even outright deception. As a result, he fled Beersheba and left the Land of promise. En route to Padan Aram he stayed at Luz, and named it Beit El (Bethel) – the House of El. The word "luz" is associated with an almond tree, and some believe that the Tree of Life was an almond tree. How appropriate then for this place to be the House of Elohim.

While Yaakob slept, he dreamed, and YHWH spoke to him in the dream. YHWH affirmed the Covenant with him. *"18 Then Yaakob rose early in the morning, and took Χ𐤀-the stone (aben) that he had put at his head, set it up as a pillar, and poured oil on top of it. 19 And he called the name of that place Bethel; but the name of that city had been Luz previously. 20 Then Yaakob made a vow, saying, 'If Elohim will be with me, and keep me in this way that I am going, and give me bread to eat and clothing to put on, 21 so that I come back to my father's house in peace, then YHWH shall be my Elohim. 22 And this stone which I have set as a pillar shall be Elohim's house, and of all that You give me I will surely give a tenth to You."* Beresheet 28:18-22.

This act had great prophetic significance. Incredibly, the Aleph Taw (Χ𐤀) is attached to the stone. This is the "aben" (𐤍𐤁𐤀) in Hebrew, which was previously mentioned. By no coincidence the word aben (𐤍𐤁𐤀) is a combination of "father" – ab (𐤁𐤀) and "son" – ben (𐤍𐤁). Yaakob then raised up the aben as a pillar in the House of El and anointed it. You anoint a king and priest – Melchizedek. Remember that the gematria value for aben (𐤍𐤁𐤀) is 53, which is the same

as "garden" – gan (𐤲𐤱), and "the jubilee" – hayobel (𐤋𐤁𐤅𐤉𐤄). All of these concepts united in the Beit El – the House of Elohim.

Yaakob raised a family and prospered greatly while living in his Uncle Laban's service as a veritable slave. When it finally came time for him to return home, he had a mysterious encounter and received a name change, like his grandfather Abraham. We read that while on his way the messengers of Elohim met with him. When Yaakob saw them he said "this is Elohim's Camp and he called the place Machenah (𐤄𐤍𐤇𐤌)" (Beresheet 32:1-2). The significance of this place might be lost, unless it is connected with the "camp" or rather "camps" (𐤌𐤉𐤍𐤇𐤌) later described in Bemidbar 5:3 which has the numerical equivalence of 153.

What happens next should be seen as a prophetic event with future implications. While Yaakob met messengers of Elohim, we are not provided any information concerning a conversation. Instead we read about Yaakob sending messengers ahead of him to speak to his brother Esau, who is coming to meet him.

Yaakob then divided his people and sent them ahead with gifts. Yaakob (𐤉𐤏𐤒𐤅) brought his family over the ford of Yabok (𐤒𐤁𐤉), which is a word play on Yaakob's name (𐤉𐤏𐤒𐤅). At this mysterious place we see the bet (𐤁), the house, replacing the ayin (𐤏). So we are being told to the "see the house."

Here is what we read in English. "*And he arose that night and took his two wives, his two female servants, and his eleven sons, and crossed over the ford of Yabok.*" Beresheet 32:22. In the Hebrew we see the Aleph Taw (𐤕𐤀) affixed to the "two" wives (𐤉𐤔𐤍 𐤉𐤕𐤔-𐤕𐤀), the "two" servants (𐤉𐤕𐤇𐤐𐤔 𐤉𐤕𐤔-𐤕𐤀) and "eleven"

sons (𐤉𐤋𐤃𐤋 𐤏𐤅𐤔 𐤊𐤇𐤀-𐤕𐤀). The Aleph Taw
(𐤕𐤀) also stands alone between "crossed over" and
"ford of Yabok." The phrase "crossed over" is "eber"
(𐤓𐤁𐤏), the same word as Hebrew - "ebriy"
(𐤉𐤓𐤁𐤏). The only difference is the yud (𐤉). In fact,
the word for "ford" (𐤉𐤓𐤁𐤌) is essentially the same
word also.

So the Aleph Taw (𐤕𐤀) is in the midst of the
"crossing over" - becoming a Hebrew. After they all
crossed over Yaakob then "sent them over the brook."
(see Beresheet 32:23). The Aleph Taw (𐤕𐤀) was
intimately involved in that process when you examine
the Hebrew. Only then, when Yaakob was alone, did he
wrestle with a mysterious Man.

Here again we see a word play with the name of
Yaakob. The word for wrestle is "yabek" (𐤒𐤁𐤀𐤉). At
the center of this wrestling event is "ab" (𐤁𐤀) - father.
The life of this man Yaakob, who wrestled with life
from the womb, was now coming full circle. He is
essentially wrestling with the "power (𐤀) of the house
(𐤁)." He is no longer wrestling with his physical family
(ie. Esau, Yitshaq, Laban), he is now wrestling with his
spiritual father.

The text describing the name change is full of
mystery. Now in an English translation it appears simple
enough. Yaakob wrestled a man until the breaking of the
day and the man said: *"Your name shall no longer be called
Jacob, but Israel; for you have struggled with Elohim and with
men, and have prevailed."* Beresheet 32:28.

When we read the text in the Hebrew, it is filled
with information that is not translated in the English.
The reason that it is not included in the English is
because the translators often do not know how to

translate mysteries. Here is a translation with some of the missing information. *"Your name shall no longer be called Yaakob, but* 𐤆𐤉 𐤅𐤊-*Yisrael; for you have* 𐤆𐤉-*struggled (*𐤗𐤆𐤓𐤅*) with* 𐤅𐤏-*Elohim and with* 𐤅𐤊-*men, and have prevailed."* Beresheet 32:28.

Now we could write a book concerning the mysteries contained in this single passage of Hebrew text. Here only a few words have been highlighted. For instance, Yaakob was not simply named Yisrael, but rather em-Yisrael. The word em (𐤅𐤊) literally means: "mother." So as with the name changes involving Abraham and Sarah, something was being birthed through Yisrael. This event demonstrated a transformation from physical to spiritual, as had occurred with Abraham and Sarah.

This fact was crystalized with the inclusion of the word "Sarai" (𐤆𐤓𐤅) followed by the taw (𐤗), which means: "covenant." The word 𐤗𐤆𐤓𐤅 is translated as "struggle," but there is the word for prince (𐤆𐤓𐤅) followed by the taw (𐤗). The focus is clear in the Hebrew. Notice that Elohim is preceded by the word "am" which means: "a flock, a people, a tribe, a nation." The same word precedes "men." This is a prophecy imbedded within the text, but it can only be seen in the Hebrew.

The word "kee" (𐤆𐤉) means: "to brand, scar or burn." The first time that kee (𐤆𐤉) is referred to in the Scriptures is when Elohim called "the Light" at the beginning "good." In fact, He called it "kee-tob" (𐤁𐤉𐤈-𐤆𐤉). So it seems hidden in the text is the branding of this man with the Light.

An important part of this wrestling event involved the name change and the blessing. It also

included a very intimate and sensitive covenant event -
circumcision. Most common English translations provide
that the man "touched the socket of his thigh." The word
used for thigh is "yarek" (Y⤸ꓵ) in Hebrew. The
"thigh" is likely a euphemism for his genitals, as was the
case with Abraham's thigh in Beresheet 24:2,9. Both
instances involve a significant Covenant event, and the
mystery here involves a circumcision of light. It was a
necessary step as he crossed over into the Promised Land
with his new name and identity. This surely would have
accounted for his limp.

Amazingly, Yaakob named the place of this event
Peniel (ㄥ⤸ꓵ⅄ꓭ). He stated "For I have seen Elohim face
to face, and my life is preserved." Beresheet 32:30. The term
"face to face" infers a deep and intimate knowledge. A
man and a woman commune intimately "face to face,"
and we will later read about a special man named
Mosheh who communed "face to face" with YHWH.

Immediately after he named the location we read:
"Just as he crossed over (eber) X⤸-Penuel (ㄥ⤸⅄ꓭꓭ-X⤸)
the sun rose on him . . ." Beresheet 32:31. Notice that the
word Penuel (ㄥ⤸⅄ꓭꓭ) is different from the previous
name Peniel (ㄥ⤸ꓵ⅄ꓭ). There is a vav (⅄) inserted in
the middle instead of the yud (ꓵ). So the man - vav (⅄)
is connected with the arm – yud (ꓵ). There is also an
Aleph Taw (X⤸) connected with Penuel.

This encounter involved his intimate parts
pointing to a birthing process which was part of the
Covenant. The change of name involved a new identity,
a blessing and the crossing over of a people, and the
Aleph Taw (X⤸) was directly involved in the process.

After this vital Covenant event, he then crossed
over into the Land and made amends with Esau. Yisrael

then went to Succot where he built a house for himself, and succas for his livestock. This was a very prophetic event as Succot is one of the important Appointed Times on the Creator's Calendar. Here again we see the Covenant people merging time and space providing prophetic pictures and patterns for future generations.

He purchased land in Shechem where things went awry. Elohim told him to go to Beit El, live there and build an altar. Interestingly, Elohim talks to him and affirms the Covenant. He confirms the name change of Yaakob to Yisrael. Yisrael built an altar and set up an aben as a pillar. He then anointed the pillar with wine <u>and</u> oil. (See Beresheet 35).

The altar of Abraham stood between man, and the House of YHWH. Now the Altar of Yisrael was erected within the House of Elohim – Beit El (Bethel). This was the place where the aben was anointed (moshiach). The aben was an unhewn stone, and the altar was built from unhewn stones. In other words it was not a creation of man, but a creation of YHWH. It was bloody and had 4 horns. It was the place where the holy fire (esh qodesh) was present and consumed the offerings of men. This was the point where a man did business with YHWH.

The altar represented the sacrifice needed to bring man into relationship with YHWH. Amazingly, an ancient breed of sheep called Jacob's Sheep have four horns. So the altar with 4 horns physically represents the Lamb of Elohim of the  Covenant patterned through the lives of the patriarchs.

We can clearly see the redemptive plan of YHWH through the Covenant, and the patterns of the lives of those who entered into that Covenant. The Covenant established through Noah was with all of creation. Those eight (8) beings in the Ark set the stage for the Covenant relationship that YHWH had in store for His people.

Ten generations from Noah led us to a man named Abram. Abram was given a promise and he acted upon that promise. His life was a pattern for the person desirous of entering into a Covenant relationship. YHWH was once again, building a House (Ark). Through the Covenant process YHWH was now building a family to fill that House.

Instead of simply creating beings and placing them in paradise, YHWH was now going to include those who freely chose Him and His ways. The Covenant process was how YHWH would communicate with mankind through a relationship. He made promises with blessings and consequences. He gave gifts and drew men to Himself. This relationship process would ultimately culminate with an assembly of people called Yisrael.

7

Yisrael

So far, we have read about YHWH entering into a Covenant relationship with certain individuals with the goal of restoring creation. He communicated with them. We even read how Abraham was actually referred to as the friend of YHWH (Isaiah 41:8). So YHWH built relationships and friendships with His Creation.

After the man Yisrael returned to the Covenant Land with his family another son was born – Benjamin. We read about the twelve sons of Yisrael in the Land, with a great emphasis on Joseph and Judah (Yahudah).[64] Joseph was actually given powerful dreams relative to his fate. In fact, this was how YHWH communicated to Joseph – through his dreams.

"[5] And Joseph dreamed a dream, and he told it to his brethren: and they hated him yet the more. [6] And he said unto them, Hear, I pray you, this dream which I have dreamed: [7] For, behold, we were binding sheaves in the field, and, lo, my sheaf arose, and also stood upright; and, behold, your sheaves stood round about, and made obeisance to my sheaf. [8] And his brethren said to him, Shall you indeed reign over us? or shalt thou indeed have dominion over us? And they hated him yet the more for

his dreams, and for his words. [9] And he dreamed yet another dream, and told his brethren, and said, Behold, I have dreamed a dream more; and, behold, the sun and the moon and the eleven stars made obeisance to me. [10] And he told it to his father, and to his brethren: and his father rebuked him, and said unto him, What is this dream that you have dreamed? Shall I and your mother and your brethren indeed come to bow down ourselves to you to the earth? [11] And his brethren envied him, but his father observed the saying." Beresheet 37:5-11.

Now if you only read this in the English you would miss something very important. When the text speaks of his brethren envying him, it also provides that his father "guarded" (shomar) "X𐤊-the Word" (𐤓𐤁𐤃𐤄-X𐤊). So we see the Aleph Taw (X𐤊) attached to "the Word." These dreams therefore had great Messianic potential.

We know that Joseph did indeed become exalted. While his brothers sold him into slavery, and he later became a prisoner in Egypt, YHWH had bigger plans. Joseph was elevated to Viceroy in Egypt, second only to Pharaoh. His family did indeed bow down to him. Incredibly they did not even recognize him at first.

The life of Joseph was a pattern for an even greater fulfillment in the future. Because Joseph suffered and overcame, the nation of Egypt, and many of the surrounding nations were spared from famine. Joseph's family ended up moving into Egypt. While they received favor at first, they eventually became slaves until the promise of the Covenant previously made with Abram

was ready to be completed. (see Beresheet 15:13-15).

The Children of Yisrael grew into a great nation while they were in Egypt. It seems as though Egypt ultimately ends up being a place of great blessing for the Covenant people, even when it does not initially appear that way. Just as Abram and Sarai went to Egypt to escape famine and Sarai had become a captive of Pharaoh, the same occurred with their descendants. Just as Abram and Sarai were released and blessed with great wealth, the same would occur with their descendants. YHWH uses the lives of the Covenant people as patterns for the future. This too is a pattern that will once again be repeated in the future.

In fact, the future fulfillment will be incredible because it involves the Nations – the Ger. Remember how Abram came out of Egypt with Hager – The Ger. So too, when the Children of Yisrael were led out of Egypt by Mosheh, they were accompanied by a "mixed multitude." (Shemot 12:38).

In Hebrew the mixed multitude is described as the "ereb rab" (𐤓𐤏 𐤓𐤏𐤏). Essentially, it is the same two words repeated except for the addition of the ayin (𐤏) to the rab (𐤓𐤏), which makes it "mixed." The ayin (𐤏) represents the eye and means "see." The gematria value of the ayin (𐤏) is 70, and 70 represents "the nations."[65] This mixed multitude represented the nations gathered into the Covenant Assembly of Yisrael. This was a prophetic event with a future fulfillment.[66]

Prior to departing from Egypt, all of Yisrael had observed the Passover. Their homes were protected by the blood of the Passover Lamb. This was another profound pattern demonstrated through the Covenant people for a future fulfillment. Those who were redeemed from Egypt were then brought to the Mountain of YHWH, where YHWH would elevate the relationship to a very intimate level – marriage.

Remember the theme of the house from "the beginning." YHWH was building a house and filling it through the Covenant. He protects the house by the blood, which represents the blood of the Covenant. This Covenant family, the soon to be Bride of YHWH, marched out of Egypt like a conquering army, carrying great wealth that was plundered from the Egyptians.

Throughout the deliverance process, YHWH used a mediator – Mosheh. Mosheh was the one who would mediate the Covenant, which was culminating into a wedding ceremony at Sinai. Here was the proposal made by YHWH: "*⁵ Now therefore, if you will obey My voice indeed, and keep My Covenant, then you shall be a peculiar treasure unto Me above all people: for all the earth is mine: ⁶ And you shall be unto Me a kingdom of priests, and an holy (set apart) nation.*" Shemot 19:5-6.

Mosheh presented the offer before the elders of Yisrael and the answer was an equivocal acceptance. The Bride, Yisrael, answered as one voice – "I do." As a bride prepares for her wedding, Yisrael was told to prepare for her Husband to meet with her. All of the people were to cleanse themselves and remain pure as YHWH appeared before them at Sinai on the third day.

It was truly an awesome and terrifying event. "*¹⁶ And it came to pass on the third day in the morning, that there were thunders and lightnings, and a thick cloud upon the mount, and the voice of the shofar (ⴶⵁⵯ) exceeding loud; so that all the people that were in the camp trembled. ¹⁷ And Mosheh brought forth the people out of the camp to meet with Elohim; and they stood at the nether part of the mount. ¹⁸ And*

mount Sinai was completely in smoke, because YHWH descended upon it in fire: and the smoke thereof ascended as the smoke of a furnace, and the whole mount quaked greatly. *19 And when the voice of the shofar (ꟼꓚYw) sounded long, and waxed louder and louder, Mosheh spoke, and Elohim answered him by a voice." Shemot 19:16-19.

There are many interesting things in this passage. Obviously, this is the first time that we are given a description of YHWH appearing and speaking in such a fashion. The fire and smoke should draw our attention to the fire and smoke that passed through the blood of the Covenant with Abram. Also, the voice of YHWH is actually described as a "shofar." This word was initially spelled ꟼꓚw.

Later when the people came out to meet with Elohim a vav (Y) was added, and it was spelled ꟼꓚYw. The vav (Y) has the numerical value of six (6), which is intimately connected with man. Remember that the sixth word of the Scriptures was v-et (XꓘY). Therefore, the voice of Elohim that speaks to the Assembly of Yisrael is the sound of a shofar likened to a man.

Now most people read the word "trumpet" in their English Bibles, but this is an important distinction. When you read "trumpet" you think of a metallic instrument, but the Hebrew word shofar (ꟼꓚw) specifically refers to a "ram's horn." So correcting the translation from Hebrew to English is important in order to gain a proper understanding of what is actually being described in the text.

YHWH then proceeded to speak to the Assembly of Yisrael.

"*1 And Elohim spoke all these words, saying, *2 I am YHWH your Elohim, which have brought

thee out of the land of Egypt, out of the house
of bondage. ³ Thou shalt have no other gods
before Me. ⁴ Thou shalt not make unto thee any
graven image, or any likeness of any thing that
is in heaven above, or that is in the earth
beneath, or that is in the water under the earth:
⁵ Thou shalt not bow down thyself to them, nor
serve them: for I YHWH your Elohim am a
jealous Elohim, visiting the iniquity of the
fathers upon the children unto the third and
fourth generation of them that hate Me; ⁶ And
showing mercy unto thousands of them that
love me, and keep My commandments. ⁷ You
shall not take the Name of YHWH your
Elohim in vain; for YHWH will not hold him
guiltless that takes His Name in vain. ⁸
Remember the Sabbath day, to keep it set apart.
⁹ Six days shalt thou labor, and do all thy work:
¹⁰ But the seventh day is the Sabbath of
YHWH your Elohim: in it you shall not do
any work, you, nor your son, nor your
daughter, your manservant, nor your
maidservant, nor your cattle, nor your stranger
that is within your gates: ¹¹ For in six days
YHWH made heaven and earth, the sea, and
all that in them is, and rested the seventh day:
wherefore YHWH blessed the Sabbath day,
and set it apart. ¹² Honor your father and your
mother: that your days may be long upon the
land which YHWH your Elohim gives you. ¹³
You shall not murder. ¹⁴ You shall not commit
adultery. ¹⁵ You shall not steal. ¹⁶ You shall not
bear false witness against your neighbor. ¹⁷ You

shall not covet your neighbor's house, you shall not covet your neighbor's wife, nor his manservant, nor his maidservant, nor his ox, nor his ass, nor any thing that is your neighbor's." Shemot 20:1-17.

After YHWH spoke what are referred to as the Ten Words we read the following account. "*[18] And all the people saw the thunderings, and the lightnings, and the voice of the shofar, and the mountain smoking: and when the people saw it, they removed, and stood afar off. [19] And they said unto Mosheh, Speak thou with us, and we will hear: but let not Elohim speak with us, lest we die. [20] And Mosheh said unto the people, Fear not: for Elohim is come to prove you, and that His fear may be before your faces, that you sin not. [21] And the people stood afar off, and Mosheh drew near unto the thick darkness where Elohim was.*" Shemot 20:18-21.

The spoken Word of YHWH was so powerful that the people actually saw the sound. The text specifically describes: "*all the people saw the thunderings and the lightenings and the voice of the shofar.*" This was probably similar to what occurred at creation, only there were no people around to hear <u>and</u> <u>see</u> the voice of YHWH.

In fact, this passage is so profound here is what you would see if you read it in Hebrew. "*[18] And all the people saw ᚷᚲ-the thunderings, ᚷᚲᚹ-the lightnings, ᚷᚲᚹ the voice of the shofar, ᚷᚲᚹ-the mountain smoking: and when the people saw it, they removed, and stood afar off.*" Shemot 20:18. Remember that this meeting was all about the Husband meeting with the Bride. The Husband was the Aleph Taw (ᚷᚲ), and the people saw the Aleph Taw (ᚷᚲ).

As a result of the enormity of this event that

clearly overwhelmed their senses, the people requested that Mosheh hear the words and transmit the words to them. YHWH agreed to this request and He would no longer speak directly to the Children of Yisrael in such a fashion. Those Ten Words stand apart from all others spoken by YHWH and recorded in written form.

YHWH spoke words on the Mountain that were then written down by Mosheh onto a Scroll. *"¹ And He said unto Mosheh, Come up unto YHWH, you, and Aharon, Nadab, and Abihu, and seventy of the elders of Yisrael; and worship you afar off. ² And Mosheh alone shall come near YHWH: but they shall not come nigh; neither shall the people go up with him. ³ And Mosheh came and told the people all the words of YHWH, and all the judgments: and all the people answered with one voice, and said, All the words which YHWH hath said will we do. ⁴ And Mosheh wrote all the words of YHWH, and rose up early in the morning, and built an altar under the hill, and twelve pillars, according to the twelve tribes of Yisrael. ⁵ And he sent young men of the children of Yisrael, which offered burnt offerings, and sacrificed peace offerings of oxen unto YHWH. ⁶ And Mosheh took half of the blood, and put it in basins; and half of the blood he sprinkled on the altar. ⁷ And he took the Scroll of the covenant, and read in the audience of the people: and they said, All that YHWH hath said will we do, and be obedient. ⁸ And Mosheh took the blood, and sprinkled it on the people, and said, Behold the blood of the covenant, which YHWH hath made with you concerning all these words."* Shemot 24: 2-8.

So we see the Marriage Covenant established with the Children of Yisrael. They were sprinkled with blood, and the Scroll of the Covenant was the Ketubah – the Marriage Contract. The Scroll of the Covenant contained the Words transmitted from YHWH to

Mosheh. Mosheh not only spoke the Words, but he also wrote all the Words on a scroll. In fact, it is those very words, written in a scroll, that we have been quoting thus far.

After that event YHWH then instructed Mosheh to come up and receive tablets. "*And YHWH said unto Mosheh, Come up to Me into the mount, and be there: and I will give you tables of stone, and the Torah, and commandments which I have written; that you may teach them.*" Shemot 24:12. So after Mosheh wrote the Scroll of the Covenant, YHWH would now inscribe the Words spoken to the Children of Yisrael onto tablets of stone.

There is a great mystery surrounding these tablets of stone, because it is the first time that we read about YHWH writing something. Not only did YHWH write words, but He was also communicating an important prophetic truth through a visual aid involving the tablets of stone. The tablets are referred to as et-lechet h'aben (ᕼᏗᛣᕪ ᚷᕼᏝ-ᚷᛣ). The Aleph Taw (ᚷᛣ) is attached to the tablets (ᚷᕼᏝ), and tablets (ᚷᕼᏝ) were made of "aben" (ᕼᏗᛣ) – stone. Now remember the aben that was raised up and anointed by Yaakob in the House of El. This is another picture of the Messiah. The picture becomes even more profound when we follow those tablets.

They represented the Marriage Contract – the words of the Marriage Covenant. While Mosheh was up on the Mountain receiving instructions, the Children of Yisrael grew impatient. They decided to construct an image, the golden calf, and declare a Feast to YHWH. They essentially began worshipping YHWH as the pagans in Egypt worshipped their gods.

As a result of their conduct, Mosheh came down

from the Mountain and broke the Tablets. Now when you view these Tablets as the Messiah, the centerpiece of the marriage Covenant, that breaking has profound implications. It would seem to reveal that the Messiah Himself would be broken. Now that is perfectly consistent with the pattern of the Lamb of Elohim, whose blood is shed to protect those in the Covenant, and the fact that YHWH would bear the penalty for the covenant made with Abram.

Interestingly, there were 2 Tablets, not just one. This would synchronize with the existence of the Aleph Taw (XⱢ) two times in Beresheet 1:1. So the Aleph Taw (XⱢ) is identified with these stones; stones that YHWH wrote upon with His own finger. He wrote the Words that He had spoken. (Debarim 9:10). These stones were intimately connected with YHWH. The Tablets were broken, and the golden calf was destroyed. It is at this point that we read about a Scroll of YHWH – a Scroll that YHWH has written. Mosheh intervenes and asks that he be blotted out of YHWH's Scroll in the event that YHWH will not forgive Yisrael.

"*32 Yet now, if thou will forgive their sin; and if not, blot me, I pray thee, out of your Scroll which you have written. 33 And YHWH said unto Mosheh, Whosoever hath sinned against Me, him will I blot out of My Scroll.*" Shemot 32:32-33. In other words, those who sinned will be responsible for their own actions. YHWH has a Scroll and your name is either in it, or not. You want your name to be in His Scroll.

We then read of a request when Mosheh asks that YHWH show him "the way" (ⱧYⱯ◁-XⱢ). YHWH then agreed to do "the Word" (ⱯⲨ◁Ⱨ-XⱢ). Mosheh then requested that YHWH show him His "glory"

(ᐊᎩƳ-Ⅹ⟨). YHWH proclaimed that He would make all His goodness pass before Mosheh. He would be *"gracious upon whom (ᎩⱲ⟨-Ⅹ⟨) He would be gracious and show mercy upon whom (ᎩⱲ⟨-Ⅹ⟨) He would show mercy."* Shemot 33:19.

YHWH told Mosheh that he could not see His face (ᘺᎩᘺ-Ⅹ⟨), but that He would cover Mosheh with His Hand. When He passed by, YHWH would take away His Hand (ᘺᎩƳ-Ⅹ⟨), and Mosheh would see His "back parts" (ᘺᎩᗷ⟨-Ⅹ⟨). During this exchange, one cannot ignore all of the allusions to the Aleph Taw (Ⅹ⟨) when describing attributes of YHWH.[67]

Immediately after Mosheh was permitted to see the "back parts" of YHWH, Mosheh was then informed how the Covenant would be renewed. YHWH would allow the Covenant to be renewed, only this time, Mosheh the mediator had to cut the stone tablets and carry them up the mountain.

> *"[1] And YHWH said unto Mosheh, Hew thee two tables of stone like unto the first: and I will write upon these tables the words that were in the first tables, which you broke. [2] And be ready in the morning, and come up in the morning unto mount Sinai, and present yourself there to Me in the top of the mount. [3] And no man shall come up with you, neither let any man be seen throughout all the mount; neither let the flocks nor herds feed before that mount. [4] And he hewed two tables of stone like unto the first; and Mosheh rose up early in the morning, and went up unto mount Sinai, as YHWH had commanded him, and took in his hand the two tables of stone. [5] And YHWH descended in the*

cloud, and stood with him there, and proclaimed the Name of YHWH. ⁶ And YHWH passed by before him, and proclaimed, YHWH, YHWH El, merciful and gracious, longsuffering, and abundant in goodness and truth, ⁷ Keeping mercy for thousands, forgiving iniquity and transgression and sin, and that will by no means clear the guilty; visiting the iniquity of the fathers upon the children, and upon the children's children, unto the third and to the fourth generation. ⁸ And Mosheh made haste, and bowed his head toward the earth, and worshipped. ⁹ And he said, If now I have found favor in your sight, O Master, let my Master, I pray thee, go among us; for it is a stiffnecked people; and pardon our iniquity and our sin, and take us for thine inheritance. ¹⁰ And He said, Behold, I make a Covenant: before all your people I will do marvels, such as have not been done in all the earth, nor in any nation: and all the people among whom you are shall see the work of YHWH. For it is an awesome thing that I will do with you. ¹¹ Observe you that which I command you this day: behold, I drive out before you the Amorite, and the Canaanite, and the Hittite, and the Perizzite, and the Hivite, and the Jebusite. ¹² Take heed to yourself, lest you make a covenant with the inhabitants of the land where you go, lest it be for a snare in the midst of you. ¹³ But you shall destroy their altars, break their images, and cut down their groves: ¹⁴ For you shall worship no other god: for YHWH, whose

Name is Jealous, is a jealous El: ⁱ⁵ Lest you make a covenant with the inhabitants of the land, and they go a whoring after their gods, and do sacrifice unto their gods, and one call you, and you eat of his sacrifice; ⁱ⁶ And you take of their daughters unto your sons, and their daughters go a whoring after their gods, and make your sons go a whoring after their gods. ⁱ⁷ You shall make you no molten gods. ⁱ⁸ The Feast of Unleavened Bread shalt you keep. Seven days you shalt eat unleavened bread, as I commanded thee, in the time of the month of the Abib: for in the month of the Abib you came out from Egypt. ⁱ⁹ All that opens the matrix is mine; and every firstling among your cattle, whether ox or sheep, that is male. ²⁰ But the firstling of an ass you shall redeem with a lamb: and if thou redeem him not, then shall you break his neck. All the firstborn of thy sons you shall redeem. And none shall appear before Me empty handed. ²¹ Six days thou shall work, but on the seventh day thou shall rest: in earing time and in harvest thou shall rest. ²² And you shall observe the Feast of Weeks, of the firstfruits of wheat harvest, and the Feast of Ingathering at the year's end. ²³ Three times in the year shall all your males appear (𐤆𐤉𐤃-𐤗𐤊) before Master YHWH, the Elohim of Yisrael. ²⁴ For I will cast out the nations before thee, and enlarge thy borders: neither shall any man desire thy land, when thou shalt go up to appear before YHWH your Elohim three times in the year. ²⁵ Thou shalt not offer the blood of My sacrifice with leaven; neither shall the sacrifice of the Feast of the Passover be left unto the morning. [26] The first of the firstfruits of your land you shall bring unto the House of YHWH your Elohim. You shall not seethe a kid in his mother's milk. [27] And YHWH said unto Mosheh, Write you these words: for after the tenor of these words I have made a Covenant with you and with Yisrael. [28] And he was there with YHWH forty days and forty nights; he did neither eat bread, nor drink water. And he wrote upon the tables the words of the Covenant, the Ten Commandments. [29] And it came to pass, when Mosheh came down from Mount Sinai with the two tables of testimony in Mosheh's hand, when he came down from the mount, that Mosheh did not know that the skin of his face shone while he talked with Him. [30] And when Aharon and all the children of Yisrael saw Mosheh, behold, the skin of his face shone; and they were afraid to come nigh him. [31] And Mosheh called unto them; and Aharon and all the rulers of the congregation returned unto him: and Mosheh talked with them. [32] And afterward all the children of Yisrael came nigh: and he gave them in commandment all that YHWH had spoken with him in mount Sinai." Shemot 34:1-32.

So YHWH wrote the same words upon those second Tablets. We also read that Mosheh told Yisrael all the Words that YHWH spoke to him on the mountain. This was previously mentioned prior to the

first set of Tablets when YHWH had told Mosheh about the Torah and the commandments.

"Torah" is another word, like "shofar," that you will likely never read in an English translation of the text. Sadly, it was one of the greatest gifts given to Yisrael through this wedding process. It is extremely misunderstood by many because it is often improperly translated as "The Law."

The word Torah (ﾈﾈﾕﾗ) in Hebrew means: "utterance, teaching, instruction or revelation from Elohim." It comes from "horah" (ﾈﾈﾕﾈ) which means: "to direct, to teach" and derives from the stem "yara" (ﾈﾈﾁ) which means: "to shoot or throw." Therefore there are two aspects to the word Torah: 1) aiming or pointing in the right direction, and 2) movement in that direction. This gives a much different sense than the word "Law."

So Mosheh wrote the words spoken to him by YHWH. He wrote those words on a Scroll. YHWH wrote the words that He spoke to Yisrael on two tablets of stone. Both of these writings signified the marriage contract. Both were kept in the Ark of the Covenant, also known as the witness, that was later constructed and placed within the Tabernacle.

The Covenant relationship now came full circle from the Garden. Just as Adam had been charged to tend and guard the Garden, the Covenant family of Yisrael was supposed to tend and guard the commandments. They were also given a sign of the seventh day. This special day was actually given a name - the Sabbath, better known as Shabbat (ﾗﾕﾔ) in Hebrew.[68]

"Therefore the children of Yisrael

shall keep the Sabbath, to observe the Sabbath
throughout their generations as a perpetual Covenant."
Shemot 31:16.

YHWH could have chosen any day, but He did not. He chose the 7th day – the day when He rested, and the day that He set apart from the very beginning. He was now connecting His set apart people, his family, with the set apart time. He was connecting this Marriage Covenant with His Creation Covenant made in the beginning. Yisrael would be the Bride of YHWH, and she would fill the House. Just as Adam was to rest from tending and guarding the Garden, so too Yisrael was to rest from their work on Shabbat.

Now the sign was not some light in the heavens or in the sky. The sign was the Covenant Children observing the set apart day. Not only was the day a sign, but so were the Children of Yisrael. They became the Children of Light.

This Covenant Family was also given instructions for building a House for YHWH. Since the Golden Calf "affair" the Levites were chosen to represent the firstborn of all Yisrael. Traditionally, the firstborn would function in the priestly role for their family. Now the Levites would fulfill that function before YHWH in the Tabernacle.

The pattern of the Passover and the Levites established that you must be a firstborn to enter in to the Covenant House. The pathway was also patterned by the seven articles of furniture: 1) The Ark; 2) The Mercy Seat; 3) The Table of Showbread; 4) The Menorah; 5) The Brazen Altar; 6) The Altar of Incense; and 7) The Laver. The entire tent structure was intended to

represent a person, with YHWH and His Commandments enthroned within them. This is the Shema. (Debarim 6:4-6).

For the time being, the Tabernacle would be placed in the center of the camp of Yisrael. It would provide a pattern for the people to learn how to dwell with YHWH. It was training camp for the return to Paradise. As with the Sabbath Day, the Covenant people were being taught by and through their actions, which were blended with both time and space.

This House would now be at the center of their relationship with YHWH. The males were commanded to meet with YHWH three times a year. Through these Pilgrimage Feasts, and the remaining Appointed Times, the people were supposed to be living set apart lives, synchronized with their Husband. Those Words written on stone, and on the Scroll, were manifesting through Yisrael.

We do not presently have the tablets of stone, because we do not know where the Ark of the Covenant is located. We do, however, have copies of the Scroll that Mosheh transcribed, known as the Torah.

So the Torah is essentially the Book, or rather, the Scroll of the Covenant. While the Torah is contained in one scroll known as a "sepher" (ᴙ𝟷ᵮ), it is understood to be divided into 5 separate books. This is why it is sometimes referred to as the Pentateuch.

The 5 books are intended for those in Covenant with YHWH, an Assembly or Congregation known as Yisrael. All who desire to be in Covenant with YHWH must join this Assembly, and walk in the way of the Torah. The Torah applies to everyone in the Covenant, regardless of where they originated. (Shemot 12:49;

Bemidbar 15:16,29).

Interestingly, the names of the 5 books reveal their emphasis and tell a story that can only be seen in the Hebrew. We already discussed the fact that the first book, commonly called Genesis, is actually "Beresheet." The messages contained in this one word are deep and profound. The "resheet" is the "first," and we saw the Aleph Taw (✗𐤊) as the first of Creation.

We then proceed to the second book commonly called Exodus, which is "Shemot" in Hebrew. Shemot means: "names." We can discern that the text is not so focused on the exodus from Egypt as it is about the revelation of the Name of YHWH.

The third book is commonly called Leviticus, which makes us think about the Levite, and the priesthood. The Hebrew name is "Vayiqra" which means: "And He called." We must recognize that it is actually a text emphasizing the set apart conduct of the called ones. The fourth book commonly called Numbers is actually "Bemidbar" in Hebrew. Bemidbar means: "In the wilderness," and this text provides incredible patterns and mysteries for the called ones to make it through their wilderness experience.

The fifth book is commonly called Deuteronomy, but it is actually "Debarim" in Hebrew. Debarim means: "words." This text reveals how the "words of Elohim" are to be written on the hearts and minds of the called, leading to blessings, rather than curses. This is a very simplistic summary, but the point should be evident. Examining the names of the texts in their original Hebrew can shed significant light on their substance, far more than the common English names.

With that understanding, we can see that the

Torah contains the instructions from the Creator for His Creation. It provides a history of Creation from the Beginning until the time when Yisrael was about to enter the Promised Land. It reveals the Covenant path for the called ones back to the Garden – the Promised Land. It is the foundation, and a framework, but there was more to come. The rest of the story is described in other texts that followed the Torah in time and scope. These other texts, combined with the Torah, collectively became known as the Scriptures.

8

Scriptures

The Marriage Covenant between YHWH and Yisrael was accompanied by some interesting and unique forms of communication. YHWH audibly and visually spoke words to the people. He then wrote those words on tablets of stone, which were thereafter broken by Mosheh. YHWH then rewrote the same words on new tablets presented by a man. This process communicated a pattern for the renewal of the Covenant.

Mosheh also wrote the Torah on a scroll. Both the Scroll and the Tablets were meant to be witnesses – two witnesses to the Covenant. This was clearly not the first time words had been written, but these writings are the foundation of the Covenant. They are special and unique as Mosheh spoke "face to face" with YHWH (Shemot 33:11), and YHWH specifically commanded the words to be written.

The Torah, also known as the five books of Mosheh or the Pentateuch, actually ends with the death of Mosheh. We read in those five texts the history of mankind, in particular, the Covenant process from the beginning of time until shortly before the bride of YHWH moves into the marital home – the Covenant Land. It is, therefore, incomplete and requires further information to see the fulfillment of the Covenant

promise. While it contains the patterns for the fulfillment, it does not provide historical confirmation of the fulfillment.

At the time that Mosheh died, Yisrael had not yet entered into the Covenant Land. That event occurred around 1,400 BCE. The history of Yisrael continues beyond the Torah through other texts known as the Prophets and the Writings. These texts are compiled in a collection known as the Tanak. Tanak is actually an acronym – TNK. It stands for the Torah, the Prophets (Nebi'im) and the Writings (Ketubim) – <u>T</u>orah, <u>N</u>ebi'im, <u>K</u>etubim.

The Tanak has collectively become recognized as "The Scriptures," with the Torah as the foundation of those texts.

"According to the Talmud (Bava Batra 14b-15a, Rashi to Megillah 3a, 14a), much of the contents of the Tanak was compiled by the Men of the Great Assembly (*Anshei K'nesset HaGedolah*), a task completed in 450 BCE, and have remained unchanged since that date. Evidence suggests that the process of canonization occurred between 200 BCE and 200 CE. A popular position is that the Torah was canonized circa 400 BCE, the Prophets circa 200 BCE, and the Writings circa 100 CE, perhaps at a hypothetical Council of Jamnia [Yavneh]. This position, however, is increasingly criticized by modern scholars. Some scholars argue that the Jewish canon was fixed by the Hasmonean dynasty (140-37 BCE). Today, there no scholarly consensus as to when the Jewish canon was set. Formal closure of the canon has often been ascribed to Rabbinic Judaism after the destruction of the Second Temple in 70 CE. Heinrich Graetz proposed in 1871 that it was concluded at a Council of Jamnia (or Yavne[h] in Hebrew), some time in the period 70-90 CE. However, Rabbinical writings seem to indicate that certain books were disputed as accepted canon (such as Ecclesiastes, Song of Songs and Esther, see also Antilegomena), but it may not necessarily be the case. The implication of the Talmud indicates that the books themselves were already accepted canon, but may have been misunderstood on philosophical or ecclesiastical grounds . . . The twenty-four books are also mentioned in the Midrash Koheleth 12:12. A slightly different accounting can be found in the book *Against Apion*, by the 1st-century Jewish historian Josephus, who describes 22 sacred books: the five books of Moses, thirteen histories, and four books of hymns to God and precepts for the conduct of human life. Some scholars have suggested that he considered Ruth part of Judges, and Lamentations part of Jeremiah; as the Christian translator Jerome recorded in the 4th century CE. Other scholars suggest that at the time Josephus wrote, such books as Esther and Ecclesiastes were not yet considered canonical."[69]

There is a lack of consensus concerning when or how the current collection of Hebrew texts became known to be "The Scriptures." Interestingly, those writings do not identify themselves to be "The Scriptures." Clearly though, with Mosheh, we see special words spoken and written. The Torah was commanded

to be written, copied by Kings and read to the Congregation of Yisrael regularly.

The Prophets provided critical information to Yisrael - past present and future - related to the Covenant. The Writings provide history, wisdom, revelation and even prophecy.

One cannot ignore the significance of the number 22 attributed to those texts. Remember that there are 22 characters in the Hebrew alephbet. So there is a sense of completion in using that number. There is also an intimate connection with the Aleph Taw (𐤗𐤀), which surrounds and includes the entire alephbet.

We already discussed the 5 books of the Torah, which are the foundation for all other texts. While the Torah describes the Covenant process beginning in the Garden and culminating with Yisrael, there are other scrolls which describe the progression and fulfillment of the Covenant process as well as the history of Yisrael – those texts are generally grouped together in a collection known as "The Writings."

The Writings, known as the "Ketubim," consist of: 1) Tehillim (Psalms); 2) Mishle (Proverbs); 3) Iyov (Job); 4) Shir Ha-Shirim (Song of Songs); 5) Ruth; 6) Eikhah (Lamentations); 7) Qoheleth (the author's name) (Ecclesiastes); 8) Esther; 9) Daniel; 10) Ezra & Nechemyah (Nehemiah) (treated as one book); 11) Dibrei Ha-Yamim (The words of the days) (Chronicles). There are 11 texts included in The Writings.

The Prophets are the other collection of writings which detail the prophecies given by YHWH through His prophets. The use of prophets is yet another way that YHWH chose to communicate with mankind. While most prophets that we read about communicated with Yisrael, or a particular House of the Divided Kingdom of Yisrael, they were also sent to other nations.

The collection of writings called the Prophets, also known as the "Nebi'im," are certainly not all of the prophets who spoke for YHWH. They are a select grouping of historical writings and prophecies consisting of the following texts: 1) Yahushua (Joshua); 2 Shoftim (Judges); 3) Shemuel (I & II Samuel); 4) Melakim (I & II Kings); 5) Yeshayahu (Isaiah); 6) Yirmeyahu (Jeremiah); 7) Yehezqel (Ezekiel); 8) The Twelve "Minor Prophets" - Hoshea, Yoel, Amos, Obadyah, Yonah, Mikhah, Nachum, Habakkuk, Zephaniah, Haggai, Zechariah, Malachi (all treated as one text).

As indicated above, the Minor prophets are often treated as one book. This leaves us with 24 books when we add the 5 Books of Mosheh, the 11 texts in the Writings and the 8 texts in the Prophets

Since Lamentations was written by Jeremiah, and describes the prophesied exile, it is often added to Jeremiah. Also, Ruth occurs during the period of the Judges so it is often added to Judges. This is how we end up with 22 books in the Tanak. There are other combinations of books suggested throughout history, but it appears that there was a concerted effort to end up with the number 22. The significance of that number and the perfection of having 22 books was clearly important.

The Torah describes the period from creation to a point when the Covenant people are about to enter into the Promised Land. This is not an arbitrary cut off point. Essentially, it provides us with a picture of the way things were meant to be, the problem of sin and subsequent fall, followed by the path of restoration through the Covenant process. Throughout the Torah we

can see the common thread of the Messiah as the ultimate solution.

Obviously, no mere man could solve the problem and restore the status of mankind, and creation, before the Creator. Mosheh himself, the deliverer of Yisrael, was not even permitted to enter into the Land.

So the Torah points to a future event - a future restoration that continued through the Prophets and the Writings. The Prophets and the Writings, while separated into different categories, progress together through the continued Covenant process of Yisrael. They are both historical in nature and they too, point to a future fulfillment.

They span the time immediately before Yisrael entered into the Covenant Land, and describe their conquering of the Land. The texts then describe a period of Judges who ruled Yisrael, during this period the people of Yisrael were fractured and divided until they were finally united into one Kingdom by David.

David ruled over the Southern Tribes, known as the House of Yahudah, for seven years. The Northern Tribes, known as the House of Yisrael, later joined under his rulership. David then ruled over the united Kingdom of Yisrael for another 33 years. This unification of the Kingdom was short lived and continued through, and briefly beyond, the reign of David's son Solomon (Shlomo).

After the death of Shlomo, the Northern Tribes seceded, and the Kingdom was divided into two distinct Kingdoms - the House of Yisrael, also known as the Northern Kingdom, and the House of Yahudah, also known as the Southern Kingdom.

The texts describe how these separate Kingdoms

both strayed from the Covenant path and strayed from YHWH. Many prophets were sent to teach and warn the people in both Kingdoms. Sometimes their message was heeded, and the people would return to YHWH. More often than not, the warnings were ignored. Ultimately, both Kingdoms were exiled from the Covenant Land. The Northern Kingdom was attacked and completely exiled by the Assyrians. The Southern Kingdom was later attacked, and partially exiled by the Babylonians.

While the Southern Tribes of the House of Yahudah retained their identity, the Northern Tribes of the House of Yisrael completely lost their identity. They were specifically told that this would happen by the Prophet Hoshea.

As a result, the House of Yisrael, often referred to as Joseph or Ephraim, was scattered throughout the world and became known as the lost sheep of the House of Yisrael. The House of Yahudah was permitted to return from their Babylonian exile, but they were never restored to their former glory, and Yisrael has yet to be reunited.

It would appear that things had actually gotten worse through the Covenant process. Mankind was no closer to the Garden, and the situation seemed hopeless. As Adam and Hawah had been ejected from the Garden, the Covenant people of Yisrael had been evicted from the Promised Land.

Thankfully, the prophets provided hope and a promise of restoration. Ezekiel, who gave specific periods for the various exiles of the House of Yisrael and the House of Yahudah, also gave hope of a future reunification and return to the Land. He told of a time when the Torah would actually be written on the hearts

and the minds of the Covenant people. (Ezekiel 11:19; Ezekiel 36:26).

This restoration would occur through the renewal of the Covenant. Yirmeyahu specifically provided that there would be a great return, and that the Covenant would be renewed.

"*10* *Hear the word of YHWH, O you nations, and declare it in the isles afar off, and say, He that scattered Yisrael will gather him, and keep him, as a shepherd doth his flock. *11* For YHWH hath redeemed Yaakob, and ransomed him from the hand of him that was stronger than he. *12* Therefore they shall come and sing in the height of Zion, and shall flow together to the goodness of YHWH, for wheat, and for wine, and for oil, and for the young of the flock and of the herd: and their soul shall be as a watered garden; and they shall not sorrow any more at all. *13* Then shall the virgin rejoice in the dance, both young men and old together: for I will turn their mourning into joy, and will comfort them, and make them rejoice from their sorrow. *14* And I will satiate the soul of the priests with fatness, and My people shall be satisfied with My goodness, saith YHWH. *15* Thus saith YHWH; A voice was heard in Ramah, lamentation, and bitter weeping; Rachel weeping for her children refused to be comforted for her children, because they were not. *16* Thus saith YHWH; Refrain your voice from weeping, and your eyes from tears: for your work shall be rewarded, saith YHWH; and they shall come again from the land of the* enemy. ¹⁷ And there is hope in your end, saith YHWH, that your children shall come again to their own border. ¹⁸ I have surely heard Ephraim bemoaning himself thus; Thou hast chastised me, and I was chastised, as a bullock unaccustomed to the yoke: turn thou me, and I shall be turned; for thou art YHWH my Elohim. ¹⁹ Surely after that I was turned, I repented; and after that I was instructed, I smote upon my thigh: I was ashamed, yea, even confounded, because I did bear the reproach of my youth. ²⁰ Is Ephraim My dear son? Is he a pleasant child? For since I spoke against him, I do earnestly remember him still. Therefore My bowels are troubled for him. I will surely have mercy upon him, saith YHWH. ²¹ Set thee up waymarks, make thee high heaps: set your heart toward the highway, even the way which you went: turn again, O virgin of Yisrael, turn again to these your cities. ²² How long will you go about, O thou backsliding daughter? for YHWH has created a new thing in the earth, A woman shall compass a man. ²³ Thus saith YHWH of hosts, the Elohim of Yisrael; As yet they shall use this speech in the land of Yahudah and in the cities thereof, when I shall bring again their captivity; YHWH bless thee, O habitation of justice, and mountain of holiness. ²⁴ And there shall dwell in Yahudah itself, and in all the cities thereof together, husbandmen, and they that go forth with flocks. ²⁵ For I have satiated the weary soul, and I have replenished every sorrowful soul. ²⁶ Upon

this I awaked, and beheld; and my sleep was sweet unto me. ²⁷ Behold, the days come, saith YHWH, that I will sow the House of Yisrael and the House of Yahudah with the seed of man, and with the seed of beast. ²⁸ And it shall come to pass, that like as I have watched over them, to pluck up, and to break down, and to throw down, and to destroy, and to afflict; so will I watch over them, to build, and to plant, saith YHWH. ²⁹ In those days they shall say no more, The fathers have eaten a sour grape, and the children's teeth are set on edge. ³⁰ But every one shall die for his own iniquity: every man that eateth the sour grape, his teeth shall be set on edge. ³¹ <u>Behold, the days come, saith YHWH, that I will make a Renewed Covenant with the X𐤊-House of Yisrael, and with the X𐤊-House of Yahudah:</u> ³² Not according to the Covenant that I made with their fathers in the day that I took them by the hand to bring them out of the land of Egypt; which My Covenant they broke, although I was a Husband unto them, saith YHWH: ³³ <u>But this shall be the Covenant that I will make with the House of Yisrael; After those days, saith YHWH, I will put My Torah in their inward parts, and write it in their hearts; and will be their Elohim, and they shall be My people.</u> ³⁴ And they shall teach no more every man his neighbor, and every man his brother, saying, Know YHWH: for they shall all know me, from the least of them unto the greatest of them, saith YHWH: for I will forgive their iniquity, and I will remember their sin no more. ³⁵ Thus saith YHWH, Who gives the sun for a light by day, and the ordinances of the moon and of the stars for a light by night, Who divideth the sea when the waves thereof roar; YHWH of hosts is His Name: ³⁶ If those ordinances depart from before Me, saith YHWH, then the seed of Yisrael also shall cease from being a nation before Me for ever. ³⁷ Thus saith YHWH; If heaven above can be measured, and the foundations of the earth searched out beneath, I will also cast off all the seed of Yisrael for all that they have done, saith YHWH. ³⁸ Behold, the days come, saith YHWH, that the city shall be built to YHWH from the tower of Hananeel unto the gate of the corner. ³⁹ And the measuring line shall yet go forth over against it upon the hill Gareb, and shall compass about to Goath. ⁴⁰ And the whole valley of the dead bodies, and of the ashes, and all the fields unto the brook of Kidron, unto the corner of the horse gate toward the east, shall be set apart unto YHWH; it shall not be plucked up, nor thrown down any more for ever." Yirmeyahu 31:10-40.

Rather than being a complete failure, as some attempt to describe the Covenant with Yisrael, it was all part of the Creator's plan to restore creation. Through the exiles, Yisrael would be mixed with the nations. Through the renewed Covenant, the Nations would be brought back to YHWH when Yisrael was regathered from the four corners of the world. It was very obvious

that this would occur through the Aleph Taw (✗✗). We can see the Aleph Taw (✗✗) literally attached to each House. Also, the Torah is an integral part of the Renewed Covenant.

So the texts of the Tanak are not just a compilation of nice sayings or scattered texts. They are not simply old historical documents. Rather, they are essential documents, which reveal the Covenant that YHWH has ordained for those who desire to dwell with Him. They also reveal how the substance and content of the Covenant will be renewed.

The Tanak historically leaves off with a remnant from the House of Yahudah returning from their Babylonian exile. They rebuilt walls, the City of Jerusalem and the House of YHWH – the Temple. Most from Yahudah did not return, and all of the House of Yisrael remained in exile – essentially lost.

The divided Kingdom of Yisrael has never been restored. Therefore, the Tanak is an unfinished work. It is incomplete until all of the prophecies are fulfilled. Indeed, most agree that the Tanak was actually compiled by Ezra as he brought the Torah back from Babylon and helped restore the House of Yahudah

According to the Prophets, there is much to be done to complete the Covenant process. Those within the Covenant would have been left with an anticipation of the Messiah because the entire Tanak speaks of the Messiah to come. Indeed, the Psalms make a clear reference to this as Elohim indicates that He is coming. *"Lo, I come: in the volumes (rolls) of the scroll."* Psalm 40:7. So the volumes of the scroll - the Torah, the Prophets and the Writings - tell us about how Elohim will fulfill and complete His Covenant through the Messiah.

9

The Messiah

The Scriptures contained within the Tanak include an unfinished story yearning for an ending. They conclude with the Covenant people, Yisrael, divided into two houses. Both were punished for their sins. The House of Yisrael was in a grievous condition. Divorced from YHWH and exiled, they have essentially been lost in history. While the prophets told of a time when the House of Yisrael would return, there is nothing in the Tanak, or any other historical document that describes their return. This is because it has not yet occurred.

The House of Yahudah returned after a 70 year exile in Babylon, but that return was incomplete. Many from Yahudah remained scattered throughout the world. They had settled into their new lives and chose not to return to the Land. Those who did return met with tremendous difficulties.

The rebuilding of Jerusalem and the Temple by the returning exiles from Babylon was hindered by delays and plagued with problems. There has never been a complete restoration of the fragmented Kingdom of Yisrael, or even the House of Yahudah for that matter. There had to be more to the story, especially in light of the imbedded promises found throughout the Scriptures concerning the Messiah. This is especially true since

history has revealed the subsequent destruction of that rebuilt Temple, and the scattering of the Yahudim from the Land by the Romans.

We already discussed the Aleph Taw (𐤗𐤀) which was at the very beginning. Indeed, the Aleph Taw (𐤗𐤀) is found throughout the Tanak, revealing hints that the texts were actually written about the Messiah. As a result, this Aleph Taw (𐤗𐤀), the untranslated Word that was present at the beginning of Creation and woven throughout the text, was linked with the solution – the Messiah.

In fact, it was not so much a hidden mystery. An analysis of all of the communication transmitted by YHWH shows that the Messiah was actually the obvious and apparent solution to the problem. The Messiah would resolve the need of mankind through the Covenant.

Just how the Messiah would solve the problem was not fully understood. People had different expectations. Some people looked at the pattern of the lives of Yitshaq and Joseph. They were looking for a Messiah "Son of Joseph" who would be a suffering servant, atone for sin and through his suffering reunite the divided Kingdom of Yisrael. This was confirmed by various Psalms and Prophecies.

It is also detailed in a text known as Gabriel's Revelation, Hazon Gabriel or the Jeselsohn Stone. This three foot tall piece of stone with some 87 lines of text dates to around the late first century BCE or the early first century CE. It would have been right around the peak of Messianic expectations based upon the information given to Daniel by Gabriel. How interesting then that this text written in ink on stone purports to be a vision from Gabriel, depicting a Messiah Son of Joseph. The notion of the Messiah Son of Joseph is also described in the Babylonian Talmud Sukkah 52a as preceding the Messiah ben David.

Likely, the most prevalent and popular Messianic expectation involved the Messiah ben David - "Son of David." This was certainly the most appealing notion to a people who had been divided, exiled and repressed. The Yahudim clearly desired a conquering King who would restore the divided Kingdom, sit upon the throne of David and rule righteously.

All of these expectations came from the Torah, the Prophets and the Writings. Both expectations were rightly based upon the patterns and the prophecies in the Scriptures. It was difficult for most to comprehend how one Messiah could accomplish all of these things. For instance, there were various prophecies that seemed to indicate the suffering servant would be killed.[70] Indeed, the patterns of Yitshaq and Joseph clearly revealed a death and resurrection for the Lamb of Elohim. This was actually shown from the pattern of atonement provided after the fall in the Garden

As a result, it is easy to discern that the Messiah would not be a mere man. Since all men were born in a fallen state, how could any man solve the problem resulting from sin. This is why it is important to recognize the Aleph Taw ($\mathsf{X}\mathsf{F}$), and make that connection with the Messiah.

Clearly a solution directly from Elohim was needed to intervene and restore Creation. This was likely understood from the signs in the heavens that clearly depict the virgin giving birth to a son.

The solution was also found within the story told

by the genealogies of the descendants of Adam. Those genealogies would suggest that the Word of YHWH would actually manifest in flesh to instruct mankind. Recall that Henoch (Enoch) was the seventh generation, and his name referred to Elohim "instructing." He was taken up to Elohim in a very mysterious way.

Remember also that Torah means "instruction." So we could expect the next revelation of YHWH along the Covenant path to involve a physical manifestation of the Torah, the Word, in "a fixed dwelling place" which was a physical body.

This is exactly what the Christian religion currently claims occurred over 2,000 years ago, precisely when Yisrael should have been anticipating the Messiah. This time has now long since past. The hope of those in Covenant with YHWH rests solely on whether the promised Messiah did, in fact, come and renew the Covenant with the House of Yisrael and the House of Yahudah. (Jeremiah 31:31).

Indeed, the only way that our sins can be permanently atoned is through the Messiah, and the Melchizedek priesthood. This is alluded to through the prophetic pattern involving Yahushua the High Priest in Zechariah 3.

"¹ *Then he showed me* X𐤊-*Yahushua the High Priest standing before the Messenger of YHWH, and Satan standing at his right hand to oppose him.* ² *And YHWH said to Satan, 'YHWH rebuke you, Satan! YHWH who has chosen Jerusalem rebuke you! Is this not a brand plucked from the fire?'* ³ *Now Yahushua was clothed with filthy garments, and was standing before the Messenger.* ⁴ *Then He answered and spoke to those who stood before Him, saying, 'Take away the*

filthy garments from him.' And to him He said, 'See, I have removed your iniquity from you, and I will clothe you with rich robes.' [5] *And I said, 'Let them put a clean turban on his head.' So they put a clean turban on his head, and they put the clothes on him. And the Messenger of YHWH stood by.* [6] *Then the Messenger of YHWH admonished Yahushua, saying,* [7] *'Thus says YHWH of hosts: 'If you will walk in My ways, and if you will keep* ✗✦*-My command, then you shall also judge* ✗✦*-My House, and likewise have charge of* ✗✦*-My courts; I will give you places to walk among these who stand here.* [8] *'Hear, O Yahushua, the high priest, You and your companions who sit before you, For they are a wondrous sign; For behold, I am bringing forth* ✗✦*-My Servant the BRANCH.* [9] *For behold, the stone (✦✦✗) that I have laid before Yahushua: upon the stone are seven eyes. Behold, I will engrave its inscription,' says YHWH of hosts, 'And I will remove the iniquity of that land in one day.* [10] *In that day,' says YHWH of hosts, 'Everyone will invite his neighbor under his vine and under his fig tree.''*
Zechariah 3:1-10.

Now this prophecy was given during a time of rebuilding, when Yahudah was returning from their Babylonian exile. Notice the Aleph Taw (✗✦) affixed to Yahushua and His delegated authority connected with YHWH. This passage was actually telling us that "The Branch," which is a clear Messianic reference would be a High Priest named Yahushua. This High Priest would not be from the Aharonic Line, since Aharon needs a Temple.

With no earthly Temple and no functioning priesthood, man stands in a very precarious position

unless the Messiah did, in fact, appear and mediate the Renewed Covenant. If the Messiah did not come when prophesied, then prophecy has failed and there is no provision for returning to the Garden.

So then how can those of us in this present day know with any degree of assurance that the Messiah did indeed come when prophesied? Thankfully we have written accounts provided within a collection of documents known as the New Testament.

IO

The New Testament

There currently exists a collection of documents, written primarily by Yisraelites, which describe the period of history after the Tanak. These writings are intended to provide information concerning the life and teachings of a man named Yahushua, as well as the movement that followed His death and resurrection.

Based upon the information provided within those texts, we can discern that Yahushua was born precisely during the time when the prophets described that the Messiah would arrive, and many believed that Yahushua was the Messiah.

According to certain New Testament texts, Yahushua taught people to repent and return to the ways of YHWH. In other words, He taught Mosheh and the Torah. When He was tempted in the wilderness, He rebuked satan by quoting Mosheh and the Torah – specifically 1) Debarim 8:2-3, 2) Debarim 6:16, and 3) Debarim 6:13. (see Matthew 4:1-11 and Luke 4:1-13).

He performed signs and proclaimed that He came for the lost sheep of the House of Yisrael. (Matthew 15:24) Toward the end of His life, He revealed that He would renew the Covenant through the Passover, and that He would actually be the Passover Lamb. He was killed on Passover Day. After 3 days and 3 nights, He

was resurrected from the dead, in fulfillment of the sign and pattern provided by Jonah.

The fact that the climax of His work was a fulfillment of the sign of Jonah is extremely significant. Recall that Jonah emerged from the depths of the seas, literally the "belly of the beast," in order to prepare Nineveh and the Assyrian Kingdom to punish and remove the House of Yisrael from the Land. Yahushua died and literally emerged from the 3 days and 3 nights to redeem and restore the House of Yisrael.

His life was lived in obedience and fulfillment of the Torah, the Prophets and the Writings. We know all of this because of New Testament texts known as "the Gospels." The word "gospel" derives from the Old English word "god spell," and is intended to mean: "good news." From these texts we can know that Yahushua was indeed the promised Messiah Who was sent to renew the Covenant. In order to do this He had to make a way for the exiles to return.

The Tanak left off with Yisrael divided and scattered. The Prophets promised a regathering and a complete return. First the divided and divorced wife, Yisrael, needed to be cleansed from her sins and reunited. Yisrael needed to have the Covenant renewed.

Therefore, the collection would be better described as "The Renewed Covenant" or the "Brit Hadashah." The proper understanding is that the Messiah came to fulfill the prophetic pattern of Mosheh as the Mediator of the Marriage Covenant between YHWH and Yisrael. Just as Yisrael had broken the Covenant and Mosheh presented new Tablets so that the Covenant could be renewed, the Messiah would fulfill that pattern. When Yisrael, once again, broke the

Covenant, the Messiah would be broken so that the Covenant could be renewed. This time, the Torah would not be written on stone tablets, but on the hearts and inward parts of the people.

Sadly, this notion of renewal, which is found throughout the Scriptures, and even creation itself, has been lost to many. Remember that in the beginning, the sun and the moon were set in place to help us tell time. The moon is primarily there to help us gauge the passage of months, which is critical for observing the Appointed Times. As the moon cycles through its phases we can demarcate the months. Each month begins when we see the first sliver. The first sliver is called the renewed moon – "rosh hodesh." It is not a brand new moon, but rather a renewed moon. This sign in the sky helps us understand the process of renewal.

Just as the moon is renewed (rosh hodesh), so is the Covenant renewed (Brit Hadashah). There is not a brand new Covenant, only a renewed Covenant as prophesied by Yirmeyahu (Yirmeyahu 31:31). The root for hodesh and hadashah is the same – hadash (W◁ℍ). Hadash (W◁ℍ) means: "to renew, rebuild or repair."

Interestingly, over time people have not necessarily understood their context, and the New Testament writings have been manipulated and mistranslated to suit the needs of various religions, sects and denominations. An obvious example of this involves the Name of Yahushua.

We have already seen that names are extremely significant in the Hebrew language, and the plan of YHWH. One would expect the Name of the Messiah to be extremely significant, and in fact His Name was hinted at throughout the Scriptures.

We know from the Prophet Malachi that Elijah was expected to precede the Messiah. (Malachi 4:5) We also know from the Scriptures that Elisha carried the mantle of Elijah and operated in a double portion of the power of Elijah. The connection between the two cannot be ignored, because it was prophetic. Elijah is actually Eliyahu (𐤟𐤄𐤆𐤋𐤀) in Hebrew. Eliyahu means: "my El" (𐤋𐤀) is "Yahu" (𐤟𐤄𐤆). Elisha means: "my El" (𐤆𐤋𐤀) is "salvation" (𐤏𐤅). When you combine these names you have "Yah is Salvation," which is Yahusha (𐤏𐤅𐤟𐤄𐤆), also pronounced Yahushua. You are also left with the conclusion that Yahushua is El.

This was, by no coincidence, the very name of the Patriarch commonly called Joshua. There is no letter "J" in either the Hebrew or Greek language. So the name Joshua that people read in English Bibles is actually Yahushua in the Hebrew. Likewise, the name Jesus that people read in their English Bibles was Ieseus in the Greek. Ieseus was not the name of the Messiah but rather has its origins in pagan sun worship. It actually appears to be the name of a child of the sun god Zeus known for powers of healing.

This is not a simple linguistic difference, it is a monumental error that is known to many. Sadly, the traditional English name of Jesus pervades most of the Christian religion, even though it is blatantly wrong. Because of its importance, this subject is dealt with in a completely separate book.[71]

So the New Testament texts describe the Messiah, but tradition has altered His correct Name which is Yahushua. As with His namesake from the Tanak, His purpose was revealed through the patterns in the Scriptures, and it was all about the Covenant with

Yisrael.

The Covenant process is laid out in the Torah, the Prophets and the Writings, as well as the plan to renew the Covenant and restore Yisrael. It is within these texts that we find the Messiah. In fact, in one of the Gospels we are told how Yahushua, after His death and resurrection and on the way to Emmaus, revealed how Mosheh (the Torah) and the Prophets spoke of Him.

"25 Then He said unto them, O fools, and slow of heart to believe all that the prophets have spoken: 26 Ought not Messiah to have suffered these things, and to enter into His glory? 27 And beginning at Mosheh and all the Prophets, He expounded unto them in all the Scriptures the things concerning Himself." Luke 24:25-27.

Interestingly, this text describes Yahushua revealing Himself as the Messiah in *"all the Scriptures."* Since there were no New Testament texts immediately following His resurrection, *"all the Scriptures"* clearly referred to the Torah, the Prophets and likely the Writings.

The early followers of Yahushua needed to understand how He fulfilled the Torah and the Prophets. They needed their eyes to be opened so they could truly know the Messiah. (see Luke 24:31). Likewise, people today need the eyes of their understanding to be opened so they can truly see and know the Messiah. Sadly, we have centuries of tradition that have been heaped upon men through religious systems, which often cloud that truth.

Indeed, the New Testament texts, which were written to aid later generations, have been laden with tradition. They are sometimes misunderstood because of

those traditions, language differences and doctrines, along with other factors. It is critical to examine what happened to the followers of Yahushua in order to see how the New Testament came into existence.

It is then necessary to examine the later formation of Judaism and Christianity as separate and distinct religions apart from the Assembly of Yisrael. As Christianity separated from Yisrael and Judaism, there was a desire to compile their own unique Scriptures. It took centuries to accomplish, and there are numerous books describing that process in detail. Here we will simply take a brief look at the history.

After the death and resurrection of Yahushua, His followers continued in the truth of the Torah. They continued to meet in the Synagogue, observe Shabbat, celebrate the Appointed Times and live according to the Instructions and commandments contained within the Torah. They also continued to read and study their Scriptures – the Torah, the Prophets and the Writings.

Initially, there was an anticipation that Yahushua would return soon to complete His mission. He had provided atonement, through His shed blood. Just as the firstborn of Yisrael were covered during the Passover in Egypt, the blood of Yahushua would offer a covering, an atonement, for the firstborn of the renewed Covenant. This was a fulfillment of the Appointed Times of Month 1. He also sent the Spirit on Shabuot, also known as Pentecost, as a fulfillment of that Feast which occurred after a count of 50 days.[72]

The Appointed Times that Yisrael had been celebrating were now understood to be a pattern for the life and work of the Messiah. While Yahushua clearly brought fulfillment to the Passover, Unleavened Bread and Shabuot, the Appointed Times of Month 7 awaited fulfillment. So the followers of Yahushua expected Him to return soon, and fulfill those Times which would usher in the Kingdom of YHWH on Earth.[73]

We can see from letters and writings circulated through the Community that His return was originally thought to be imminent. We read letters from certain individuals making statements about His return such as *"it is the last hour"* (1 John 2:18) and *"the day is near."* (Romans 13:12). We also read instructions from a man commonly called Paul. In his first letter to the Corinthians he encouraged people not to get married because *"time has been shortened"* and *"the form of this world is passing away."* (1 Corinthians 7:27-31). In many of his earlier letters he repeatedly expressed an expectation that Yahushua would soon be returning. (see 1 Thessalonians, Romans 13, 1 Corinthians 7).

Certainly, with the dramatic events occurring in the world at that time, the end would have appeared to be imminent. These individuals were generally writing their thoughts and opinions. Rarely do they claim to be relating specific words directly from YHWH, as was customary for a prophet to do. The letters lack the trademark foundation often ascribed to prophecies such as "the Word of YHWH appeared to me and said . . ."

They were, without question, mortal men writing letters to people who they cared for. It is possible that they were wrong, and they later changed their position. In fact, it is possible that they assumed Yahushua would return at the Jubilee of 65 CE. After all, the Messiah would be the One to set things straight, unite the divided Kingdom and restore Yisrael to their inheritance. The Jubilee on Day 10 of Month 7 would have seemed ideal.

It was a time that they were "rehearsing" with anxious anticipation. This is similar to the expectation that Yahushua will be returning at the approaching 120th Jubilee on Day 1 of Month 7.

When that event came and went, they may have realized that His return was no longer imminent. As a result, the method of preserving and transmitting their testimony appeared to have changed. Information concerning Yahushua was originally simply transmitted by eye witnesses who testified to what they saw and explained how Yahushua was the Messiah according to the Torah and the Prophets.

This was actually the procedure revealed by Yahushua to the two witnesses on the way to Emmaus. They returned to Jerusalem and gave their testimony, and Yahushua then appeared to the eleven remaining disciples (Talmidim), as well as the others who were with them. Yahushua then appeared and ate with them. He also repeated what He had told the two, only now He revealed Himself in the psalms - the Writings.

"[44] And He said unto them, These are the words which I spoke unto you, while I was yet with you, that all things must be fulfilled, which were written in the Torah of Mosheh, and in the Prophets, and in the Psalms, concerning Me. [45] Then He opened their understanding, that they might understand the Scriptures, [46] And said unto them, Thus it is written, and thus it behooved Messiah to suffer, and to rise from the dead the third day: [47] And that repentance and remission of sins should be preached in His Name among all nations, beginning at Jerusalem. [48] And you are witnesses of these things. [49] And, behold, I send the promise of My Father upon you: but tarry in the city of Jerusalem, until you be endued with power from on high." Luke 24:44-49.

So Yahushua further explained His purpose according to the Scriptures - the Torah, the Prophets and the Writings (the Psalms). Therefore Yahushua Himself was affirming that the Scriptures were the Tanak. This was the pattern repeated by His Talmidim, they gave their testimony and revealed the truth of the Messiah through the Scriptures – the Torah, the Prophets and the writings. There were no other Scriptures, nor does it appear that there was any immediate perceived need for additional Scriptures. It appears many believed that Yahushua would soon be returning and their objective was to convey this truth to the exiles of Yisrael.

This may be why the earliest writings contained in the New Testament from that time period are some letters from Paul. Again, there may not have been a perceived need to formally compile and preserve the testimony of Yahushua, because there were numerous eye-witnesses throughout the Community of Believers, particularly the Talmidim, and the information was readily available.

Since the followers of Yahushua were primarily native Yisraelites, they remained a part of the Community of Yisrael. They were, after all, within the Covenant and had recently witnessed how YHWH, through the Messiah, would renew the Covenant with the two Houses of Yisrael and Yahudah.

A major problem began to develop when those who followed Yahushua refused to conform to the religious traditions of the religious leaders. Yahushua had spent much of His time rebuking the religious leaders for their traditions that were contrary to the Torah. Certainly His followers were not going to follow those traditions. They were now under the authority of

Yahushua as their Master, and they rejected the authority of the religious leaders. This was an underlying source of contention that existed within the community of Yisrael.

This situation only got worse as the Good News of Yahushua was spread to the Gentiles. The word Gentiles refers to "the nations" or "the heathens." In other words, those outside the Covenant Assembly of Yisrael. As the Gentiles heard the Good News of Yahushua, many began joining the Covenant Community. They were essentially joining and becoming part of the Assembly of Yisrael. Of course, those who believed that Yahushua was the Messiah understood that the Gentiles were joining Yisrael through faith in Yahushua. This was obviously not an satisfactory "conversion" according to the religious leaders who did not accept Yahushua as the Messiah.

As a result, there was a great division that occurred between the "sects." Those Yisraelites who did not believe in Yahushua did not accept those Gentile converts. They required a complex circumcision process which they believed was a prerequisite to joining the Covenant Assembly – the "qahal" (𐤋𐤄𐤒). They failed to understand the pattern provided through the life of Abram as he originally entered into Covenant while he was uncircumcised, and was only later circumcised when the Covenant of Circumcision was established.

Great disputes broke out and more divisions formed within the already divided Assembly of Yahudim. Eventually, those who followed The Way of Yahushua, became known as the Natzrim or Natzarenes. The name derives from the word "natzar" (𐤓𐤑𐤍) which means "branch." This was a declaration that Yahushua was the Messiah according to the Prophecy given by Isaiah: "*There shall come forth a Rod from the stem of Jesse, and a Branch* (𐤍𐤑𐤓) *shall grow out of his roots.*" Isaiah 11:1. Those of the Yahudim who preferred their traditions over Yahushua went on to form the religion of Judaism, after the destruction of the Temple in Jerusalem.

Both of these sects continued to consider the Torah, the Prophets and the Writings as their Scriptures. The Natzrim surely had eyewitness accounts and oral teachings concerning Yahushua. Essentially, the Good News would have been transmitted orally by those witnesses who explained how Yahushua was the Messiah - according to the Scriptures (The Torah, the Prophets and the Writings). The oral tradition, after all, is quite common and accepted in those cultures. Especially when dealing with largely illiterate people.

When the Talmidim of Yahushua understood that Yahushua would not be returning immediately, they apparently changed their outlook. This seems to be the case from other letters likely written later. In his letter to Timothy, Paul actually encouraged young widows to get remarried, have children and manage households. (1 Timothy 5:14) Interestingly, that letter is typically dated around 66 to 67 CE.[74]

This also coincides with the timeframe when the Gospels were believed to be written. Again, while there apparently was originally no perceived need to document the accounts of Yahushua for future generations, that seemed to have changed. By no coincidence, that occurred after the Jubilee. Once it was recognized that Yahushua would tarry, that appears to be the time when witnesses began to compile their testimony into writings that are commonly called Gospels. There are currently 4

such Gospels contained in the New Testament: namely Matthew, Mark, Luke and John. There are various other "Gospels" not contained in the New Testament, but that will be discussed further on.

It is generally recognized that the Gospels contained in the New Testament were written around 70 CE to 100 CE. That has baffled many who wonder why we have letters from Paul that predate the Gospels. You would think that the Gospels would have been written first. If indeed, the expectations of the Talmidim changed then the timing makes perfect sense.

The Talmidim recognized that their mission involved more than simply visiting Synagogues around the Mediterranean, and giving their testimony to the Yahudim still in Diaspora. It would focus on reaching out to the lost sheep of the House of Yisrael scattered throughout the world. That is where the outcasts of Yisrael were located, throughout the entire world – not just to the west throughout the Roman Empire. It also would be a mission that would span into the future.

According to the Prophet Hoshea, the House of Yisrael would be scattered and completely lose their identity with YHWH and His Covenant. (Hoshea 1). Just as Joseph was unrecognizable to his brothers, so the House of Yisrael was unrecognizable to the Yahudim. Those of the House of Yisrael (Joseph) had been mixed and scattered throughout the Nations. They were mixed with the Nations, because that was the pattern and method that YHWH used to regather His people.

This was actually how YHWH intended to bring all of the Nations into the Covenant. So over time, native Yisraelites came to believe in Yahushua. They also understood that there was a need to transmit this message to the Nations, and part of that involved documenting their testimony. Now this was not necessarily determined at a meeting, but there is an amazing and unique focus to the individual Gospels.

The 4 Gospels called Matthew, Mark, Luke and John are, without a doubt, the most important portion of the New Testament. They provide the testimony of the appearance of the Messiah. They provide an actual account of the words spoken by "the Word of YHWH in the flesh." These are the critical writings that provide the testimony of Yahushua, so people can understand that He did, indeed, come as prophesied throughout the Scriptures.

There was also a historical account, known as the Book of Acts, which outlines the "acts" of the apostles, after the death and resurrection of Yahushua. It primarily focuses on Peter and Paul, and it clearly only mentions a fraction of the events that occurred. As with the Gospels, there are numerous "non-canonized" acts, such as The Acts of John, The Acts of Paul, The Acts of Thecla, The Acts of Thomas and The Acts of Peter. Most people are completely unaware of these texts because long ago in history past, certain people decided to only include one "Acts" account, which obviously placed the focus on Paul and his travels within the Roman Empire.

Now it must be stated that my mention of these different "acts" is in no way an endorsement of their content - nor is my mention of other Gospels, letters or texts outside the Bible or the New Testament. The point of mentioning the texts is to show that there were many different writings, and at some point people made a decision regarding which ones made the cut and which

ones did not. It is helpful to examine the motives and beliefs of those individuals to understand why certain texts may have been selected over others.

Aside from the Gospels and the Book of Acts, the New Testament also contains a collection of letters, some of which have already been mentioned. These letters, known as "Epistles," were written to various assemblies from different authors. These letters are addressing certain issues, some known while others not so clear. These letters are probably only a fraction of the letters that were transmitted by the early Talmidim.

Finally, most versions of the New Testament conclude with the Book of Revelation. This was the Revelation of Yahushua, written by Yahanan, while on the Isle of Patmos.

There are currently 27 unique texts contained in the most popular and accepted version of the New Testament. All of these documents were written separately, and at different times. They all followed their own unique course through the various assemblies where they were delivered, copied and preserved. Some were copied and transmitted into different languages. All of them were maintained as unique and separate texts for centuries. We actually do not have any originals, called "autographs" and none of those documents were immediately considered to be Scriptures.

It is important to understand that there was initially no uniform method of collecting, compiling, copying and preserving all of those writings. As a result, the texts currently contained in the New Testament provide a very small amount of information concerning the Messiah and those who spread the Good News of His appearance and message.

In fact, we are specifically told that the Gospels only tell a fraction of the words and deeds spoken by Yahushua. *"And there are also many other things that Yahushua did, which if they were written one by one, I suppose that even the world itself could not contain the books that would be written."* John 21:25.

So the Gospels provide a small, but necessary, portion of the information concerning Yahushua. Each of the Gospels is generally understood to show the Messiah in different roles. They are clearly not a complete account of the life of Yahushua, only a brief summary.

We also must understand that the New Testament only provides a small measure of the events that occurred before and after the first coming of the Messiah. Interestingly, the Book of Acts, commonly known as the Acts of the Apostles, begins by describing an incredible event in Jerusalem.

It details the Day of Pentecost, better known as Shabuot in Hebrew. Shabuot is an important Appointed Time, believed to be the same day when the Torah was given to Yisrael at Mount Sinai. In obedience to the Torah, men from all over the world had gathered in Jerusalem just 48 days after the resurrection of Yahushua. (Acts 2:5). Many were from the east, Parthians, Medes, Elamites, dwellers in Mesopotamia and Asia. (Acts 2:9). These individuals all heard the Good News of Yahushua in their own tongue and many believed. These individuals would have returned to their homes and spread the Good News, yet we read little to nothing of what occurred with those from the east.

Remember that Yahushua spent His ministry teaching, training and equipping twelve Talmidim. After

the death of Judas, they felt compelled to maintain that number, and selected Matthias to replace Judas. (Acts 1:26). They cast lots, which was a very traditional and accepted method of deciding a matter. The priests would actually cast lots each day to delegate their duties.

Those twelve did indeed spend their lives spreading the Good News of Messiah. (Acts 6:2-4, 8:4). According to extra-Biblical sources, many journeyed to the east. Yet again, you will not read about the majority of those acts in the New Testament. In fact, the single Book of Acts is focused primarily on Peter and John at first. It then transitions a bit to Philip, then on to Paul, who was not one of the twelve, for most of the remainder of the text.

Therefore, the New Testament actually provides a very limited view of history and the expansion of the Good News. Clearly there was more. Surely there must have been incredible testimonies, miracles and letters to the Assemblies from the east, yet the New Testament is essentially a collection of texts focused on the Assemblies of the west – those within the Roman Empire. So the Book of Acts, and the New Testament, are incomplete and unfinished texts, telling a portion of the story that continues to this day.

A majority of the documents contained within the New Testament are letters. In fact, of the 27 documents contained therein, 21 are letters, known as Epistles. This differs greatly from the Tanak which includes the Torah, the Prophets and Writings. In the Tanak, the Writings are essentially history, psalms and proverbs. The Tanak does not contain any correspondence, which actually seems out of place when we consider the texts traditionally considered to be

Scriptures.

These selected Epistles are only half of a conversation. We do not always know what prompted their writing, which sometimes leads to their misapplication or misunderstanding. Further, this collection of 21 letters is likely only a sampling of the letters sent between the Assemblies. You might reasonably expect to read letters from all of the eleven remaining Talmidim specifically trained by Yahushua, as well as Matthias.

Incredibly, we only have letters from two, namely Peter and John. They are noticeably placed toward the end of the New Testament, as are the other letters allegedly written by James, the brother of Yahushua, and Jude. We do not know exactly who Jude (Yahudah) was, or whether this was merely a pseudonym.

James, on the other hand, was a different matter. We know that James was the undisputed leader of the Natzrim Sect after the death and resurrection of Yahushua. As a result, one would expect his Epistle to be preeminent. Instead, it is relegated toward the end.

The fact that it was written *"to the twelve tribes which are scattered abroad"* is of particular note since Yahushua said He came for *"the Lost Sheep of the House of Yisrael."* James was writing to all of Yisrael. He was not making a distinction between the Yahudim and the Gentiles. He was presenting a unified message. There are possibly other political factors that led to James being minimized in the New Testament that we will explore in the next chapter.

So the majority of the Epistles contained in the New Testament, 13 to 14 in all, are actually attributed to Paul. They are given priority and immediately follow the

Book of Acts, which is mostly about Paul. His writings were supposed to be helpful revelation, teaching, instruction and advice written to those whom he had transmitted the good news of Messiah. Again, these writings are letters, and it is highly questionable whether a letter should ever be categorized as "Scripture." In fact, while Paul did indicate that he was teaching mysteries, he never purported that his letters were "Scriptures."

Over time, men have taken these select letters and elevated them to be equal, and even above the Words of Mosheh, Yahushua and YHWH. Because the letters are easily misunderstood by the untrained, many have fallen away from the path blazed by Yahushua. Multitudes have entered into a life of lawlessness, ignorantly believing that it was what Paul taught, as if Paul had the authority to change the commandments of YHWH, and the recently revealed Messiah Yahushua.

This is nothing new. In fact, the writings of Paul created confusion in the days when they were written, copied and distributed. This became such an issue that Peter specifically addressed the issue and referred to the difficulties created by those letters. Read what he says:

"¹⁴ Therefore, beloved, looking forward to these things, be diligent to be found by Him in peace, without spot and blameless; ¹⁵ and consider that the longsuffering of our Master is salvation - as also our beloved brother Paul, according to the wisdom given to him, has written to you, ¹⁶ as also in all his <u>*epistles, speaking in them of these things, in which are some*</u> <u>*things hard to understand, which untaught and unstable people*</u> <u>*twist to their own destruction, as they do also the rest of the*</u> <u>*writings*</u> *(γραφὰς)."* 2 Peter 3:14-16.

Now many Bibles translate the Greek word "grafes" (γραφὰς) as Scriptures, which leads people to believe that Peter is actually classifying Paul's letters as "Scriptures." This is clearly not the case. The Greek word "grafes" (γραφὰς) simply means: "something written" or "writings." So Peter is simply indicating that people are twisting Paul's writings, as they do the other writings that were circulating among the Assemblies.

While Paul was apparently highly intelligent, his letters can only be properly understood when read in context, and with a thorough knowledge of the Torah, the Prophets and the Writings – the very Scriptures from which he was intending to reveal certain "mysteries."

Peter said the writings of Paul were hard to understand, and they were twisted. We can clearly see that this happened in Christianity, and continues to this day. Paul has been elevated to such a degree that his teachings often eclipse those of Yahushua. As a result of this emphasis in the New Testament, we will take a closer look at those writings and the man named Paul.

II

Paul

Apart from the writings called the gospels, a large portion of the New Testament consists of letters referred to as the Epistles. In reality these are simply correspondence from certain individuals to other individuals, groups or assemblies. These letters are attributed to certain people. Sometimes the authorship is verifiable, but not always. There are sometimes questions regarding who wrote certain texts, as we previously discussed concerning the letter of Jude (Yahudah).

In ancient times, it was not uncommon for people to write texts, and attribute them to certain authors. This may have been done to perpetrate a fraud, but more often it was meant as a compliment. For instance, a student might have written something and attributed it to his teacher, as a matter of honor and respect. They would, of course, have attempted to write something that reflected the ideas or teachings of the namesake. This is referred to as pseudonymous writing.

Determining genuine authorship of ancient texts, especially when they are copies, is a question that many scholars endeavor to determine. It is, at times, a daunting task - more a question of educated guesswork than it is an exact science. By far the letters attributed to Paul constitute the largest collection of texts in the New Testament, and these letters are no exception when scholars question authorship.

It is generally understood that these letters were written in the early 50's CE to the mid 60's CE. As already mentioned, this is likely earlier than the Gospels. The letters where Paul's authorship is undisputed by scholars are: Romans, I and II Corinthians, Galatians and Philippians.

I Thessalonians and Philemon are disputed by some, but generally recognized to be written by Paul. There is general consensus in scholarship that Paul did not write I and II Timothy and Titus. Scholars debate Colossians, Ephesians and II Thessalonians. The book of Hebrews is also highly contested, in part because it is anonymous.

The reason for these debates in scholarship is because there is evidence that Paul did not write all letters written in his name. There are, in fact, actualy pseudonymous letters written in his name such as The Epistle to the Laodiceans and III Corinthians.

So these debates concerning the Epistles contained within the New Testament are not without justification, and are based upon a number of factors. For instance, the writing style in I Thessalonians is different than II Thessalonians. I Thessalonians contains short choppy sentences only seen in the Greek, and also asserts that the end is imminent. II Thessalonians, on the other hand, is written in a different style in the Greek with long convoluted sentences. Also, the end is not imminent

in the text.

"E.J Goodspeed argued that the vocabulary of the Epistle of the Ephesians showed a literary relationship with the First Epistle of Clement, written around the end of the First Century. Similarly, E. Percy argued that the speech and style of Colossians more strongly resembled Pauline authorship than not."[75]

This is a very brief sampling, and none of this is proof positive for whether or not Paul actually wrote the texts. As for writing style, he may have simply used a different scribe. Sometimes, people change their writing style over time. Often the arguments are simply speculation.

These are issues that scholars investigate, and there is no harm in these examinations. Ultimately, though, regardless of proof of authorship, it is important to insure that the context of these letters are understood, and that they are not used to support any doctrines or teachings that are contrary to the Torah. The writings of Paul, and the other authors in the New Testament, were teachings intended to address certain issues and were, for the most part, Torah teachings.

Many people struggle with the letters attributed to Paul. This is largely because they fail to understand his role, and the context in which his letters were written. Further, they often read his writings within the framework of certain Christian preconceived theologies, and those theologies do not align with the requisite Torah based perspective from which Paul was addressing the problems of certain assemblies.

As we saw, the Roman Christian religion, largely responsible for the development of the New Testament, placed a significant emphasis on Paul to the point where many see Paul as the founder of Christianity. In fact, so much emphasis has been placed on this man that his letters often distract from the purpose of Yahushua the Messiah. It has gotten to the point that many in Christianity have essentially "deified" Paul and his writings.

I am astounded when I hear people quote from these various letters, and then boldly declare "These are the very words of God." My first response is: "Where ever did you get that idea?" Paul certainly never said that his letters were "the Word of God." In fact, I strongly doubt he ever approved of classifting his letters as Scriptures. I believe he would be shocked to see what has been done with his writings; at least he should be.

First of all, they are letters – period. They often deal with both important and mundane issues within certain assemblies. The problem is we are only reading one side of the conversation, so we do not actually have the complete perspective.

Second, just because something is written or contained in the Bible does not mean it is "the Word of God." Typically, this sort of statement is simply made out of ignorance, but it is very misleading. A perfect example of this is found in the Garden, and the so-called temptations of Yahushua. Clearly the words spoken by the nachash to the woman, and those spoken by hashatan to Yahushua are not "the Word of God," unless they were verbatim quotes from the Scriptures attributed to YHWH.

Therefore, simply because words are written in the text, does not make them "the Word of God." The Words of Elohim are those words spoken directly by Elohim, spoken through a prophet on behalf of Elohim,

or spoken by the Messiah. Most times when spoken by a Prophet it is clear that he is transmitting a message from YHWH.

So just because Paul wrote a letter does not mean that every word in that letter can be deemed "the Word of Elohim." Now this may sound shocking to someone raised believing that the Bible is the inerrant Word of Elohim that was essentially dropped from heaven onto the lap of King James, completely translated into the English language.

We will examine the process of compiling the Bible further on in this discussion, but for now we will continue to focus on Paul. No doubt, Paul was a very intelligent man. By his own account he was: "*a Yahudim, born in Tarsus of Cilicia, but brought up in this city at the feet of Gamaliel, taught according to the strictness of our fathers' law, and was zealous toward God as you all are today.*" Acts 22:3. He was: "*⁵ circumcised the eighth day, of the stock of Yisrael, of the tribe of Benjamin, a Hebrew of the Hebrews; concerning the Torah, a Pharisee; ⁶ concerning zeal, persecuting the assembly; concerning the righteousness which is in the Torah, blameless.*" Philippians 3:5-6.

Paul had great intellectual credentials, the only problem was that he was originally on the wrong side. As smart as he was regarding the Torah, he was hindering the work of the Messiah. This resulted in a personal visit by Yahushua. He was confronted by Yahushua on the road to Damascus. He was told to stop persecuting the Talmidim, and start spreading the Good News. Many refer to the Road to Damascus experience as a conversion.

This is incorrect, Paul did not change religions. He did not become a Christian. He may have changed sects from the Pharisees to the Natzrim, but that was the extent of it. He was still a man, and he was clearly Torah observant, which he was well versed in. He simply understood that Yahushua was the promised Messiah. We know from the Book of Acts that Paul went teaching and preaching the Good News of Yahushua.

He was responsible for overseeing those people whom he taught. He would visit them and build relationships with them. He would also send and receive letters. Again, we do not have any of the verbal or written communications sent to Paul, only his responses or correspondence that he initiated. Those letters are often addressing very specific issues, but we do not always have the complete context.

The letters are filled with instructive information and revelation, but they were not doctrinal statements made by an authoritative body. Paul was not even a part of the leadership established in Jerusalem. This is evident from accounts in the Book of Acts that describe times when Paul would travel to Jerusalem. Jerusalem was the center of authority for the Natzrim, and this is where issues were discussed and settled by the elders.

In Acts 15 we read an account when Paul and Barnabas visited Jerusalem, and a decision was made on a pervasive issue – physical circumcision as a prerequisite for salvation.

"*¹ And certain men came down from Judea and taught the brethren, 'Unless you are circumcised according to the custom of Mosheh, you cannot be saved.' ² Therefore, when Paul and Barnabas had no small dissension and dispute with them, they determined that Paul and Barnabas and certain others of them should*

go up to Jerusalem, to the apostles and elders, about this question. ³ So, being sent on their way by the church, they passed through Phoenicia and Samaria, describing the conversion of the Gentiles; and they caused great joy to all the brethren. ⁴ And when they had come to Jerusalem, they were received by the assembly and the apostles and the elders; and they reported all things that Elohim had done with them. ⁵ But some of the sect of the Pharisees who believed rose up, saying, 'It is necessary to circumcise them, and to command them to keep the Torah of Mosheh.' ⁶ Now the apostles and elders came together to consider this matter. ⁷ And when there had been much dispute, Peter rose up and said to them: 'Men and brethren, you know that a good while ago Elohim chose among us, that by my mouth the Gentiles should hear the word of the good news and believe. ⁸ So Elohim, who knows the heart, acknowledged them by giving them the Set Apart Spirit, just as He did to us, ⁹ and made no distinction between us and them, purifying their hearts by faith. ¹⁰ Now therefore, why do you test Elohim by putting a yoke on the neck of the Talmidim which neither our fathers nor we were able to bear? ¹¹ But we believe that through the grace of the Master Yahushua Messiah we shall be saved in the same manner as they.' ¹² Then all the multitude kept silent and listened to Barnabas and Paul declaring how many miracles and wonders Elohim had worked through them among the Gentiles. ¹³

And after they had become silent, James
answered, saying, 'Men and brethren, listen to
me: ¹⁴ *Simon has declared how Elohim at the*
first visited the Gentiles to take out of them a
people for His name. ¹⁵ *And with this the words*
of the prophets agree, just as it is written: ¹⁶
'After this I will return and will rebuild the
tabernacle of David, which has fallen down; I
will rebuild its ruins, and I will set it up; ¹⁷ *So*
that the rest of mankind may seek YHWH,
even all the Gentiles who are called by My
name, says YHWH who does all these things.'
¹⁸ *'Known to Elohim from eternity are all His*
works. ¹⁹ *Therefore I judge that we should not*
trouble those from among the Gentiles who are
turning to Elohim, ²⁰ *but that we write to them*
to abstain from things polluted by idols, from
sexual immorality, from things strangled, and
from blood. ²¹ *For Mosheh has had throughout*
many generations those who preach him in
every city, being read in the synagogues every
Sabbath.' ²² *Then it pleased the apostles and*
elders, with the whole assembly, to send chosen
men of their own company to Antioch with
Paul and Barnabas, namely, Judas who was
also named Barsabas, and Silas, leading men
among the brethren." Acts 15:1-22.

So here we read a formal reply to the question:
"Unless you are circumcised according to the custom of
Mosheh, you cannot be saved." Some were teaching that
you could not be saved unless you were circumcised
"according to the custom of Mosheh."

First of all, there is no act or work of the flesh

that can save a man. Circumcision is important, but it is only an outward sign of the Covenant, and it cannot save a person. Salvation only comes from the shed blood of the Messiah, the One who circumcises the heart.

This was a hot issue since circumcision was the traditional entry point into the Assembly of Yisrael. There were elaborate conversion ceremonies associated with circumcision, and this boiled down to an issue of authority. Did a person first need to follow the circumcision rituals of the Yahudim to enter into the Renewed Covenant, or was it solely reliant upon immersion in the name of the Messiah. The Name of Yahushua was His "authority."

The important thing to emphasize is that there was an authoritative body in Jerusalem, and it did not include Paul. It was Peter who spoke the truth to the matter, and James (Yaakob) who settled the matter. In fact James, whose actual Hebrew name was Yaakob, was the undisputed leader – he decided the matter. (Acts 15:19). The center of the Natzrim assembly was in Jerusalem. This, of course makes perfect sense since Jerusalem was the location of the House of Elohim, and the place where YHWH chose to put His Name. Aside from the Gospels, you can hardly discern that fact from the New Testament texts though.

There are other sources that clearly indicate the fact that Yahushua chose his brother Yaakob before His ascension, with Peter and John under Yaakob. The leadership was followed by the remaining of the 12 Talmidim, then seventy elders. How amazing that Yahushua chose His brother, it almost reminds us of Mosheh and Aharon, brothers leading the 12 Tribes of Yisrael. This is a fact, rarely acknowledged or even

known by most people.

Clement of Alexandria, Eusebius and Hegesippus all attest to this fact – Yaakob was the leader specifically chosen by Yahushua. Interestingly, the non-canonized Gospel of Thomas, in saying number 12, actually describes the account of Yahushua appointing Yaakob.

Paul himself testified that James, Cephas (Peter) and John were the "pillars" of the assembly. (Galatians 2:9). It is difficult to discern whether he was being sincere when he provided the observation. A common text provides: ". . . James, Cephas, and John who *seemed to be* pillars . . ." Some interpret the Greek as saying: ". . . James, Cephas, and John, *so-called pillars* . . ."

We know that when Paul was in Jerusalem at a later time, he appeared before Yaakob and the elders to answer the rumors surrounding his teachings. He also followed the directives of Yaakob. (Acts 21). The reality is Yaakob was in charge, but this is rarely understood or acknowledged by Christians. This should cause one to wonder why there is so little emphasis on Yaakob, and so much attention on Paul in the New Testament. It is almost as if there was a purposeful diminishment of Yaakob, and an intentional emphasis on Paul.

We know that there were many disputes centered around the teachings promoted by certain men. (1 Corinthians 1:12; 3:4). Apparently, this resulted in rivalries, divisions and factions based upon authority and leadership. There was a particular sect of Natzrim, later called the Ebionites, who actually rejected the Epistles of Paul, and considered him to be an apostate. In the Pseudo-Clementine literature we read that they esteemed Yaakob as the leader of the Assembly centered in Jerusalem.

Their position is not so hard to understand. After all, Paul was originally an enemy of Yahushua. He later claimed to have an encounter with Messiah, but would that elevate him above the Twelve hand selected Talmidim who walked, lived and learned from the Messiah for years. Yahushua obviously chose the Twelve Talmidim for a reason, and they were trained for a purpose.

There were many others like the Ebionites who did not revere Paul. They did not agree with his teachings, many of which had been twisted and misconstrued. The Ebionites, along with other sects, were later branded as "heretics" by Christians who obviously followed Paul. History has a very interesting way of choosing sides, and diminishing or destroying those who end up in the minority.

Again, Yaakob was the brother of Yahushua. He was highly revered and the undisputed leader of the Jerusalem Assembly, the center of the Natzrim sect. As a result, one would think that much information would be provided about this individual and the growth of the Assembly in Jerusalem.

Instead, after reading about the great outpouring on Shabuot, the Book of Acts provides some information about Peter and then very obviously the emphasis turns almost exclusively to Paul. The Book of Acts actually ends off with Paul in Rome. The New Testament then focuses on Paul's letters to Assemblies and people within the Roman Empire. The emphasis on Paul and Rome must be acknowledged, since it was the Roman Church that later compiled and canonized the New Testament texts, which placed a major emphasis on Paul and his teachings.

Now, let us look back to the issue presented at the Jerusalem Council in Acts 15. Yaakob judged the matter and rendered a decision. The solution was Torah based and involved obeying the heart of the Torah, because Mosheh is taught in the synagogue every Shabbat.

So the point was clear, not to overwhelm the unlearned Gentile converts. Give them the essentials by keeping them out of the idolatrous pagan temple worship system. Then get them into the synagogue every Shabbat so they could hear Mosheh - the Torah. The purpose was that they could continue to hear, learn and obviously obey.

Coming out of paganism is a process, and circumcision was not even appropriate until they learned the Torah, understood the Covenant and made an informed decision to become circumcised. It was not a salvation issue. The distinction is really when and why a person becomes circumcised, not whether they became circumcised. Remember that Abram was not immediately circumcised when he came out of Babylon and entered into Covenant with YHWH. (see Beresheet 15).

Paul obviously understood that circumcision was important, otherwise he would not have circumcised Timothy. (Acts 16:3). Many believe that he taught against circumcision, and some of his letters clearly give that impression. If he ever taught against circumcision, the sign of the Covenant, then he must give an account to YHWH on that matter.

He actually spent much of his time addressing this issue, because that was the primary argument being used to bring people under the bondage of the law - man's law. His letters are attacks on those who he called

"The Circumcision," and he was also defending himself through those letters. A good portion of the content of these letters was of a personal nature. For instance, the entire final chapter of 1 Corinthians was a closing.

"¹ Now concerning the collection for the saints, as I have given orders to the assemblies of Galatia, so you must do also: ² On the first day of the week let each one of you lay something aside, storing up as he may prosper, that there be no collections when I come. ³ And when I come, whomever you approve by your letters I will send to bear your gift to Jerusalem. ⁴ But if it is fitting that I go also, they will go with me. ⁵ Now I will come to you when I pass through Macedonia (for I am passing through Macedonia). ⁶ And it may be that I will remain, or even spend the winter with you, that you may send me on my journey, wherever I go. ⁷ For I do not wish to see you now on the way; but I hope to stay a while with you, if the Lord permits. ⁸ But I will tarry in Ephesus until Shabuot. ⁹ For a great and effective door has opened to me, and there are many adversaries. ¹⁰ And if Timothy comes, see that he may be with you without fear; for he does the work of the Master, as I also do. ¹¹ Therefore let no one despise him. But send him on his journey in peace, that he may come to me; for I am waiting for him with the brethren. ¹² Now concerning our brother Apollos, I strongly urged him to come to you with the brethren, but he was quite unwilling to come at this time; however, he will come when he has a

convenient time. *¹³ Watch, stand fast in the faith, be brave, be strong. ¹⁴ Let all that you do be done with love. ¹⁵ I urge you, brethren - you know the household of Stephanas, that it is the firstfruits of Achaia, and that they have devoted themselves to the ministry of the saints - ¹⁶ that you also submit to such, and to everyone who works and labors with us. ¹⁷ I am glad about the coming of Stephanas, Fortunatus, and Achaicus, for what was lacking on your part they supplied. ¹⁸ For they refreshed my spirit and yours. Therefore acknowledge such men. ¹⁹ The assemblies of Asia greet you. Aquila and Priscilla greet you heartily in the Master, with the assembly that is in their house. ²⁰ All the brethren greet you. Greet one another with a holy kiss. ²¹ The salutation of me Paul with my own hand. ²² If anyone does not love the Master Yahushua Messiah, let him be accursed. O Maranatha! ²³ The grace of our Master Yahushua Messiah be with you. ²⁴ My love be with you all in Messiah Yahushua. Amen."* 1 Corinthians 16:1-24.

We read from this passage some personal and travel information, along with instructions concerning the method of collecting money for Jerusalem. We are provided much historical and logistical data, including the fact that Paul penned the salutation with his own hand. This is all well and good, but this information is clearly not "the Word of Elohim."

We can read the same with the last chapter of the letter to the Romans, as well as in other letters. These are

very personal comments made for the recipients of the letter. The letters typically have greetings and closings with instructions and personal information. Of course, this is normal and to be expected in a letter.

Other examples of the specific and personal nature of these letters is found in a letter written to Timothy wherein he is instructed not to drink anymore water, but to drink some wine for his stomach (1 Timothy 5:23). This is advice to a friend, not some commandment from YHWH to drink wine. In another passage Timothy is asked to bring a cloak that was left behind. (2 Timothy 4:13). Again, reminding someone to retrieve a garment that was left at someone's house is not the Word of Elohim. To classify it as such simply diminishes the significance of the True Word that was spoken directly from Elohim.

The entire portion of 2 Corinthians 11 involves Paul talking about himself. In fact, he mentions "I" or "me" no less that 50 times in that passage. While he proclaims his humility, he spends a great deal of time "boasting" about his accomplishments. In fact, this is actually a trademark of Paul's writings and the reason why most scholars contend that Paul did not write the book of Hebrews. The author of the book of Hebrews actually spends far less time talking about himself than Paul typically does.

The reason for all of the personal references seems to be because he was contending with the other "apostles." Paul was clearly trying to distinguish and establish himself and his authority. He tells how when he was first called, he did not confer with flesh and blood, nor did he go to Jerusalem. (Galatians 1:16). He specifically points out that he corrected Peter and

Barnabas, thus giving the impression that he is above them. (Galatians 2:11-16). Indeed, he specifically stated: *"For I consider that I am not at all inferior to the most eminent apostles."* 2 Corinthians 11:5.

He seemingly makes an allusion to himself as a Mosaic figure when he states: *"Even though I am untrained in speech, yet I am not in knowledge."* 2 Corinthians 11:6 (see also Galatians 1:15). Again, Paul was apparently well learned in the Torah. By his own account, he sat at the feet of Gamaliel, a well respected Sage. (Acts 22:3). He may have known the Torah better than any of the other early Talmidim, but the fact that he initially persecuted and killed them shows the distinction between knowledge and Spirit led understanding.

It was only when he met the Messiah on the Road to Damascus that his physical eyes were blinded and his spiritual eyes were opened. According to his own testimony, he was a chosen vessel, hand selected by Yahushua, to bear His name *"before the Gentiles, and kings, and the children of Yisrael."* Acts 9:15.

He taught those truths to his Yisraelite brethren as well as to the Gentiles. We know from the book of Acts, which is largely focused on his life and ministry, that he continually taught that Yahushua was the Messiah through the Scriptures. He considered the Scriptures to be the Torah of Mosheh and the prophets. (see Acts 28:23). So Paul was constantly using the Torah and the Prophets to teach the truth of the Messiah.

Amazingly, there are many people who use the words in his letters in an attempt to negate the Torah. Some Christian sects use passages such as 1 Corinthians 11, to create new doctrines regarding women and head coverings. At the same time they completely ignore the

Torah commandments requiring men to wear tzitzit.

When you view the New Testament and the Scriptures in their proper context, it is plain to see that Paul could not add to or take away from the Torah – that is strictly prohibited. (Debarim 12:32).

The writings of Paul cannot contradict the Torah, the Prophets or the Writings if they purport to teach truth. If they are truly inspired by the Set Apart Spirit then it is impossible – period. If Paul did contradict the Scriptures then he was a false prophet – period. That is really the bottom line on this subject.

I know many people are invested in Paul and his letters, because they need them to justify their lawless behavior. Yahushua was crystal clear on this subject. He specifically stated: *"Do not think that I came to destroy the Torah or the Prophets. I did not come to destroy but to fulfill."* Matthew 5:17.

Yahushua made this statement at the beginning of His ministry so that there would be no mistake about the issue. While Yahushua repeatedly violated the man-made laws of the religious leaders, He never violated the Torah. He came to "fulfill," which was the opposite of "destroy." He came as the Living Torah to reveal the Spirit of the Torah, and to show men how to walk in Spirit and in Truth.

Yahushua went on to state: *"Whoever therefore breaks one of the least of these commandments, and teaches men so, shall be called least in the kingdom of heaven; but whoever does and teaches them, he shall be called great in the kingdom of heaven."* Matthew 5:19. Accordingly, if Paul taught people to disobey the commandments then he will be called "least" in the kingdom. These are the words of Yahushua the Messiah and not to be ignored.

Incredibly, many people actually use the writings of Paul to support the notion that the Torah has been done away with. This would be in direct contravention to the words of Yahushua, but they believe that Paul, through his letters, is somehow advocating for the abolition of the Torah. If you believe that Paul had the authority to do something that Messiah Himself said would not be done, then you have placed the man Paul above the Messiah. You have made Paul your god, and you are an idolater.

Many in the Christian religion have done just that. They have essentially made Paul their god by endowing him with the power, through his letters, to usurp and overrule Mosheh, the Prophets and Yahushua. The irony is that what they believe Paul taught is often not what he taught. Rather, it is a twisted or distorted interpretation of his teachings.

The problem generally stems from a failure to understand the Scriptures, and the writings of Paul. Since most in Christianity look at the original Scriptures - the Torah, the Prophets and the Writings - as "old," they do not have the Scriptures as their foundation. As a result, when they read the letters from Paul, they not only lack cultural and subject matter context, they also lack Scriptural context.

It is questionable whether Paul intended to teach or advocate many of the doctrines that people attribute to him. If you understand the Scriptures properly, then you will truly understand that Paul was often simply explaining the Scriptures, not trying to change them.

Again, the only Scriptures in existence when he wrote his letters were the Torah, the Prophets and the Writings. Paul described these Scriptures as: "[15] . . . *able*

to make you wise for salvation through faith which is in Yahushua Messiah. *[16] All Scripture is given by inspiration of Elohim, and is profitable for doctrine, for reproof, for correction, for instruction in righteousness, [17] that the man of Elohim may be complete, thoroughly equipped for every good work.*" 2 Timothy 3:15-16.

Some people attempt to use this statement to apply to Paul's letters, but that was not his intent. He was clearly referring to the Torah, the Prophets and the Writings. So Paul states that the Scriptures make you wise for salvation through faith, which is in Yahushua Messiah.

Again, the Scriptures are able to reveal Messiah. Those Scriptures are what Paul used to prove that Yahushua was the Messiah. This was the case for all who believed in Yahushua. "*. . . for he vigorously refuted the Yahudim publicly, showing from the Scriptures that Yahushua is the Messiah.*" Acts 18:28. Paul did not need his letters to prove the Good News of Yahushua. He only needed the Scriptures. The same holds true for all of those who follow Yahushua, both past and present.

Those in Berea searched out the Scriptures to confirm what they were told about Yahushua. "*[10] Then the brethren immediately sent Paul and Silas away by night to Berea. When they arrived, they went into the synagogue of the Yahudim. [11] These were more fair-minded than those in Thessalonica, in that they received the word with all readiness, and searched the Scriptures daily to find out whether these things were so.*" Acts 17:10-11.

So the writings of Paul must be viewed in their proper context. Back in the day, before there was a codex called the Bible, these writings were simply separate scrolls and texts that were circulated, copied and shared.

If you can grasp this realization, you will be able to work through many of the false beliefs and doctrines that have influenced people.

We will look at one example of how the writings of Paul have been misconstrued. There is a famous quote from Paul that proclaims: *"you are not under the law but under grace."* Romans 6:14. Many interpret this to mean that the Torah is done away with, and therefore, no one has to observe the Torah any longer. This, of course, is not what Paul meant. Let us look at the passage in context.

> *"¹ What shall we say then? Shall we continue in sin that grace may abound? ² Certainly not! How shall we who died to sin live any longer in it? ³ Or do you not know that as many of us as were immersed into Messiah Yahushua were immersed into His death? ⁴ Therefore we were buried with Him through immersion into death, that just as Messiah was raised from the dead by the glory of the Father, even so we also should walk in newness of life. ⁵ For if we have been united together in the likeness of His death, certainly we also shall be in the likeness of His resurrection, ⁶ knowing this, that our old man was crucified with Him, that the body of sin might be done away with, that we should no longer be slaves of sin. ⁷ For he who has died has been freed from sin. ⁸ Now if we died with Messiah, we believe that we shall also live with Him, ⁹ knowing that Messiah, having been raised from the dead, dies no more. Death no longer has dominion over Him. ¹⁰ For the death that He died, He died to sin once for all; but*

the life that He lives, He lives to Elohim. *[11]* *Likewise you also, reckon yourselves to be dead indeed to sin, but alive to Elohim in Messiah Yahushua our Master. [12] Therefore do not let sin reign in your mortal body, that you should obey it in its lusts. [13] And do not present your members as instruments of unrighteousness to sin, but present yourselves to Elohim as being alive from the dead, and your members as instruments of righteousness to Elohim. [14] For sin shall not have dominion over you, for you are not under law but under grace. [15] What then? Shall we sin because we are not under law but under grace? Certainly not! [16] Do you not know that to whom you present yourselves slaves to obey, you are that one's slaves whom you obey, whether of sin leading to death, or of obedience leading to righteousness? [17] But Elohim be thanked that though you were slaves of sin, yet you obeyed from the heart that form of doctrine to which you were delivered. [18] And having been set free from sin, you became slaves of righteousness. [19] I speak in human terms because of the weakness of your flesh. For just as you presented your members as slaves of uncleanness, and of lawlessness leading to more lawlessness, so now present your members as slaves of righteousness for holiness.*" Romans 6:1-19.

When it is read in context the meaning should be evident. We all have been tainted by sin. Sin is defined as lawlessness – a violation of the Torah. The Torah points the righteous path, and refusal to live a righteous

life is sin and lawlessness.

When we are immersed (baptized) in Yahushua, we die to sin and are no longer subject to the penalty of death. We come out of Babylon and "cross over" according to pattern of Abram. Because of the work of Messiah, we are made clean. This is the "grace" or rather "unmerited favor" of Elohim.

Once we receive this free gift that we did not earn, we are then supposed to stay clean. This has everything to do with the Torah. The Torah, after all, provides us with the instructions for righteous living. We are not supposed to continue in lawlessness. Paul emphasized that point by proclaiming *"[15] What then? Shall we sin because we are not under law but under grace? Certainly not!"*

So when we have a proper understanding of the Scriptures we realize that Paul was not saying we do not obey the Commandments found within Torah. To the contrary, He was saying that we are set free and made clean from our lawlessness and no longer under the penalty of death prescribed for that lawlessness.

Yahushua paid that price, and when we immerse in His Name we die with Him. Having been set free from our death sentence we do not turn back to lawlessness. Certainly not! We no longer walk in sin, we have been freed from the curse that began at the Garden.

Yahushua took the written list of accusations and charges against us and nailed them "to the cross," or rather, "the execution stake." Paul never advocated the abolishment of the Torah, the Appointed Times or the Dietary Instructions as so many attempt to imply. (Colossians 2:14-17). In fact, we repeatedly read in the Book of Acts about his efforts to get back to Jerusalem in

time for the Feasts.

The reason why Paul is often misunderstood is because English New Testaments use the word "law" for both the Torah, and the Pharisaic Laws that Yahushua opposed. Also, Paul is making a very fine, but important distinction regarding Torah observance. Many felt that they were justified by their Torah observance, and Paul was trying to clarify that Torah observance does not bring about salvation.

We cannot earn our salvation by being obedient. This was a major theme of his writings, and the disputes with those Pharisees who he called "The Circumcision." They were advocating circumcision, and a traditional "conversion process" as a prerequisite to salvation. There was much dissension brewing within and between the various assemblies.

This was not simply a dispute occurring with Paul, but it created hostility between Gentile converts and Yisraelites who did not follow Yahushua. The Natzrim were stuck in the middle. Paul was under attack by many, and we can clearly see this antagonism reflected in some of his letters.

No doubt Paul provided helpful guidance, and revelatory knowledge for believers struggling to follow the Messiah in a very complicated religious environment. He wrote most of his letters to Gentile converts who were coming out of a pagan background, joining Yisrael, but rebuffed by the Yahudim. It was quite a hostile situation, and it was progressively getting worse.

This is a very important point to remember when we look at the dominant role that Paul and his writings have held in the New Testament and the Christian religion. When examining the development of the New Testament and the Bible, it is imperative to understand the history of the Natzrim in the decades and centuries that followed the death and resurrection of Yahushua.

The first three centuries are likely the most obscure, yet definitely the most important. It was during this period that the greatest divisions occurred. We briefly touched upon the different sects revolving around different men and their teachings. False teaching abounded, and false gospels were even being preached during the life of Paul. (Galatians 1:6-9).

Remember that all of the early followers of Yahushua were primarily native Yisraelites. They all shared a common tradition and community. Things were not so complicated in the early years as the Talmidim of Yahushua taught their Yisraelite brethren that Yahushua was the promised Messiah.

After time, it became apparent that the Good News of the Messiah was intended for the Nations - the Gentiles. This was always the case, but Yisrael had failed miserably in their mission to the Nations. Yisrael was supposed to shine as a light to the pagan peoples who surrounded them, and draw the Nations to YHWH. Instead, Yisrael was repeatedly led astray into the very pagan practices that they were supposed to help deliver people from. Remember, Yisrael was called to be a Nation of Priests. (Shemot 19:6).

As a result of her adultery, Yisrael was divided, exiled and scattered to the four corners of the earth. Through this exile and prophesied regathering, YHWH would accomplish through the punishment of Yisrael that which was not accomplished through the blessing of Yisrael. It would have been easier if Yisrael had obeyed

and been blessed, but either way, the will of YHWH was going to be accomplished. The Covenant Promises made to Abram, and later Abraham, would be fulfilled.

So the Message of Yahushua, the High Priest according to the Order of Melchizedek, was meant for the nations. The conduit for this was through the regathering of the outcasts of Yisrael - just as the nations had been delivered from Egypt by Mosheh, an even greater deliverance would occur through the Messiah. The net was being cast and Messiah would be fishing for the sons of the living Elohim. (Yirmeyahu 16:16). This included the House of Yisrael, which had been scattered to the four corners of the planet.

When Gentiles (the Nations) began converting and joining Yisrael, it created problems for the native Yisraelite community. Those who did not follow Yahushua did not understand or accept what was happening. They refused to accept the Gentile converts into their synagogues, because they did not acknowledge the authority of Yahushua.

The Gentile converts were not converting according to the man-made laws and traditions of the religious leaders, which included an elaborate circumcision procedure. This also created a schism between the Yisraelites in the Natzerene sect, and their unbelieving brethren. After all, it was the Natzrim who were creating the "problem" by bringing all of these "pagans" into the synagogues.

Jerusalem was the center of the Natzrim sect until Titus razed the city around 70 CE. While the Natzrim returned and reassembled on Mt. Zion, their Assembly was once again disrupted around 135 CE when the Bar Kochba revolt was crushed. At that time Hadrian established Jerusalem as a pagan city known as Aelia Capitolina.

Yet again, the Natzrim returned and set up their assembly on Mt. Zion, although divisions and disputes continued to abound. While the Natzrim in Jerusalem maintained the Syriac language, many of the converts outside of Jerusalem predominately spoke in Greek. In fact, those who spoke Greek frowned upon those who spoke the native tongue.

The Syriac language was actually despised by those who spoke Greek. It was considered to be "the barbarian language."[76] Indeed, Eusebius, an early Christian historian, called the "men of Galilee, despicable and rustic who knew naught except the Syriac dialect" and the "poor and obscure, ignorant of literature, who used the Syriac tongue."[77]

As a result, language became a major point of division. Calendar issues also became a basis for contention as the Natzrim held to the Creator's Calendar, described in the Torah. The Gentile converts, began changing the calendar and celebrated Easter, rather than Passover.

Because of these differences, the congregations communed in different locations, based upon their particular beliefs. For instance, in Jerusalem, the Natzrim maintained their center on Mt. Zion, while the Gentile converts settled into the site of the Temple of Aphrodite (Easter), which was eventually renamed The Church of the Holy Sepulcher.

So what does all this have to do with Paul? Ultimately, the Gentile converts became the majority in the Assembly. Their numbers grew much faster because they were drawing from a much larger pool of people.

They essentially grew into their own "sect," and later developed a separate and distinct religion, using many of the letters from Paul as a doctrinal foundation. They became known as Christians, as opposed to the Natzrim, who remained a sect of Yisrael.

The center of their new Christian religion was relocated to Rome, as Christianity became the official State Religion of the Roman Empire. This is similar, in many ways, to how many perceive America to be a Christian nation. Religion became intimately tied to politics and the state. Interestingly, the links between America and Rome are by no means coincidental, but that is for another discussion.[78]

What is important to understand is that the original language, faith and traditions of the early Talmidim was continued on by the Natzrim, not the Christians. The Christians ultimately dominated the faith and controlled the history and the texts. That is why we do not read much in the New Testament concerning the Jerusalem Assembly, Yaakob or the Twelve. They could not be completely ignored, but they could be minimized.

The Talmidim of Yahushua all travelled throughout the world spreading the Good News of the Messiah, and seeking out the Lost Sheep of the House of Yisrael. Surely they all wrote or transcribed letters to others, yet very little remains regarding those individuals whe were hand selected by Messiah.

When you understand the dominance of Rome and the pagan infiltration of Christianity at its inception, all of these things become much clearer. There was surely an incredible history with many great miracles and accounts of the Talmidim of Yahushua who are described in the Gospels. They were already given power and sent out once while Yahushua was alive. (See Matthew 10). They were well trained, and I have no doubt that the eleven who remained true to Yahushua, along with Matthias, fulfilled their purposes. Sadly, we do not read about their adventures, primarily only Paul, who was not one of the Twelve.

Again, this is best understood when one recognizes the fact that the Gentile converts created the Christian religion, and they controlled the later compilation process of the Bible. Obviously, they would have easy access to the letters of Paul, which were written to, and accepted by Roman congregations. They were also predisposed to those teachings, since Paul spent a lot of his time preaching and teaching to the Gentiles, and attempting to bring them into the Assembly of Yisrael. He also spent much of his time arguing against certain Yahudim who he called "The Circumcision." Accordingly, he became an important spokesperson for the Christian religion that ultimately became opposed to the Yahudim and their religion called Judaism.

Some believe that Paul intentionally separated himself from the Twelve Talmidim, and specifically professed a different Gospel based upon his "special" or "better" revelation. In his letters one can, in fact, sense attitude which some describe as "sarcasm," "disdain" and even "arrogance." It is hard to judge a person's character from simply reading letters and brief accounts of their missionary journeys.

We could likely spend a lot of time picking on Paul, and there are many who have. That is not the purpose of this chapter. The simple fact is that Yahushua hand selected Twelve Talmidim. He was betrayed by

one of them, who was later replaced. After His death and resurrection, Yahushua told His Talmidim to go to Jerusalem and wait for the Comforter – the Spirit.

The Spirit did indeed come and filled the Talmidim on Shabuot. Paul would have surely been there, as a Torah observant Yahudim, but he was not filled at that time. That would not occur until later, after he had persecuted and killed the followers of Yahushua.

So the Talmidim of Yahushua listened and obeyed. They were working in direct obedience to the Messiah. They were taught by Him and could give direct testimony regarding Him. Naturally, we should expect these Talmidim to be the pillars of the faith, and the ones teaching doctrine. Instead, the New Testament clearly defers to Paul for doctrine, and Paul essentially eclipses the Twelve Talmidim of Yahushua and Yaakob, the undisputed leader of the Natzrim.

Now many Christians have elevated Paul to the level of infallibility, and forgotten that he was a man - not the Messiah. This, I believe is largely due to the fact that his letters have been canonized, and viewed to constitute the authoritative Word of Elohim. As a result, when his letters are taken out of context or misinterpreted they are used to lead people away from the Torah and the Covenant Assembly of Yisrael.

Due to the predominate inclusion of his letters in the Bible, and the confusion surrounding their meaning, those Epistles have been used to justify the change from the Natzerite sect of Yisrael to the Christian religion. The change was not immediate. It took time and was accomplished, in large part, through the process of compiling the book that we know as The Bible.

12

The Bible

It is important to understand that throughout written history, and particularly Yisraelite history, people viewed "The Scriptures" not as a book, or even one collection of writings. Rather, "The Scriptures" were separate texts located on individual scrolls. These scrolls would have been  stored on shelves or in containers along with other writings. It is important to conceptualize that these writings were not originally bound together into a unified "canonized" collection. In fact, the only real unified text would have been the Torah Scroll, which was often treated different from the other texts.

The various scrolls looked upon as Scriptures were divided into three collections already discussed: the Torah, the Prophets and the Writings. These were not one scroll or book, nor were they even contained in three scrolls or books. They were many individual scrolls kept and maintained separately and individually. If a person wanted to read the Prophet Yeshayahu, they would take

the Scroll of Yeshayahu off the shelf, open the Scroll, find where they wanted to read and then begin reading.

It was not until the development of the codex, bound volumes in book form, that these individual scrolls were gathered and joined. The separate collections began to be combined together. Exactly which texts were combined was determined by who was doing the combining. Different religions, sects or denomination might have different collections that they referred to as their "Bible."

We will now examine how the "Bible" came into existence. The observant reader has probably noticed that the word "Bible" is enclosed with quotation marks as was done with the word "gospel." The word "Bible" has become so commonplace that it is hard not to use it, although the origins of the word are questionable. That subject will be examined further in the text.

The "Bible" is a compilation of various writings that men in the past canonized and bundled together into one volume. Most Christian "Bibles" are divided in two parts with a clear indicator between what is called the "Old Testament" and the "New Testament." The word Bible is not found anywhere in the text of the book itself. In other words, nowhere in the "Bible" will you ever find the word "bible," and nowhere in the "Bible" does it ever describe itself as the "Bible." "Bible" is a name given by men to a book of inspired and sacred writings which are traditionally described as Scriptures.

The "Bible" has been traditionally been defined defined as "a collection of books that have been considered authoritative by the Christian church and have been used to determine its beliefs and doctrines. The Bible, comprised of sixty-six books from more than forty authors, was called 'the divine library' (bibliotecha divina) by Jerome, the translator of the Latin Vulgate in the fourth century . . . The Bible is primarily God's revelation to mankind concerning that which would otherwise be unknown unless He revealed it. Revelation is the process by which God makes truth about himself known to man . . ."[79]

The word "Bible" "derives from the Latin translation of the Greek word biblion ("book"), itself a derivation of the word byblos, one of the names of papyrus . . . Latin-speaking Christians . . . borrowed the word biblia . . . The earliest recorded instance of the term biblia applied to the documents of the Christian church is found in 2 Clement 14:2 (dated at about A.D. 150), which states 'the books (biblia) and the apostles declare that the church . . . has existed from the beginning.'"[80]

Many of the manuscripts contained in the "Bible" were made of papyrus, which was a popular medium for scrolls. Byblos was actually the name of a Phoenician port city that exported papyrus. "The Phoenicians worshipped a triad of deities, each having different names and attributes depending upon the city in which they were worshipped, although their basic nature remained the same. The primary god was El, protector of the universe, but often called Baal. The son, Baal or Melqart, symbolized the annual cycle of vegetation and was associated with the female deity Astarte in her role as the maternal goddess. She was called Asherar-yam, our lady of the sea, and in Byblos she was Baalat, our dear lady. Astarte was linked with mother goddesses of neighboring cultures, in her role as combined heavenly mother and earth mother."[81]

"This seaport was also known to be a city which

was founded by Baal Chronos, as well as the real seat of Adonis, where a large temple of Adonis once stood. Isis and Osiris, both sun-deities, also became popular in this city."[82] Further study reveals that "the City Byblis, in Egypt, was named after the female sun deity Byblis, also called Biblis and Byble. This female sun deity was the grand-daughter of Apollo, the well known Greek sun-deity."[83]

It is quite apparent that Byblia and Byble are the same pagan sun deity in two different cultures. This fertility goddess was apparently a nymph.[84] Since there is no letter "y" in Latin, the word was later spelled "biblia" in Latin. Therefore, the word used to describe the most important writings in the Christian faith are collectively referred to under the same name as a pagan fertility goddess.

Due to the foregoing, I am reluctant to refer to the writings containing the Words of YHWH and related anointed texts as the "Bible." I prefer to use the word Scriptures, but the collective writings contained in the "Old Testament" and the "New Testament" have traditionally been called "The Bible." English translations of the "New Testament" repeatedly refer to the Tanak as the Scriptures. As a result, for clarity, we will continue to use these labels through the discussion. Having made these cautionary statements, the word Bible will no longer be enclosed in parenthesis.

You may have noticed the parenthesis around "Old Testament" and "New Testament" as well. The reason for this is because neither is an appropriate label for the texts that they presume to describe. The use of the words "old" and "new" imply that the old is outdated and obsolete, while the new has replaced the old. This is simply untrue.

Some use the terms "old covenant" and "new covenant." These are equally problematic, in my opinion. There are not two covenants in the Bible. The Covenant described in the Tanak is with Yisrael, and that Covenant was prophesied to be renewed with the House of Yisrael and the House of Yahudah. (Yirmeyahu 31:31). Therefore, I believe that the "old" and "new" division is improper and misleading, and I will avoid the use of those terms whenever possible.[85] If it is used, it will only be for the sake of describing the collection of writings contained therein.

Whatever the source of the name, it is now commonplace to label religious collections of writings with the term "Bible." Interestingly, there are many different collections which have this label applied to them. For instance, many refer to the collection of the Torah, the Prophets and the Writings (Tanak) as "The Jewish Bible."

There are also a variety of Christian Bibles containing differing collections of writings. It is the development of those Christian Bibles that we will now briefly examine. It was a long and complex process that many have filled volumes attempting to describe. It was a process that occurred over great periods of time, involved politics, contention and bloodshed. To say that there was a lack of consensus on the matter is an understatement.

There still is no universal agreement over the contents of a Christian Bible. That depends upon each particular Christian denomination or sect. Thus far we are only referring to the process of selecting the writings that were included within the collection, not the actual

translation of those texts, which is an altogether different matter.

At this point in the discussion I must make a confession – I was not present during the creation of the Bible, nor do I know anyone who was. It was a process that spanned centuries and, as a result, no one is able to assess with certainty the integrity or spirituality of those involved in the process. I also am not privy to all of the manuscripts that were considered, accepted or rejected by those involved in the compilation process, or the criterion used for admitting and rejecting certain texts.

Recognizing the tumultuous period in which this process occurred, it would behoove us all to scrutinize the events leading up to the actual "canonization" of the Bible. This may actually be a good time to look at the term "canon." Many who adhere to the truth of the contents of The Bible consider those texts to be reliable and authoritative. This is largely due to the fact that the Bible contains texts that were "canonized." As a result, there is an apparent "seal of approval" from the Creator on those writings. Those texts which are not canonized are thought to be not so reliable or authoritative.

It should be understood that the concept of a "canon" and "canonization" is not restricted to the Jewish and Christian texts. For the purposes of this discussion we will be limiting our examination to that context, particularly the Christian canonization process.

Canon is commonly defined as follows: ". . . the definitive list of inspired, authoritative books which constitute the recognized and accepted body of sacred scripture of a major religious group, that definitive list being the result of inclusive and exclusive decisions after serious deliberation." It is further defined as: ". . . the definitive, closed list of the books that constitute the authentic contents of scripture."[86]

While many believe that the use of the term is ancient, others trace it to more modern times, and while the term is Christian, the idea is Jewish. "The term is late and Christian . . . though the idea is Jewish . . . We should be clear, however, that the current use of the term 'canon' to refer to a collection of scripture books was introduced by David Ruhnken in 1768 in his *Historia critica oratorum graecorum* for lists of sacred scriptures. While it is tempting to think that such usage has its origins in antiquity in reference to a closed collection of scriptures, such is not the case. The technical discussion includes Athanasius's use of 'kanonizomenon=canonized' and Eusebius's use of *kanon* and 'endiathekous biblous=encovenanted books' and the Mishnaic term *Sefarim Hizonim* (external books)."[87]

When examining the history and development of canons we have in the 39th Letter from Athanasius of Alexandria, written in the Fourth Century (367 CE), an itemization of texts that he referred to as the Scriptures. His reference is quite telling. It is actually the first instance of someone detailing the 27 writings that currently make up most New Testaments, although it certainly did not settle the matter.

> "4. There are, then, of the Old Testament, twenty-two books in number; for, as I have heard, it is handed down that this is the number of the letters among the Hebrews; their respective order and names being as follows. The first is Genesis, then Exodus, next Leviticus, after that Numbers, and then Deuteronomy.

Following these there is Joshua, the son of Nun, then Judges, then Ruth. And again, after these four books of Kings, the first and second being reckoned as one book, and so likewise the third and fourth as one book. And again, the first and second of the Chronicles are reckoned as one book. Again Ezra, the first and second are similarly one book. After these there is the book of Psalms, then the Proverbs, next Ecclesiastes, and the Song of Songs. Job follows, then the Prophets, the twelve being reckoned as one book. Then Isaiah, one book, then Jeremiah with Baruch, Lamentations, and the epistle, one book; afterwards, Ezekiel and Daniel, each one book. Thus far constitutes the Old Testament. 5. Again it is not tedious to speak of the [books] of the New Testament. These are, the four Gospels, according to Matthew, Mark, Luke, and John. Afterwards, the Acts of the Apostles and Epistles (called Catholic), seven, viz. of James, one; of Peter, two; of John, three; after these, one of Jude. In addition, there are fourteen Epistles of Paul, written in this order. The first, to the Romans; then two to the Corinthians; after these, to the Galatians; next, to the Ephesians; then to the Philippians; then to the Colossians; after these, two to the Thessalonians, and that to the Hebrews; and again, two to Timothy; one to Titus; and lastly, that to

Philemon. And besides, the Revelation of John. 6. These are fountains of salvation, that they who thirst may be satisfied with the living words they contain. In these alone is proclaimed the doctrine of godliness. <u>Let no man add to these, neither let him take ought from these</u>. For concerning these the Lord put to shame the Sadducees, and said, '<u>Ye do err, not knowing the Scriptures</u>.' And He reproved the Jews, saying, '<u>Search the Scriptures, for these are they that testify of Me</u>."[88]

Notice what Athanasius does, he references quotes which are specifically referring to the Tanak as the Scriptures, and he uses them to define his collection of New Testament writings as "Scriptures." This is a very important distinction to make because there was a time when only the Torah, the Prophets and the Writings were considered to be Scriptures.

In fact, Hegesippus, referred to earlier, was a writer of the 2nd century likely from the Natzerite sect. When providing a history of leadership in various assemblies he stated: ". . . everything is taught by the [Torah], the Prophets and the [Master]."[89]

Hegesippus referred to the guiding texts of the Torah, the Prophets and the Teachings of Yahushua as the prevailing texts. So what happened between Hegesippus and Athanasius involved more than the passage of time, it was the division that was already mentioned between the Natzrim and Christians. The divisions did not stop there. Each of these sects then began to splinter, and follow various differing doctrines.

You cannot understand the development of the

New Testament and the Christian Bible without understanding the culture, the politics and the languages of the time. As was already mentioned, the Modern Hebrew language essentially appeared after the House of Yahudah returned from their Babylonian exile. At that time, there were various languages spoken in the Land of Yisrael, Aramaic being one of the primary languages that replaced Akkadian as the official language of the Assyrian Empire.

Both Hebrew and Aramaic are considered eastern languages, although Aramaic has variations, including both eastern and western Aramaic. As previously mentioned the Natzrim spoke the eastern dialects, and their culture was eastern. Yahushua came primarily to those "orthodox" Yisraelites, and therefore, most of His teachings would have been in their native tongue. There are minimal accounts of Him dealing with Hellenists - those Yisraelites who adopted a Hellenistic lifestyle. These Yahudim would have spoken Greek, a western language.

As the Good News of Yahushua spread, it went beyond eastern speaking cultures, and information was transmitted in different languages to various nations and peoples. There was much diversity with no central organization. So while the message flourished, it was not always a uniform message. As time continued, there were numerous diverse writings spread about, many of which contained conflicting doctrines.

There were clearly many Gnostic writings that were far-fetched and not profitable. There were also many valuable writings. It appears that there was an attempt to "circle the wagons" and compile a closed set of writings, post-Messiah, that would be included within and classified as Scriptures.

Those proponents of canonization were essentially claiming that there was only a finite set of writings categorized as Scriptures that could never be added to or taken away. Anyone familiar with the Torah will recognize that language was spoken to Yisrael concerning the commandments of YHWH. (Debarim 12:32). Athanasius was extending that particular commandment of YHWH to texts.

This formal canonization of texts mentioned by Athanasius was largely an endeavor of the Christian religion that was established by the western oriented Roman Empire. That deserves examination because it explains the veritable absence of any mention of the eastern assemblies beyond the Assembly of Jerusalem.

It is vital to recognize the east-west dichotomy that existed in Christianity from the very beginning. Jerusalem itself was an eastern culture, controlled by a western civilization – the Roman Empire. To the east were the Parthian and Persian Empires. Great tension existed between these different empires, and this resulted in a division between the faithful who dwelled in those empires.

"The [assemblies] which spread so rapidly in Syria and the Persian Empire were shut off from many of the influences which affected the Western [assemblies] by difference of language and by political circumstances. Aramaic being spoken in Palestine and Palmyra and used as the commercial language down the Euphrates valley, and the mutual jealousy and mistrust of the Roman and Persian Empires acted as a further bar to contact."[90]

As a result of the separation between the eastern

and western assemblies, stark and dramatic doctrinal differences emerged between these two groups. Matters such as the Calendar, the Sabbath, the Appointed Times, and the Torah, among others, continued to divide them for centuries. This ended up playing a major role in the formation of the "Bible." It is important to examine these circumstances as we see how the "Bible" came into existence.

Sadly, I was raised in an environment where such a thought was considered to be bordering on heresy. As far as my particular Christian denomination was concerned, the Bible constituted the infallible Word of God - period. It was not to be questioned, and only those hostile to Christianity would consider such a thing.

This is surely the same thing that many Christians believe today, and it is sad that people are discouraged from examining the origins of a text which provides such a foundation for their faith. If indeed, heaven and hell rested upon the truths contained in the Christian Bible, then anyone concerned with their eternal future should be very interested in how the Bible came into existence.

It is by no means my desire to diminish the importance of the writings found in the Bible. Indeed, it is a vital and incredible compilation that enriches our faith, and helps guide us in the Ways of YHWH. Because all of the texts are compiled together in one collection instead of separate scrolls, many have developed an unhealthy and unbalanced understanding of YHWH and His Covenant. All texts are not created equal and there are surely portions that carry greater weight than others. Yahushua specifically spoke to that when He chastised the Scribes and the Pharisees for neglecting *"the weightier matters of the Torah."* (Matthew 23:23)

If the reader walks away from this examination retaining only one concept, I would hope that they would remember that we must take a balanced view of the documents found in the Bible. As with constructing a building, the foundation holds the rest of the structure. Here too, we must remember that the beginning is the foundation upon which everything that follows is built. If you remove the foundation, the entire structure collapses. Through the texts found in the Bible, the building that is being constructed is the House of Elohim

We already discussed the Renewed Covenant mentioned in the Book of Yirmeyahu. It was a renewal of the former Covenant made with Yisrael. Therefore, the Renewed Covenant was for Yisrael, both the House of Yisrael and the House of Yahudah. The text is very clear on that point. Anyone could join into this Covenant, but to do so they must join the Commonwealth of Yisrael.

This is where we start to see some problems with the Bible. While the Tanak divides itself into different categories, with the Torah as the foundation, the Bible mistakenly calls the Tanak "old" and the Messianic Writings "new." This tends to taint a persons opinion of the text from the very beginning. After all, what would you rather have – a new car or an old car, a new suit or an old suit, etc? Obviously most want the new so they often bypass the "old" entirely, and get right to the "new" stuff which is deemed better than the old.

Along with this division has come an enormous misrepresentation and misunderstanding of the people of YHWH. The Renewed Covenant was for a people called

Yisrael, but it is hard to find mention of Yisrael in the New Testament. As a result, most believe that the Renewed Covenant was not renewed. Instead, they think that a brand new Covenant was established by the Messiah. Since it is believed to be brand new, it only makes sense that it was made with a brand new entity called the Church.

To anyone reading an English translation of the Bible, this appears to be perfectly consistent since the Bible speaks repeatedly of "the Church." In fact, most people recall the Messiah proclaiming to Peter (Kepha) that *"upon this rock I will build My church."* (Matthew 16:18). The problem is that He did not say "church," but rather "House of Prayer" or "Congregation," based upon what source text you are using.[91]

In fact, no one referenced in the New Testament ever said the word church. There was no such thing as the Church. It is an English word (cirice) that derives from Teutonic and Slavic origins (kirk).[92] It means "circle" and would refer to the buildings or meeting places where people would assemble. It did not refer to a people who entered into a New Covenant with YHWH separate and apart from Yisrael. Only Yisrael was chosen to be in Covenant with YHWH. If you desire to enter into the Renewed Covenant mediated by the Messiah, you must join the Assembly of Yisrael <u>not</u> the Church.

The word "church" is a complete fabrication that only perpetuates the divide between Christians and Jews. It distances the Christian religion from its Yisraelite origins. The people of Elohim, Yisrael, were generally always referred to as the "qahal" (ℓℱ𐤐) in Hebrew, which meant "assembly or congregation." When the

Tanak was translated into the Greek, in what is referred to as the Septuagint, the Hebrew word qahal (ℓꟼ9) was translated as "ekklessia" (ἐκκλησίαν). So the Hebrew "qahal" (ℓꟼ9) is equivalent in meaning to the Greek "ekklessia" (ἐκκλησίαν), and they both refer to Yisrael.

Now you may be asking: What is the point? We are still talking about the Tanak so of course the Assembly refers to Yisrael. What you need to understand is that the word "ekklessia" is found all throughout the Greek New Testament, but in those texts the word "ekklessia" is translated into English as "the Church" which directs people away from Yisrael and the Tanak. Just as we saw with the Matthew 16:18 example above, the word "church" has been used throughout the New Testament. This is a very simple error which has resulted in centuries of division and confusion concerning the identity of the people of YHWH, and the application of the Renewed Covenant.

Only when you understand this very important distinction does a passage such as Acts 7:38 make any sense. If you read the King James Version it states: *"This is he that was in the church in the wilderness with the angel which spake to him in the mount Sina, and with our fathers who received the lively oracles to give unto us."*

The passage is clearly talking about Mosheh and the children of Yisrael. (see Acts 7:37). So why on earth would the text refer to *"the church in the wilderness."* It does not make sense, because we know that Yisrael was in the wilderness. When we look into the Greek we see the word "ekklessia" (ἐκκλησίαν), and we then understand that it is not referring to a new entity called "the church," but rather the "qahal" (ℓꟼ9) – the congregation of Yisrael.

So throughout the New Testament the set apart Assembly is Yisrael, not the Church. That is why Yahushua chose 12 Talmidim, and went to the Yisraelites to Renew the Covenant. He did not renew the Covenant with Gentiles, that could not happen since they were not parties to the original Covenant. When you see past Christian tradition and understand that the New Testament is describing the Messiah and the Renewed Covenant with Yisrael, it places things in an entirely different light – all because of the mistranslation and insertion of one fabricated word.

With that basic understanding let us take a closer look at how the Bible came into existence. As we mentioned, what initially began as a Hebrew Messiah appearing to some of the exiles of the House of Yahudah who had returned to the Land, eventually exploded throughout the entire world. While one would assume that the earliest teachings and writings would have been in an eastern language (i.e. Aramaic or Hebrew), most popular New Testaments are not based upon eastern language texts, but rather western Greek manuscripts.

Now there is an Aramaic New Testament, known as the Peshitta, which has a long tradition of being used in Eastern Christianity. Even so, some question whether the Peshitta is a translation from the Greek, and later than the Greek. It is most often dated to around the 5th century CE. The fact that it includes all of the Epistles of Paul that are found in the Western Christian canon might tend to show that it is a translation from a predetermined compilation of texts, although it does not include all of the same texts.

In fact, the Peshitta only contains 22 books, which is quite profound since that would match perfectly parallel the accepted notion that there are 22 books in the Tanak. Obviously, those who compiled the Peshitta had an eastern mindset, and knew the significance of the number 22.

Whether we are examining the New Testament in an eastern language or a western language, neither language has original documents. There are only copies of various texts, and not all agree. So there are a variety of issues associated with determining source texts. Now I am clearly stressing the eastern/western diametric, because the importance cannot be overemphasized.

The difference between eastern and western languages and cultures is profound and significant. While eastern language is very concrete and active, western language is very abstract and passive. While eastern thought tends to be cyclical, western thought is linear. Therefore, a person's language and culture actually determine how they think and act. Eastern and western cultures are in many ways opposite from one another. This is actually quite apparent by the fact that eastern languages read from right to left, while western languages read from left to right.

These differences show up in religions and religious texts. So when we are looking at source texts, the language that they are written in tells a lot. The very fact that the life of a Hebrew Messiah is so often transmitted as a Greek Christ can be troubling.

For instance, the western Christian religion has no problem replacing the Hebrew Name of Yahushua with the English name Jesus, or the Greek name Iesus. The western Christian religion also has no trouble espousing that their Christ did away with the Torah, because the Torah is considered to be something eastern

and specifically applicable to the Yisraelites, who were of Hebrew origin.

Of course, both of these notions would be unthinkable to a person of eastern descent, specifically a Yisraelite. Names are very important, and they are given special meaning to individuals. In the case of the Messiah, His Name was critical to express that "YHWH" (Yahu) "saves" (shua). It was also meant to connect with the Commander of Yisrael who bore the same name, although often incorrectly called Joshua.

So then, we can clearly see that language, culture and doctrine were important factors in determining what texts made it into the New Testament, and how those texts were translated. In the period building up to the destruction of Jerusalem around 70 CE, we know that a major rift was developing within the Yisraelite community - between those who followed Yahushua and those who rejected Him as the Messiah. This essentially determined whether or not a Yisraelite joined in the Renewed Covenant mediated by Yahushua.

While there remained an operating Temple, this distinction may not have seemed like a critical problem for most. All of the Yisraelites still dwelled in the same community and assembled to worship at the same Temple. After the destruction of Jerusalem, Yahudim were essentially forbidden from being in Jerusalem. Those who rejected Yahushua as Messiah moved their headquarters to the Mediterranean coast to a place called Yavneh. It was at Yavneh that the new religion of Rabbinic Judaism was established.

Rabbinic Judaism was the natural result of Pharisaic Judaism without a Temple, or other competing sects. It was through Rabbinic Judaism that a new calendar was developed and the oral law was refined and encoded. This is also when certain affirmative acts were taken to separate from the Natzrim. They actually developed a daily malediction, or curse, recited in the synagogues and directed at "the minim" which was a derogatory term applied to the Natzrim. This is clearly revealed in fragment T-S.8.H.24 of the Birkat ha-Minim which includes the Hebrew word "Notzrim" or rather Natzrim.

The daily malediction essentially guaranteed the fact that the Natzrim would no longer assemble in the synagogues. Without an operating Temple or community, the division between the Natzrim and the new religion of Rabbinic Judaism widened.

Now this was only part of the fracture that was occurring within the Set Apart Community. The Natzrim community was also experiencing problems. With the great influx of Gentile converts also came a lot of pagan "baggage." Most of the converts came from polytheistic, Babylonian derived, sun worship. This resulted in differing doctrines and practices within these various assemblies. This was something that occurred from the very start, and we have letters, known as Epistles, from various leaders that attempt to correct these problems. Ultimately, the Gentile converts outnumbered and overran the Native Yisraelites. They essentially hijacked the faith and the Messiah, mixed in some sun worship, and rebranded it as Christianity.

So the Natzrim, were native Yisraelites, and originally they were the sect that followed Yahushua. They maintained their identity with Yisrael, and the Covenant. Ultimately, they ended up getting squeezed in between the new religion of Rabbinic Judaism created at

Yavneh, and the burgeoning western Gentile dominated religion that would eventually become known as Christianity.

The Christian religion was not a new religion created by Yahushua. Remember, He specifically stated that He did not come to destroy the Torah or the Prophets, but to fulfill. That fulfillment consisted of repairing and restoring the Covenant. He mediated the Renewed Covenant prophesied by Yirmeyahu. He was the Messiah of Yisrael provided by the Tanak. He specifically stated that He came for the Lost Sheep of the House of Yisrael. As the Son of David, He was on a mission to restore the divided Kingdom of Yisrael.

That was understood by the early Talmidim, who were Yisraelites and recognized the role of Yisrael in the Creator's redemption plan for mankind. Sadly, as divisions crept in, so did the identity of the faith with Yisrael. Instead, the culture of Yisrael was turned over to the Yahudim and the religion of Judaism. The Gentile Converts pushed back, adopting their own familiar pagan ways that fit into their Western Roman lifestyle and culture. At first, this was a slow process, but it accelerated rapidly once the Roman Empire became involved.

After the passage of centuries, the Roman Empire began to make Christianity a state religion. Through various councils and decrees many changes were instituted to make it into a religion more palatable to a sun worshipping polytheistic populace.

One of the first "official" changes made by the State of Rome was the abolition of the sign of the Covenant – the Sabbath. From the beginning of Creation the seventh day Sabbath was a set apart day. It was a

sign for Yisrael and was something that the Covenant people were supposed to live out and "rehearse" each week.

Here is the enactment of Sun Day observation made by Emperor Constantine in March 321 CE. "On the venerable Day of the Sun let the magistrates and people residing in cities rest, and let all workshops be closed. In the country, however, persons engaged in agriculture may freely and lawfully continue their pursuits; because it often happens that another day is not so suitable for grain-sowing or for vine-planting; lest by neglecting the proper moment for such operations the bounty of heaven should be lost. (Given the 7th day of March, Crispus and Constantine being consuls each of them for the second time [321 CE].)[93]

Later at the Council of Laodicea, around 364 CE, Christians were forbidden from observing the Sabbath. According to Canon XXIX "Christians must not Judaize by resting on the Sabbath, but must work on this day, rather honouring the Lord's Day; and, if they can, resting then as Christians. But if any shall be found to be Judaizers, let them be anathema from Christ."

So very clearly, the Christian religion had become hostile to the Yahudim, and anything associated with them. Christianity rejected Yisrael, the Covenant and the sign of the Covenant – the Sabbath. Is it any wonder why they latched onto the teaching of Paul, believing that he rejected another Sign of the Covenant – Circumcision. They also established the "venerable day of the sun" as their "rest day." This was the day that sun worshippers honored the sun, so it was very appropriate that Christianity would adopt that day. It was, after all, a hybrid form of Babylonian sun worship.

The Council of Laodicea made many other poor doctrinal decisions such as, setting up a religious hierarchy and forbidding feasting with Jews, among other things. A great deal of the Canons were clearly opposed to the Tanak. Ironically, this was the time when we can see Christianity begin to officially canonize certain documents by determining which ones were acceptable and which ones were prohibited.

According to Canon LX: "These are the Books of the Old Testament appointed to be read: 1) Genesis of the World; 2) The Exodus from Egypt; 3) Leviticus; 4) Numbers; 5) Deuteronomy; 6) Joshua, the son of Nun; 7) Judges, Ruth; 8) Esther; 9) Of the Kings, First and Second; 12) Esdras, First and Second; 13) The Book of Psalms; 14) The Proverbs of Solomon; 15) Ecclesiastes; 16) The Song of Songs; 17) Job; 18) The Twelve Prophets; 19) Isaiah; 20) Jeremiah, and Baruch, the Lamentations, and the Epistle; 21) Ezekiel; 22) Daniel. And these are the books of the New Testament: Four Gospels, according to Matthew, Mark, Luke and John; The Acts of the Apostles; Seven Catholic Epistles, to wit, one of James, two of Peter, three of John, one of Jude; Fourteen Epistles of Paul, one to the Romans, two to the Corinthians, one to the Galatians, one to the Ephesians, one to the Philippians, one to the Colossians, two to the Thessalonians, one to the Hebrews, two to Timothy, one to Titus, and one to Philemon."

So the council included 22 books in the Tanak, although Ezra and Nehemiah were replaced by Esdras, First and Second. We can see that Baruch and the Epistle of Jeremiah varied from the current Tanak. Also, some of the content of the individual book varied from what we see today. There were 26 texts included in the New

Testament. The Book of Revelation is noticeably absent.

Later, at the Synod in Hippo in 393 CE, the previous list provided by Athanasius was accepted. This was later affirmed at the Third Synod of Carthage, around 397 CE, which issued a canon providing: "Besides the Canonical Scriptures, nothing shall be read in Church under the name of divine Scriptures. Moreover, the canonical Scriptures." The Council then goes on to list the Tanak and defines the New Testament as: "the Gospels, four books; The Acts of the Apostles, one book; the Epistles of Paul; thirteen; of the same to the Hebrews, one Epistle; of Peter, two; of John, apostle, three; of James, one; of Jude, one; the Revelation of John." The Council of Carthage includes the Book of Revelation, making a total of 27 books in the New Testament.

These Councils were very political events, and certain individuals were known to influence the proceedings. There was never complete universal acceptance of the 27 books promoted by Athanasius, although the majority of Christianity accepts them as "canonized," which can now be seen as more of a religious and political process than anything else.

It is purported that the Council of Laodicea banned certain books, although there is no list of banned books in any of the Canons. By selecting certain books in their Canon, the various councils effectively excluded other popular books, which I suppose could then be considered "banned." A list of some of those books would include: Barnabas; I Clement; II Clement; Christ and Abgarus; The Apostles' Creed; The Shepherd of Hermas; I Infancy; II Infancy; Mary; Magnesians; Nicodemus; Correspondence of Paul and Seneca; Acts of

Paul; Acts of Thecla; The First and Second Book of Adam and Eve; The Secrets of Enoch; The Psalms of Solomon; The Odes of Solomon; The Fourth Book of Maccabees; The Story of Ahikar; The Testament of Reuben; The Testament of Simeon; The Testament of Judah; The Testament of Levi; The Testament of Issachar; The Testament of Zebulun; The Testament of Dan; The Testament of Naphtali; The Testament of Gad; The Testament of Asher; The Testament of Joseph; The Testament of Benjamin.

Interestingly, Paul's letter to the Laodiceans did not even make the cut. Although there were some issues concerning Marcionite forgeries being circulated, it is found in Latin manuscripts of the New Testament from the middle ages.

The above is by no means an exhaustive list of texts that did not find their way into the canonized Bible. We will mention more of them as the discussion continues. Again, the mention of these texts should not be seen as an endorsement of any of them - it is not. I clearly do not agree with the doctrines represented in many of the texts, particularly the Gnostic texts.

The point of mentioning them here is to show that these texts were in circulation, and people were reading and studying them. They were then excluded by decisionmaking bodies, such as the Council of Laodicea. This was the same Council that also assumed the authority to prohibit Sabbath observance. Imagine that. The Sabbath was a commandment etched in stone by the very finger of Elohim, and this Council flippantly cast it aside. Based on that alone, I recognize that their judgment and understanding was seriously flawed. As a result, I take their decisions with a grain of salt.

It is important to understand that Constantine was a politician, and he desired to unify the fractured sects of this religion that would become Christianity. This new state religion would serve as a unifying force in his fractured state. To do this he needed to completely separate the new religion from Yisrael. Rome needed to be the center, not Jerusalem and the Land of Yisrael.

Obviously changing the Sabbath to the Venerable Day of the Sun was an important separation. He had to distinguish Christians from Yahudim and the Church from Yisrael. Changing the "sign" of their respective covenants was essential. The separation continued when he changed the Appointed Times. For instance, instead of observing Passover, the special Appointed Time when the blood of the Lamb of Elohim is shed, Christianity adopted the celebration of Easter, a pagan fertility celebration named after a fertility goddess. This, of course, was nothing but Babylonian sun worship.

In commenting on the decision to celebrate Easter instead of Passover Constantine wrote the following: "We ought not, therefore, to have anything in common with the Jews, for the Savior has shown us another way; our worship follows a more legitimate and more convenient course (the order of the days of the week); and consequently, in unanimously adopting this mode, we desire, dearest brethren, to separate ourselves from the detestable company of the Jews, for it is truly shameful for us to hear them boast that without their direction we could not keep this feast."[94] After writing this letter, at the Council of Antioch, Christians were prohibited from celebrating the Passover with the Yahudim.

This is only a sampling of the anti-Semitic

rhetoric that came out of Constantine and was embedded in the Roman Catholic Christian Church from the onset. It stemmed from the roots of division and strife already mentioned, and was clearly evident at what was known as the Council of Nicea.

Nicea was a Hellenic city in northwestern Anatolia. It is generally understood that there were around 318 leaders present at the first council held in 325 CE. Most of them were Greeks, and none of them were from the Natzrim sect. So there were no participants from the Yahudim. They were not wanted. It was known that they adhered to the Scriptures – the Torah, the Prophets and the Writings. They stayed true to the Calendar of YHWH, the Appointed Times and Covenant, all of which were essentially being rejected by Christianity. While the Natzrim remained part of Yisrael, Christianity was going the way of Babylon.

The Council of Nicea was also a political event, with opening ceremonies involving Emperor Constantine decked in gold and jewel studded attire, seated upon a golden throne. This would have certainly precluded attendance from those outside of the Roman Empire. For a citizen of another empire to attend a Roman state sponsored political and religious event, it clearly would have been seen as treasonous.

We can see that the Council of Nicea was the place where Christianity started to become an organized state sponsored religion tied politically with the Roman Empire.[95] A creed was agreed upon and Canons were issued. Interestingly, at no point were the Scriptures specifically quoted in support of any statements in the creed or canons. This clearly reveals that there was no official compilation of New Testament texts at that time.

In fact, it was not until later in the 4th Century CE, as we saw from Laodicea, Hippo and Carthage, that the acceptance of 27 New Testament texts was essentially formalized. Now obviously these texts had circulated for centuries, along with others. It was a process combining time and tradition that resulted in those texts being accepted as canonized texts, although there has never been any absolute and universal acceptance or uniformity.[96]

What is particularly interesting is the fact that the western assemblies adopted a New Testament with 27 books, while the eastern assemblies adopted a New Testament with 22 books. The eastern assemblies clearly acknowledged the importance of the number 22 associated with the Aleph Bet and The Word.

The western assemblies, on the other hand, did not have that connection with the language. Imagine the significance of combining 22 books from the Tanak with 22 books from the New Testament. Remember that blood "dam" (𐤌𐤀) has the Gematria value of 44, and "the life of the flesh is in the blood." Vayiqra 17:11. So the emphasis of the eastern assemblies was to make the point that when you combine the Messiah with the Tanak there is completion and life.

The New Testament of the western assemblies was based upon Greek manuscripts while the eastern assemblies New Testament was based upon Aramaic manuscripts, also possibly Hebrew manuscripts. So the western Christian Church ended up with a Bible that was divided into both east and west. The Tanak, which they called The Old Testament was of Hebrew origin – an eastern language. The New Testament was of Greek

origin – a western language. Notice how the Hebrew was considered "old" and the Greek was considered "new." This clearly reflects a language and cultural bias that continues to permeate Christianity to this day.

Having very briefly examined the process of compiling the Bible, we then look at those underlying texts, because the Bible, as most are aware, has become a much translated book. We then need to ascertain the source texts from which those translations derive. We have already mentioned language difference and bias of various Christian assemblies, but the New Testament texts are not the only ones with conflicting source languages.

There are actually three primary source texts for the Tanak namely: 1) The Masoretic Text; 2) The Septuagint, also referred to as the LXX; and 3) The Samaritan Pentateuch.

The Masoretic text and the Septuagint are those primarily in use today. The Masoretic text was adopted by the Rabbis in the Third Century to Eighth Century CE.

> "Almost all modern English translations of the "Old Testament" are based on a single manuscript, the Leningrad Codex, which was copied in 1008 CE and is our earliest complete copy of the Masoretic (or Rabbinic) Text of the Hebrew Bible. The Leningrad Codex is used by most biblical scholars in its published edition, Biblia Stuttgartensia (or the earlier Biblia Hebraica). Another important manuscript is the Aleppo Codex .. [which] was copied in about 925 C.E. and is thus earlier than

the Leningrad Codex . . . both the
Leningrad Codex and the Aleppo Codex
are part of what is known as the
"Masoretic Text." This term is quite
complicated, since it covers many
manuscripts rather than a single one."[97]
The Septuagint is written in Koine Greek and is
dated to the late second century BCE. It is commonly
known as the Greek Old Testament or the LXX. The
word Septuagint actually derives from Latin *versio
septuaginta interpretum*, "translation of the seventy
interpreters." This is also the reason it is called the LXX,
which is 70 in Roman numerals. There is a legend
surrounding the translation which claims that 72 Hebrew
elders were brought together by King Ptolemy to create a
Greek text that Alexandrian Jews could study. Flavius
Josephus, a first century Yisraelite historian testifies to
the existence and process of translating the Septuagint.
This Greek translation was a very detailed process
described by Josephus in his book, Antiquities of the
Jews, Book XII, Chapter 2.

The Septuagint was older than the Masoretic
text(s) and was even quoted in the New Testament. As a
result, the Septuagint has been used primarily by
Protestants.

So we have diverse translations in various
languages with different source texts. Aside from the
obvious language differences, there are some significant
textual differences between the Septuagint and the
Masoretic text. At first glance it might seem that there
are only minor variations, the biggest being that they are
arranged in different order. A closer look reveals more
profound differences.

If a person did not know any better, they would likely choose the Masoretic text as a more reliable text, simply based upon the fact that it is written in Hebrew. Obviously, if you want to understand the Tanak which was originally spoken and written in Hebrew, you would likely look for a Hebrew text for the best understanding. This is not necessarily true because the Septuagint pre-dates the Masoretic text by centuries. So the argument is that the Septuagint derives from a more ancient, and arguably more reliable, Hebrew text.

Indeed, it is a pre-Messianic text written and used before the appearance of Yahushua, so it may provide a better understanding of the religious thought and beliefs during that period of time.

"It was held in high esteem until the time of Aquila (120 CE), and in fact, was used to spread the Messianic message."[98] In response to being rebuffed by the early Talmidim of Yahushua, Aquila developed a corrupted version of the Septuagint, essentially erasing clear prophetic references to Yahushua as the Messiah.

Recognizing its past value and history, we should not be too quick to disregard the Septuagint simply because it is written in Greek. There are times that it can provide insight, and more accurate renderings than the Hebrew Masoretic text. In fact, there are a number of issues with the Masoretic text that should be considered. To begin, it is believed that the Masoretic text was originally pieced together from approximately 3,400 differing scrolls and codices.

It is also believed by some that Rabbi Akiva was the one who compiled the original source text. This is important because although Rabbi Akiva is highly esteemed in Judaism, his credibility was tarnished due to his incorrect assertion in 130 CE that Bar Kochba was the Messiah. It is also known that he altered the "Jewish Calendar" in order to confirm the Messiahship of Bar Kochba, which resulted in a loss of approximately 250 years from the current Rabbinic Calendar.[99]

It is well recognized that the Masoretic text was developed by Rabbinic Judaism. "This monumental work was begun around the 6th century [CE] and completed in the 10th by scholars at Talmudic academies in Babylonia and Palestine."[100]

So the Septuagint is far older than the Masoretic text. First century Yisraelites clearly used and quoted the Septuagint, and the text was later used by Christianity. Some believe that the Masoretic text was actually translated in an attempt to attack the Septuagint and undermine Christians.

Here is an example. One of the most famous examples of how the Jews attacked the Greek Septuagint involved the word "virgin." Obviously, a great claim of the Natzrim, and later Christianity, was the fact that Yahushua was born from a virgin in fulfillment of prophecy. What better way to diminish that claim than to diminish the prophecy.

The particular verse in question is Isaiah 7:14. The English translation of the Septuagint text states: "*Therefore, the Master Himself will give you a sign: Behold, a virgin will conceive in the womb, and will bring forth a Son, and you will call His Name Emmanuel.*"

In the Greek, the word for virgin is "parthenos," and it literally means: "a virgin." In the Masoretic Text, however, the Hebrew word is "almah" which means: "a young girl." The usual Hebrew word for virgin, and the word in every case translated virgin in the Revised

Version, is "bethuwlah." This verse is quoted from Isaiah in the Christian Bible in Matthew 1:23.

It is clear from the Septuagint that the intention of the text is to relate that a virgin would conceive. It is not a miraculous sign for a young maiden to conceive. In fact, that is no sign at all. Clearly, those who developed the Masoretic text understood the claim that Yahushua was born from a virgin in fulfillment of the sign in Isaiah 7:14.

So the word "bethuwlah" would have been the correct Hebrew word to use for this sign. Remember, that it is also the name of the mazzaroth depicting the virgin, called Virgo in modern astronomy. So the sign in the text is connected to the sign in the sky. They both point to a virgin conceiving, and the son would be El with us – Emmanuel.

It is now known that the Masoretic text altered the Name of YHWH on 134 occasions in direct violation of the commandments. It appears that the Masorite translators made many other alterations to the Scriptures, especially to those dealing with the Messiah. They added vowel pointing which changed the pronunciation of YHWH, and they scrambled the order of the Book of Daniel in order to confuse those seeking to confirm the timing of the Messiah's appearance.[101]

Over the centuries, the differences between the Septuagint and Masoretic texts continued without any definitive resolution. With the discovery of the Dead Sea Scrolls, it is now possible to flesh out some of these differences and confirm the accuracy of a particular passage. The Scrolls were given their name based upon the geographical area where they were found. Long ago, scrolls were stored or hidden in clay jars which were placed in caves around the Dead Sea region. They were found between the years 1946 and 1956.

The largest collection of Dead Sea Scrolls were found in 11 caves in the region of Khirbet Qumran located in the modern State of Israel. At Qumran "nearly 900 manuscripts were found in some twenty-five thousand pieces, with many no bigger than a postage stamp. A few scrolls are well preserved, such as the Great Isaiah Scroll from Cave 1 (1QIsa^a) and the Great Psalms Scroll from Cave 11 (11QPs^a) . . . The earliest manuscripts date from about 250 BC[E]."[102]

There were also manuscripts found in other vicinities around the Dead Sea. The manuscripts were written in Hebrew, Aramaic and Greek. They were written prior to the destruction of the Temple in Jerusalem in 70 CE, and from those texts we have the oldest copies of the Hebrew Scriptural texts. The Dead Sea Scrolls provide near contemporary Hebrew texts with the Greek Septuagint, and the Dead Sea Scrolls tend to confirm the accuracy of the Septuagint.

The Dead Sea Scrolls were an incredible find. They can help us discern variances and provide the oldest known version of a passage. An example can be seen in Debarim 32:8. In the Hebrew Masoretic text we read: ". . . *He established the boundaries of the people according to the number of the sons of Yisrael.*" Sons of Yisrael in the Hebrew is "beni Yisrael."

In the Septuagint text we read: ". . . *He established the boundaries of the people according to the number of the sons of El.*" Sons of El in the Greek is translated as "uion theos." In the Dead Sea Scrolls fragment 4QDeuteronomyJ we read: ". . . *He established the boundaries of the people according to the number of the sons of*

<u>El</u> (beni El)."

This simple example shows that the Septuagint is a valid translation, and the Masoretic text is a true variant of the Older Hebrew.[103] It does not tell us which version is ultimately correct, but it does provide us with the oldest known Hebrew witness of the passage.

This reference to the "sons of El" should make us recall Beresheet 6:4 when the text described the conditions before the flood involving the "sons of Elohim."

Now there are some who allege that the Masoretic text contains intentional alterations. In the above text some believe that "sons of Yisrael" was intentionally inserted in place of "sons of El." If so, it could be another reason why people fail to make the prophetic connection between the work of the Messiah and the return of the House of Yisrael. In a clear Messianic reference in Hoshea 1:10, the prophecy tells that the House of Yisrael (Children of Yisrael) will be called "sons of the living El" (**ヿH-ノメ ヿЧ⅁**), before they are gathered together with the Children of Yahudah under one Head.

There are other examples from the Masoretic text which seem to hide or deflect the fact that Yahushua is the Messiah. Some point to Psalms 22:16 where the English translation of the Masoretic text reads: *"For dogs have compassed Me. The assembly of the wicked have enclosed me. They seize my hands and feet like a lion."* This Psalm clearly represents a Messianic reference, which described the death of Yahushua precisely. The only problem is there is no historical record of anyone seizing His hands and feet "like a lion." In fact, it is not clear what it even means to seize someone's hands and feet like a lion.

The reason why this passage does not seem to fit with the rest of the Scripture is because of a mistranslation in the Masoretic text. The word "kaari" in Modern Hebrew Script (כארי) means: "like the lion." It is inserted instead of the word "kaaru" (כארו), which means "they pierced." An accurate rendition of the passage reads: *"For dogs have surrounded Me. The congregation of the wicked has enclosed Me. They pierced My hands and My feet."* Psalm 22:16.

Clearly, history tells us that the hands and feet of Yahushua were pierced when He was crucified. It would appear that by replacing a vav (ו) with a yud (י) the scribes potentially deflect the reader from identifying Yahushua as the subject of this passage.

The correct translation "kaaru" (כארו) meaning "they pierced" is confirmed by the Dead Sea Scrolls. This is why the Dead Sea Scrolls are so important. They provide us with an opportunity to test the source texts that we have relied upon, but which are potentially wrong. Was this an intentional act or a simple mistake? No one can say for certain, but this is one of many examples that have raised suspicion over the accuracy of the Masoretic text.[104]

Another simple example of an issue with the Masoretic text is found in Shemot 1:5. The Masoretic text reads: *"All those who were descendants of Jacob were seventy persons (for Joseph was in Egypt already)."* Both the Dead Sea Scrolls and Septuagint read *seventy-five*. This is also consistent with Acts 7:14 which states: *"Then Joseph sent and called his father Jacob and all his relatives to him, seventy-five people."* In fact, there are actually many texts from the New Testament that are quoted from the Septuagint.

The Dead Sea Scrolls can sometimes even provide us with better translations of texts. For instance, the Messianic prophecy in Isaiah 53:11 from the Masoretic text as translated in the King James Version provides: *"He shall see of the travail of his soul, and shall be satisfied: by his knowledge shall my righteous servant justify many: for he shall bear their iniquities."* There is a textual problem with the "of" that confuses the text.

When examining the Dead Sea Scrolls we see a new word in Isaiah 1QIsa[a]. The additional word that is not found in the Masoretic text is "owr" (𐤀𐤅𐤓) – light. Remember the light at the beginning. It is now being connected with the Messiah – the suffering servant. Thanks to the Dead Sea Scrolls we have a better, and more understandable translation of Isaiah 53:11 as follows: *"Out of the suffering of His soul He shall see light, and find satisfaction. And through his knowledge my servant, the righteous one, will make many righteous and He will bear their iniquities."*[105]

So from the Dead Sea Scrolls we see "light." This was not an anomaly found in only one scroll. In every fragment where Isaiah 53:11 was preserved, "light" is found in the text. It was found in the smaller Isaiah Scroll in Cave 1, and the Isaiah Scroll from Cave 4 (4Q58).

The Dead Sea Scrolls help us to improve our understanding of certain verses by filling in words. They also provide us with missing verses. Psalm 145 provides a wonderful example, because it is an acrostic Psalm. In other words, it has verses that begin with aleph, bet, gimel, dalet, etc. in progressive order through the entire alephbet. It is a Psalm based upon the alephbet, and since it is written in Hebrew, we would expect to find 22 verses. Instead, in the Masoretic text there are only 21 verses. The nun ($\mathbf{Y}$) verse is missing. It actually skips from mem ($\mathbf{Y}$) to samech ($\mathbf{\overline{T}}$) in the Masoretic text. So there is a verse missing between verse 13 and verse 14. For centuries, those relying upon the Masoretic text have sought to find spiritual meaning in the missing nun ($\mathbf{Y}$) verse, all the while it was simply lost.

Incredibly, Psalm 145 was found in the Dead Sea Scrolls, along with the missing nun ($\mathbf{Y}$) verse in fragment 11QPs-a. In Modern Hebrew the nun (נ) verse reads: "נאמן אלוהים בדבריו והסיד מעשוי" In English it reads: "*Elohim is faithful in His words, and gracious in all His deeds.*" So if you have a Bible with only 21 verses in Psalm 145, you can now make a scribal correction by adding the nun verse between verses 13 and verses 14. You will then have a complete translation of Psalm 145 with 22 verses.

Another example of a complete omission from the Masoretic text was discovered in 1 Samuel 11:1. An entire paragraph was omitted from the Masoretic text, although the paragraph was contained in the Septuagint. That paragraph was also found in the Dead Sea Scrolls 4QSam[a] which supported the fact that the paragraph was original, and that the Septuagint was accurate.

Another omission in the Masoretic text is found in Beresheet 4:8 which provides: "*And Qayin said (vayomer) to his brother Hebel, and it came to pass . . .*" The only problem is that the text fails to provide what Qayin actually said. As a result, many translators changed the word "said" to "talked."

The Septuagint, the Aramaic Targums, the Samaritan Pentateuch and the Aramaic Peshitta all provide: "*And Qayin said to his brother Hebel 'Let us go out*

to the field.'" So there are texts that actually reveal what Qayin said to Hebel. Not only does the Masoretic text fail to include the information, but the translation is altered to accommodate the omission. Interestingly, the Dead Sea Scrolls do not include what Qayin said, so they have not provided an absolute solution to the problem of variances between the texts.[106]

So we have seen from these simple examples that there are different versions of different texts. What we now see in modern religious systems is an attempt to develop uniform and accepted texts as they "canonize" their Scriptures. We must always remain cognizant of the fact that these are ancient documents that contain variances.

This chapter provides only a very brief review of the issues. The development of the Bible involved numerous factors. It was a process that very much involved men with varying interests. This may explain why some of the most popular Bibles, used by western Christianity, focus on the west. It also likely explains why the primary source texts for these Bibles were, and remain, documents written in western languages.

As a result of the canonization process, we often think of the texts as static and unchangeable, but this was not always the case. While the Torah is described as being transmitted directly from YHWH through Mosheh, this is not the case with other Scriptures. The compilation of writings known as the Tanak was not dropped from the heavens in codex form. They were written at different times, by different authors who had different sources.

Scribes might attempt to illuminate texts, and certainly as texts were translated from one language to another there would be some elaboration, bias or influence from the translator. A good example of this is found in the Targums, which are considered to be translations or interpretations – not word for word copies.

Currently we see people getting upset over variances between English translations, attempting to claim that one English version is "the inspired" version as opposed to others. Again, it seems that some believe in 1611, the year attributed to the King James Version, an English version of the Bible was dropped from the heavens. It was apparently fully translated into the fairly new language of English, in a form that can never be altered, corrected or modified in any way. This was clearly not the case, and that perspective is far removed from the days when the Dead Sea Scrolls were written and maintained.

Now there are clearly arguments to be made regarding one English Translation being better than another. These arguments are futile unless a person is willing to examine all these translations. Since the King James Version is based upon the Masoretic text, we know that it certainly contains some variances. A person must be willing to examine these variances if they want the truth.

The exercise that we just went through with some of the examples above is called textual criticism. The object of textual criticism is not intended to "criticize" the Bible, as some might think. The objective is to critique various texts, and attempt to discern the most original and therefore the most authentic and accurate text.

Now granted there are many who do desire to

criticize the Bible and prove it inaccurate. Their actions are usually motivated by a desire to diminish the authority of the text and question the existence of the creator. That practice is commonly described as "higher criticism." Those who endeavor upon "higher criticism" are typically bent on discrediting and disproving the Bible.

Scholarship is supposed to have neutral and unbiased motivations. If that is the case, then anyone searching for truth should welcome such a review. Again, we are dealing with very ancient documents and we have no originals, known as autographs. There are variances between texts and translations, and it is very desirable to find answers to these variances and get back, as much as possible, to the original texts.

This is also helpful, because it assists us in examining and evaluating other texts that were not "canonized." You see, aside from those texts that were canonized, there are actually seventeen extra-canonical books that are mentioned in the Tanak.

The following is a list of the Books and the portions of Scripture in which they were written.

(1) The Book of the Wars of YHWH referenced in Bemidbar 21:14;

(2) The Book of Yasher referenced in Joshua (Yahushua) 10:13 and 2 Shemuel 1:18;

(3) The Book of the Acts of Solomon referenced in 1 Kings (Melakim) 11:41;

(4) The Book of the Annals of the Kings of Israel referenced in 1 Kings (Melakim) 14:29, 15:31, 16:5, 16:14, 16:20, 16:27, 2 Chronicles 20:34;

(5) The Book of the Annals of the Kings of Judah referenced in 1 Kings (Melakim) 14:29, 15:7, 15:23, 22:45, 2

Kings (Melakim) 8:23, 12:19;

(6) The Book of the Annals of King David referenced in 1 Chronicles 27:24;

(7) The Chronicles of Samuel the Seer, the Chronicles of Nathan the Prophet, the Chronicles of Gad the Seer referenced in 1 Chronicles 29:29;

(8) The Records of Nathan the Prophet, the Prophecy of Ahijah the Shilonite, and the Visions of Iddo the Seer referenced in 2 Chronicles 9:29;

(9) The Histories of Shemaiah the Prophet and of Iddo the Seer referenced in 2 Chronicles 12:15;

(10) The Commentary of the Prophet Iddo referenced in 2 Chronicles 13:22;

(11) The Commentary of the Books of the Kings referenced in 2 Chronicles 24:27;

(12) The Acts of Uzziah referenced in 2 Chronicles 26:22;

(13) The Book of the Kings of Judah and Israel referenced in 2 Chronicles 32:32;

(14) The Records of the Kings of Israel referenced in 2 Chronicles 33:18;

(15) The Book of Chronicles referenced in Nehemiah 12:23;

(16) The Book of the Chronicles referenced in Esther 2:23; 6:1;

(17) The Book of the Chronicles of the Kings of Media and Persia referenced in Esther 10:2.

Now I take no position on these texts, but it is worth noting that they are referenced in the Tanak – the Scriptures. One might think that the mention would effectively be a seal of approval of those texts, but that is not necessarily the case. Certainly, people would have had these scrolls, read them and given them different

weight. That was a very common and well accepted practice. A writing could be deemed valuable and useful without necessarily being considered to be a Scripture.

The above is a list of Books referenced in canonized Scripture, yet they are not included in the Scriptures. If they are mentioned in canonized Scripture doesn't that lend some credibility to the writing and make it worthy of our study at the very least.

Take for example the Book of Yasher. It is not just referenced one time, but rather two times in the Tanak. *"Is this not written in the Book of Yasher?"* Yahushua 10:13. We also read the following: *"¹⁷ Then David lamented with this lamentation over Saul and over Jonathan his son, ¹⁸ and he told them to teach the children of Yahudah the Song of the Bow; indeed it is written in the Book of Yasher."* 2 Shemuel 1:17-18.

Even Paul writes: *"⁸ Now as Jannes and Jambres resisted Mosheh, so do these also resist the truth: men of corrupt minds, Disapproved concerning the faith; ⁹ but they will progress no further, for their folly will be manifest to all, as theirs also was."* 2 Timothy 3:8-9. He is not referencing the Tanak, but rather the Book of Yasher at Chapter 79 verse 27.

These examples tend to lend quite a bit to the credibility of the Book of Yasher, but I would guess that most people have never even heard of that text.

There are yet other works not referenced in Tanak, which are included in what is known as the Apocrypha. The word "Apocrypha" generally refers to the collection of religious writings that are found in the Septuagint and the Latin Vulgate, but not in the Hebrew Scriptures or most Protestant canons.

"There is good evidence that none of the

apocryphal or pseudepigraphal works were included in the Old Testament Hebrew canon used by Jews and early Christians. However, it is interesting that the earliest manuscripts of the Septuagint include several of them (with the exception of 2 Esdras, which was never part of the Septuagint). There is no evidence that these books were ever accepted by the Alexandrian Jews to form an Alexandrian canon in contrast to a Palestinian canon."[107]

The Protestant titles for the Apocryphal writings are as follows: 1) The Wisdom of Solomon; 2) Ecclesiasticus; 3) Tobit; 4) Judith; 5) 1 Esdras; 6) 1 Maccabees; 7) 2 Maccabees; 8) Baruch; 9) The Letter of Jeremiah; 10) 2 Esdras; 11) Additions to Esther; 12) The Prayer of Azariah; 13 Susanna; 14) Bel and the Dragon; and 15) The Prayer of Manasseh.

There has been much debate whether or not the Apocryphal writings are canon. It is not my intention to prove that they are, but simply to point out that there are other books which have been considered to be inspired. There are arguments regarding inaccuracies in these books which certainly have merit. The important thing is that the reader is aware of their existence.

There are also a body of "Old Testament" writings called the Pseudepigrapha, a word of Greek origin which means false writings "denoting writings with false superscriptions . . . There is no set list of pseudepigraphal works, but the most recent collection contains sixty-three books . . . Many new pseudepigraphal works were discovered among the Dead Sea Scrolls and are helpful to gain insight about the thoughts and ideas circulating at this time."[108]

The Dead Sea Scrolls offer some interesting

insight into the use of pseudepigraphal texts. It is also interesting to examine what they considered to be "Scriptures." For instance, there were multiple copies of Jubilees written in Hebrew. In the Damascus Document, Column 16 the Book of Jubilees is considered authoritative. There were also multiple copies of the Book of Enoch written in Hebrew and Aramaic. Indeed, the Dead Sea Scroll Community used the Book of Enoch to justify a solar calendar, rather than the luni-solar calendar established in the Torah.

Again, as with the Apocryphal writings, I am not trying to advocate their canonization. In fact, there are clear errors in some of these texts. The point is to recognize their existence, and potential importance to earlier communities of faith. There is also valuable information contained in some of these texts. Clearly there are other writings outside of the canonized Scriptures that are important and revelatory in nature.

For example, The Book of Jude, found in the New Testament, actually quotes from the Book of Enoch as follows: "*[14] Now Enoch, the seventh from Adam, prophesied about these men also, saying, 'Behold, the Lord comes with ten thousands of His saints, [15] to execute judgment on all, to convict all who are ungodly among them of all their ungodly deeds which they have committed in an ungodly way, and of all the harsh things which ungodly sinners have spoken against Him.'*" Jude 14-15 NKJV.

So the Book of Jude, which Christians canonized, cites the Book of Enoch, which is not canonized. "The Abyssinian Church in Ethiopia has actually preserved 1 Enoch as an authoritative work and as an object of commentary and theological reflection."[109] Some speculate that its length (108) chapters, as well as its difficulty to understand, read and transcribe may be some factors that have resulted in its exclusion from canonization. There are clearly errors with the calendar found in that text.

There were also a variety of Gospels, Acts, Epistles and Apocalypses, all of which were purported to be written by followers of Yahushua, that were not included within the canonized New Testament. Here is a list of some of the non-canonical Gospels: 1) The Gospel of the Nazarenes, 2) The Gospel of the Ebionites, 3) The Gospel According to the Hebrews, 4) The Gospel According to the Egyptians, 5) The Coptic Gospel of Thomas, 6) Papyrus Egerton 2: The Unknown Gospel, 7) The Gospel of Peter, 8) The Gospel of Mary, 9) The Gospel of Philip, 10) The Gospel of Truth, 11) The Gospel of the Savior, 12) The Infancy Gospel of Thomas, 13) The Proto-Gospel of James, 14) The Epistle of the Apostles, 15) The Coptic Apocalypse of Peter, 16) The Second treatise of the Great Seth, 17) The Secret Gospel of Mark.

The following is a list of non-canonical Acts of the Apostles: 1) The Acts of John, 2) The Acts of Paul, 3) The Acts of Thecla, 4) The Acts of Thomas, 5) The Acts of Peter. The following is a list of non-canonical Epistles and writings: 1) The Third Letter to the Corinthians, 2) Correspondence of Paul and Seneca, 3) Paul's Letter to the Laodiceans, 4) The Letter of 1 Clement, 5) The Letter of 2 Clement, 6) The Letter of Peter to James and its Reception, 7) The Homilies of Clement, 8) Ptolemy's Letter to Flora, 9) The Treatise on the Resurrection, 10) The Didache, 11) The Letter of Barnabas, 12) The Preaching of Peter, 13) Pseudo-Titus.

The following is a list of non-canonical

Apocalypses and Revelatory Treatises: 1) The Shepherd of Hermas, 2) The Apocalypse of Peter, 3) The Apocalypse of Paul, 4) The Secret Book of John, 5) On the Origin of the World, 6) The First Thought in Three Forms, 7) The Hymn of the Pearl.

Some of these were previously mentioned and again, my providing these lists should in no way be seen as an endorsement of the texts. The point is not to advocate for the inclusion of any of these texts in the canon, but to merely reiterate that there were other texts outside the canon which were circulated, esteemed and revered as sacred and inspired by certain communities of faith.

There are a variety of canonical lists found throughout history regarding the New Testament and we discussed the Councils that essentially resolved the matter for Christianity. The oldest surviving New Testament canon list is known as the Muratorian Fragment. It lists 22 books and excludes Hebrews, James, 1 Peter, 2 Peter and 3 John.

The author of the Muratorian Fragment accepts as canonical the Wisdom of Solomon and the Apocalypse of Peter. The Shepherd of Hermes is also accepted for reading. There were a variety of other canon lists that can be gleaned from Origen, Eusebius, and as we already saw with Athanasius, Laodicea, Hippo, and the Third Synod of Carthage.[110] Again, there has never been a universal acceptance of a single accepted New Testament canon by the early Assembly or from Christianity for that matter.

There are many who hold to the belief that the entire process of compiling the Bible, as flawed as it may seem, was nevertheless coordinated and controlled by the

Holy Spirit. That may very well be the case, and it is not my intention to dispute that argument. I believe YHWH is ultimately in control, although there is nothing anywhere to confirm the belief that YHWH specifically chose the books that are in the Bible. Just as pagan doctrines have infiltrated man-made religion, there is also the likelihood that errors can be littered within translated texts.

An appalling example can be found in the New Testament promoted by the Gideons in Indonesia. In that version the translators replaced the title "God," with the name "Allah." So not only have they lost the Hebrew understanding of Elohim, as most English Bibles do, but they now actually represent Allah as the Elohim of Yisrael instead of YHWH.[III]

Clearly man has tampered with and profaned the truth throughout history. There is no reason to assume that the process of the Roman Catholic Church compiling texts to support their new state religion was somehow immunized from that reality. In fact, there is every reason to believe that the process was flawed, when viewed in the greater context of the anti-Torah, anti-Covenant, anti-Yisrael doctrines endorsed through the same councils, and by the same people, who canonized the New Testament.

Now I know that there are those who refuse to believe that their Bible is anything but divinely inspired. They would do well to determine where they first obtained that belief.

When we allow the pendulum to swing back and the plum to hold true, we see that it points to the foundational Scriptures of the Tanak. For instance, we have the words of Messiah indicating that He did not

come to destroy the Torah or the Prophets, but to fulfill them. (Matthew 5:17). For me, that is an important affirmation of the Tanak.

When asked by a scribe: *"What must I do to inherit eternal life" Yahushua responded with a question: 'What is written in the Torah?'"* (Luke 10:25-26). Some translations provide "What do the Scriptures say?" Again, Yahushua was directing people back to the only Scriptures in existence. He repeatedly used those Scriptures to answer questions, and direct people to the path of eternal life.

Early followers of Yahushua did not have Bibles. Their Scriptures were the Torah, the Prophets and the Writings. Many had seen or heard Yahushua before and after His death and resurrection. They understood His work in the context of the Scriptures – the Torah, the Prophets and the Writings. While they likely passed on testimonies and eye witness accounts, there were probably no formal Gospels for decades.

While they certainly passed around letters, writings, instructions and the like, none of those were deemed "Scriptures." They were likely looked upon as we view a good spiritual book, teaching or sermon. Those under the authority of Paul clearly held his letters in high esteem, although they certainly would not have viewed his letters as Scriptures when they arrived. Further, it can safely be said that Paul would not have considered his letters to be Scriptures.

It was only some time later that certain individuals decided to compile texts, and those people determined which texts to include. So the Bible, as we know it, is a collection of what were historically known to be the Scriptures (Tanak), along with a selection of writings that did not exist for a time, and which were not originally viewed as Scriptures.

Only hundreds of years later was the Bible compiled, and the process was initiated and controlled by the Christian religion. With this understanding it should help to understand the hierarchy of the texts. Hopefully the reader can discern that the Torah, the Prophets and the Writings were, and remain, the foundation of the faith. We then have the Gospels, which are the testimony of Yahushua followed by the Revelation provided by Yahushua to John. After that we have the Epistles which provide instruction, guidance, revelation and even prophecy. Nothing in any of those Epistles can change the foundational texts.

Nothing in this chapter should be construed as a criticism of the texts included within the New Testament portion of the Bible. It is only an analysis of the historical context of the process. Whether more texts should have been included in the New Testament or whether some of the texts should have been excluded is not the point of this book. The purpose is to reveal the priority of the texts, so the reader can gain a balanced perspective regarding the Scriptures, and the Covenant message contained therein.

There are some who do, in fact, criticize the texts because of what are perceived as translation problems. We will now look at some of those issues and see how translation issues can lead to certain matters getting lost in translation.

13

Lost in Translation

Up to this point we have examined the fact that YHWH specifically chose five texts to be written by Mosheh. These texts were transcribed from YHWH to Mosheh. There were other texts that eventually became known as the Tanak, and these were called The Scriptures. There were other texts not included in the Scriptures and this was a process determined by men and tradition. When we examine the creation of the New Testament we see that Christianity set out to develop a canon to add to the Scriptures. Some texts were accepted while other texts were rejected.

So we have seen that there has been a selection process directed at including and excluding writings. Now we will briefly examine some issues concerning those texts that were included within the canon. While it is evident that the Tanak was originally written in Hebrew, it is also important to remember that the New Testament writings were penned by First Century Yisraelites.

Many people pick up an English New Testament and attempt to read this ancient text, which describes an ancient eastern faith and culture in a very modern western language. While the story of the Good News is fairly simple, people often get into trouble when they attempt to read and interpret those texts out of context. You must read and understand those texts within their Hebrew context, understanding the language and culture of that time. Failure to do so can be problematic to say the least.

A very simple example is the existence of idioms and figures of speech. An idiom is an expression or a phrase whose meaning cannot be deduced from the literal definitions of the words, but instead refers to a figurative meaning that is known only through the conventional use of a specific language.

For instance in the English language you might hear statements such as: "It's raining cats and dogs," "I'm feeling under the weather" or "I have a bone to pick with you." None of these statements make sense if taken literally. You simply must understand their inherent meaning.

The same holds true with the Hebrew language. The Hebrew Scriptures are filled with idioms which must be recognized and understood to be idioms. Otherwise, the translation into another language simply makes no sense.

For instance, some well known Hebrew idioms include the following: "A Land flowing with milk and honey." This statement often refers to the Promised Land and it means that it is a good and fertile land. It does not mean that there is actually milk and honey flowing like rivers.

Another idiom refers to someone as "stiff necked" or with a "hard forehead." This is not referring to the rigidity of their anatomy, but rather the fact that they are stubborn. When a person is described as having a "good eye" it does not mean that they have 20/20 vision, but

rather that they are generous.

There are ample resources to learn about idioms and figures of speech. Understanding these culture specific phrases can help us better understand the meaning of the text, and even the thought process behind the language. Even when words appear to translate directly from one language to another, it is not always the case.

For instance, the notion of "salvation" to a modern Evangelical Christian is much different than "salvation" to a Yisraelite. While an Evangelical Christian considers salvation to be the guarantee of a persons soul going to heaven, a Yisraelite viewed salvation as a deliverance from oppression.

The notion of being "saved" can have a variety of meanings, some of which are not religious at all. For instance, when the English declare "God save the Queen" they are not praying for the eternal state of the queen's soul, rather they are referring to her health and the peaceful continuation of her throne and her kingdom. The statement is spoken as a celebration of British patriotism, a plea to protect the monarchy and preserve the political order, not a call for her conversion or spiritual salvation. Similarly in ancient [Y]israel, talk of being saved or redeemed had a physical/political meaning rather than a spiritual one, as evidenced in numerous Bible passages about salvation and redemption."[112]

While we have words in the English that seem to equate with ancient words, you must always consider the active/passive contrast between eastern and western thought. There is no doubt that Hebrew was the language of the Tanak, it was the language of Yisrael, and it is the language that pervaded the Yisraelite culture in which the Messiah taught. At that time in history, the Land of Yisrael was subjugated to the Roman Empire at that time, and there were multiple languages being spoken, but those concerned with the Messiah and His ministry primarily spoke an eastern Semitic dialect such as Hebrew or Aramaic.

Even Paul, "the Apostle to the Gentiles" spoke Hebrew to the Yisraelites, because that was the language that they spoke. (Acts 21:40-22:2). So it is within the context of the Hebrew language, and the Hebrew culture, that we must examine the Hebrew Messiah, and the texts written by His Hebrew Talmidim.

The problem is that the Hebraic context has been diluted and veritably lost through time. For instance, aside from the Scriptural texts themselves, one of the prominent histories in Christianity is found in "The History of the Church" by Eusebius.[13] Sadly, by the time this history had been written, centuries of division and tradition had already taken root. In fact, the division between the Natzrim and Christians was essentially complete. Eusebius, a contemporary of Constantine, was therefore writing with considerable bias. He was, after all, compiling a History of the Catholic Church, and was clearly opposed to the Jews.

In fact, some of his first words in his treatise indicate his desire to describe "the calamities that immediately after their conspiracy against our Savior overwhelmed the entire Jewish race."[14] Those are strong words and the fact that he separates the entire "Jewish race" into a category of apparently cursed people because of their "conspiracy" actually set the tone for later persecution. It also reinforced the division between the

Natzrim and Christians, later defined as between Jews and Gentiles.

If you can write history and then canonize, control and interpret truth you have the power. This is what occurred when the Roman Empire created the Christian Religion, and established the Catholic Church. Constantine's decision to "convert" and then make Christianity the official state religion of the Roman Empire was a political decision.

Christianity was a way to synchronize the familiar worship of the sun with the belief in the Christ. An important part of the development of this new religion was the selection and translation of the texts to be considered "sacred texts" of the religion.

The Christian religion felt it needed more than the Tanak. In fact, Christianity essentially rejected the Torah, believing it was exclusively for the Jews. While the early Talmidim, Paul and the Natzrim exclusively used the Torah, the Prophets and the Writings as their Scriptures, Christianity needed more.

This is why we see Christianity as the driving force to add to the Scriptures by developing the New Testament. The power to codify and canonize meant the ability to determine what goes in and what stays out. Christianity wanted desperately to separate from the Jews, and the New Testament was critical to that separation. They needed their own unique Scriptures to justify their new religion. Without new Scriptures, they could not advocate the changes that they professed had occurred with the Covenant.

Interestingly, despite their canonization of the New Testament, the Catholic Church was primarily opposed to the laity actually reading that canon. In fact, the Church prohibited the laity from owning and reading the texts.

Here is a quote from Pope Innocent III: "As by the old law the beast touching the holy mount was to be stoned to death so simple and uneducated men were not to touch the Bible or venture to preach its doctrines."[115]

Pope Innocent III was referring to the time when the Children of Yisrael stood before Mount Sinai. YHWH clearly commanded that no one touch the mountain, but that was not to prohibit anyone from reading the Bible. Nothing had been written at that point, although YHWH spoke directly to everyone. It was the day of Shabuot, often referred to as Pentecost, and it was not meant to restrict the Word from anyone. In fact, quite the opposite occurred on that day. The Word was spoken directly from YHWH to all of the people.

The Roman Catholic Church restricted access to the Scriptures. As a result, most never had an opportunity to read the Scriptures. As a result, they relied upon the Church for the contents and interpretation of the texts. This, of course, gave the Church power to determine and control "truth." The laity were subject to those interpretations and doctrines, because they had no way to read and challenge those positions.

The Catholic Church actively persecuted groups such as the Waldenses and the Albigenses, who did not follow church doctrine, but instead followed the Scriptures. Interestingly, just exactly what those Scriptures said was still subject to debate.[116]

After determining what texts were to be included in the canon, the Church itself had to grapple with the

translation of those contents. This is an incredibly vast area of study that traces many centuries, languages and translations.

Texts originally written in Hebrew, Aramaic and Greek were eventually translated into Latin, the language of the Roman Empire.  Initially written in the Old Latin, the four Gospels were later revised by Eusebius Hieronymus, known as Jerome. His translation was completed around 384 CE, and later became known as the Latin Vulgate. It is not certain whether Jerome revised the rest of the New Testament, but after 384 CE he moved to Bethlehem where he translated the Tanak into Latin.

It is from this translation that we see Jerome essentially creating the name Lucifer, which now has become a common name for "satan." Interestingly, it did not exist before Jerome inserted it into Isaiah 14:12. The text actually reads: "*How you are fallen from heaven, Heylal, son of the morning! How you are cut down to the ground, you who weakened the nations!*"

The name that Jerome changed to Lucifer is actually spelled hey (ﬡ), yud (ﬠ), lamed (ﬥ), lamed (ﬥ) in Hebrew - ﬥﬥﬠﬡ. Since names are transliterated, Jerome should have spelled a Latin word that would be pronounced the same as it is in Hebrew. Instead, Jerome decided to translate "Heylal," which means: "brightness."

Lucifer is a derivative of two words: "lux" (light) and "ferrous" (to bear or carry). Thus "Lucifer" in Latin means: "light bearer." As a result of it being inserted in place of a proper noun, the translated word "lucifer" is now used as a proper name. There now exist powerful traditions revolving around the name "Lucifer." It is a complete fabrication due to Jerome altering the text.

This is a good example of the problem with translating names, rather than transliterating names. When you speak someone's name, you do not state the translation of the name – you simply speak the name. Therefore, names do not change from one language to another. While they may be spelled differently from language to language, names are transliterated so that they are pronounced the same anywhere in the world.

If I travel to Rome, I do not seek out the Latin equivalent of the meaning of my name. My name is still pronounced the same regardless of the fact that I am in a country that speaks a different language. We will examine this issue further, but for now it is worthy to note the importance that translators have had in developing the texts.

It is also significant to note that these people had personal doctrinal beliefs that influenced the texts they translated. For instance, Jerome in *Against Helvidius* defended the doctrine of perpetus virginitate, which advocated the perpetual virginity of Mary. The doctrine also espouses that Joseph lived a celibate life. As a result of this belief, it is asserted that the New Testament texts referencing the brothers of Yahushua were altered to fit this doctrine. Instead of calling them brothers, they were referred to as "stepbrothers."[117]

No doubt, texts have been altered, and we can state with certainty that there were problems with the Latin Vulgate. As centuries followed certain individuals

examined the Vulgate and attempted to refine and retranslate the text. Around 1384 John Wycliffe translated the Latin into Middle English.

Around 1454 to 1455 Johannes Gutenberg of Germany, used his invention of removable type, to print a Latin Bible based upon the Latin Vulgate. This was a pivotal time as the text was now made more accessible to the masses. This allowed for greater scrutiny, and it led to refinements and the ability to develop translations into other languages.

Between 1516 and 1522 Desiderius Erasmus Roterodamus, known as Erasmus, developed various editions of a parallel version of the New Testament with both Latin and Greek translations side by side. Erasmus determined that the Latin was so corrupt that he retranslated the Latin from the Greek.

For instance, the Latin used words such as "penance" while the Greek used "repentance." Penance was tied to the Church Sacrament that requires absolution through a priest. This notion places the pope or the priest in the position of absolving people from their sins. Repentance, on the other hand, derives from the Hebrew word "shuwb" (𐤔𐤅𐤁), which involves returning to YHWH. When we repent, we acknowledge that we have strayed from YHWH and His commandments. We return to YHWH and His ways when we repent.

From the work begun by Erasmus, we see a flow of translations, particularly into English beginning with

William Tyndale around 1526. Tyndale actually developed the first Bible printed in English. Thereafter, the Coverdale Bible was completed in 1535 followed by the Matthew's Bible in 1537, The Great Bible in 1539, The Geneva Bible in 1557 and The New Geneva Bible in 1560. "The Geneva Bible was the first English Bible to use verse numbers based on the work of Stephanus (Robert Estienne of Paris). It also had an elaborate system of commentary in marginal glosses."[118]

In 1611, likely the most famous Bible in History was printed –The King James Bible. It appears that something different occurred with this translation of the Bible. While most previous versions were men's best efforts to attain the original meaning of the text, with acknowledged shortfalls, the King James Version made very powerful claims. In the Preface to the Reader it provided that: "The original thereof being from heaven, not from Earth, the author being God, not man, the Editor, the Holy Spirit, not the wit of the Apostles or Prophets."

So this text was elevated above all others and was claimed to be divinely inspired, ordered and even edited. This is where we get the modern notions of inerrancy. Interestingly, a subsequent version was not well received. "The new translation of the Bible was no huge success when it was first published. The English preferred to stick with the Geneva Bibles they knew and loved. Besides, edition after edition was littered with errors. The famous Wicked Bible of 1631 printed Deuteronomy 5:24 – meant to celebrate God's "greatnesse" – as "And ye said, Behold, the Lord our Good hath shewed us his glory, and his great asse." The same edition also left out a crucial word in Exodus 20:14,

which as a result read, 'Thou shalt commit adultery.'"[119]

One very poignant mistake in the 1611 translation can be found in Acts 12:4. Here is the verse in the King James Version: "*And when he had apprehended him, he put him in prison, and delivered him to four quaternions of soldiers to keep him; intending after <u>Easter</u> to bring him forth to the people.*"

Many people probably do not see a problem with this text, because Easter has become a very popular Christian Holiday. It is important to recognize that Easter is a pagan fertility rite that derives from Babylon. It often occurs around the Scriptural Appointed Time known as Pesach, commonly called Passover in English.

What makes the passage in Acts 12:4 so problematic is that the Greek texts use the word "pascha." So the point is absolutely clear that the Greek texts are referring to the Appointed Time of Pesach, not the pagan holiday Easter. In fact, the previous verse specifically states that it was during "the Days of Unleavened Bread." Acts 12:3. Often, the word Pesach was used to describe not just the meal that occurred on Day 14 of Month 1, but also the Feast of Unleavened Bread that occurred between Day 15 and Day 22 of Month 1. So the entire span is commonly referred to as Pesach.

Now this is a very straightforward and easily correctable mistake. One would think that it would not be a big deal once recognized. In fact, the New King James version corrected the mistake as follows: "*So when* *he had arrested him, he put him in prison, and delivered him to four squads of soldiers to keep him, intending to bring him before the people after <u>Passover</u>.*" Acts 12:4 NKJV.

Incredibly, there are those who will perform intellectual acrobatics to justify the use of Easter in the 1611 KJV. It is these people who are essentially turning a translation into an idol. They feel the need to believe that the translation is perfect, and divine. This is sad, because they are living in a self imposed delusion, and they are completely missing the point. No English translation will ever be perfect, because it is a translation! It is not the original text written in the original language.

Now, after all of the centuries of struggles by certain men to provide an accurate translation for the masses we have quite the opposite of the problem that motivated them to translate the texts. The masses now have the texts readily available. Regrettably, most people do not read them, or they do not know how to read them and interpret them because of preconceived theologies that often take precedence over the actual text.

As was stated at the beginning of this chapter, context is important. Sadly, Christianity has esteemed its "New Testament" as a newer and better set of Scriptures than the "Old Testament." This division and labeling has essentially placed the two portions in opposition to one another - east versus west.

I have witnessed many occasions when Christians would hold evangelistic events, and offer salvation to those in attendance. Those who accepted the invitation were often given a single text of the Gospel of John. Now while it is a wonderful thing to give a gift, they may unwittingly be sending these new converts on a very precarious journey.

Remember that the formula for training new converts originally began in the synagogue "where Mosheh (Torah) was read each Sabbath." (Acts 15). So once a convert who was not raised a Yisraelite heard the Good News of Yahushua, they started observing Shabbat and they started hearing and learning the Torah. This is the foundation necessary to fully understand the work of the Messiah.

If you are simply handed a Gospel of John, without the foundation of the Torah, the Prophets and the Writings, you may be left with more questions than answers. This may also explain the lack of identity between Christians and the Assembly of Yisrael. Christians do not see themselves as joining the Renewed Covenant with Yisrael. Rather, they believe that they are in a new covenant, exclusively made with Christians. That, of course is a myth. There is no Covenant for Christians, but because new converts do not have an adequate foundation, this is often misunderstood.

I sometimes think that Christianity is so concerned with numbers that they make it too easy to convert. Often, it is simply an act of raising your hand – "while every eye is closed" or by saying a simple prayer - "repeat after me." Many times the decision to convert is made in response to an emotional pitch given during a crusade or outreach. Believe me, I have been there and done that, so I am critiquing my own past conduct and experience.

Typically, only after a decision is made at one of these events is the convert given any written information. You would think that there would be much information provided to the person before they make a decision. Sadly, most enter this journey of faith with a very poor understanding of the Creator, the Covenant and the Messiah. While they exercise and express faith, it is usually not based upon much Scriptural understanding.

A good example of not understanding the Scriptures can be seen in Acts 2, an event that many Christians believe was the start of "the Church." Yisraelites from a variety of nations were gathered at Jerusalem for the Appointed Time of Shabuot. It was a Feast, and it was specifically for all of those in the Covenant.

In fact, this was a Covenant event and only those in the Covenant would gather at the House of YHWH. It was the Feast of Firstfruits (Bikkurim), and it occurred 50 days following Day 16 of Month 1. It was specifically connected with the Feast of Unleavened Bread which occurred between Day 15 of Month 1 and Day 22 of Month 1. In fact, this was often considered to be the "atzeret" of Passover.[120]

This was a rehearsal that Yisraelites had been participating in for centuries. It would be a time of fulfillment concerning a previous Shabuot, when the Children of Yisrael had left Egypt, and were entering into a Covenant relationship with YHWH at Mount Sinai. This was the context of the event described in Acts 2. You must understand it in relation to Sinai, when YHWH spoke the Words to the people. It was on the same day, and it was to fulfill a pattern.

On the Day of Shabuot described in Acts 2 we read the following: "*¹ When the Day of Pentecost had fully come, they were all with one accord in one place. ² And suddenly there came a sound from heaven, as of a rushing mighty wind, and it filled the whole house where they were*

sitting. *³ Then there appeared to them divided tongues, as of fire, and one sat upon each of them. ⁴ And they were all filled with the Set Apart Spirit and began to speak with other tongues, as the Spirit gave them utterance.*" Acts 2:1-4.

The "house" that the passage is referring to is the House of YHWH – the Temple. Yisraelites were supposed to gather at the House of YHWH on Shabuot, not some "upper room" that has been the subject of Christian tradition. That is why so many Yisraelites were gathered together to witness the event. The passage begins by stating that "*they were all with one accord in one place*" Acts 2:1. It ends with the fact that they were "*continuing daily with one accord in the Temple.*" Acts 2:46. So the passage confirms that the place where they were of one accord was in the Temple.

The rushing wind, the fire and the sound should all make us think of Sinai. Now, thanks to the Messiah, the Spirit was speaking through men, and they spoke in languages that could be understood. The rest of the passage in Acts 2 details how Peter stood up and explained what was happening in relation to the prophecies. Particularly, he explained that Yahushua was the Messiah, and that He had been resurrected from the dead. Resurrection was one of the greatest debated topics of the day. Peter explained to the people that Messiah had to come from the seed of David, and that He needed to die and be resurrected.

Many believed and repented that day, because they understood the significance of the event within the context of the Appointed Time. They recognized it as a fulfillment of the prophecies, and the patterns of the Appointed Times. They were in the right place at the right time, because they were obeying the

commandments. As a result, they were in a position to receive the promise of the Spirit. This should be seen as an explicit endorsement of the Appointed Times. This event, after all, was a fulfillment of a Covenant promise. It was the renewal of the Covenant as described by the prophets.

The connection could not be any clearer as the text describes: *"those who gladly received his word were immersed and that day about three thousand souls were added to them."* Acts 2:41. The number 3,000 is no arbitrary figure. In fact, it is the number of people who were slain after the Golden Calf incident that occurred after Shabuot at Sinai. (Shemot 32:28). So instead of 3,000 being killed for breaking the Covenant mediated by Mosheh, 3,000 were saved when they joined the renewed Covenant mediated by Messiah.

So the Gospels and the Book of Acts historically pick up where the Tanak left off. The divided Kingdom of Yisrael was expecting the Messiah Who would bring together the divided Houses of Yisrael and Yahudah. Those who were in the Covenant were anticipating one like Mosheh as promised. *"I will raise up for them a Prophet like you from among their brethren, and will put My words in His mouth, and He shall speak to them all that I command Him."* Debarim 18:18.

The reason they were anticipating One like Mosheh was because they knew they needed One who could mediate the Renewed Covenant with Yisrael as prophesied by the prophet Yirmeyahu.

"[31] Behold, the days are coming, says YHWH, when I will make a Renewed Covenant with the House of Yisrael and with the House of Yahudah [32] not according to the Covenant that

I made with their fathers in the day that I took them by the hand to lead them out of the land of Egypt, My Covenant which they broke, though I was a husband to them, says YHWH. ³³ But this is the Covenant that I will make with the House of Yisrael after those days, says YHWH: I will put My Torah in their minds, and write it on their hearts; and I will be their Elohim, and they shall be My people. ³⁴ No more shall every man teach his neighbor, and every man his brother, saying, Know YHWH, for they all shall know Me, from the least of them to the greatest of them, says YHWH. For I will forgive their iniquity, and their sin I will remember no more. ³⁵ Thus says YHWH, Who gives the sun for a light by day, The ordinances of the moon and the stars for a light by night, Who disturbs the sea, And its waves roar YHWH of hosts is His Name: ³⁶ If those ordinances depart from before Me, says YHWH, Then the seed of Yisrael shall also cease from being a nation before Me forever."
Yirmeyahu 31:31-36.

This was not a brand new Covenant. It was a renewed Covenant exactly as was foreshadowed by the Renewal at Sinai when Mosheh cut two tablets to replace the ones that had been broken. At Sinai, YHWH renewed the Covenant on the tablets presented by the mediator Mosheh. It was the same Covenant written on the second set of tablets. That pattern was to reveal a future renewed Covenant. Only now, YHWH would remove the hearts of stone, and replace them with hearts of flesh.

"14 Again the Word of YHWH came to me, saying, 15 Son of man, your brethren, your relatives, your countrymen, and all the House of Yisrael in its entirety, are those about whom the inhabitants of Jerusalem have said, Get far away from YHWH, this land has been given to us as a possession. 16 Therefore say, Thus says the Master YHWH: Although I have cast them far off among the Gentiles, and although I have scattered them among the countries, yet I shall be a little sanctuary for them in the countries where they have gone. 17 Therefore say, Thus says the Master YHWH: I will gather you from the peoples, assemble you from the countries where you have been scattered, and I will give you the land of Yisrael. 18 And they will go there, and they will take away all its detestable things and all its abominations from there. 19 Then I will give them one heart, and I will put a new spirit within them, and take the stony heart out of their flesh, and give them a heart of flesh, 20 that they may walk in My statutes and keep My judgments and do them; and they shall be My people, and I will be their Elohim. 21 But as for those whose hearts follow the desire for their detestable things and their abominations, I will recompense their deeds on their own heads, says the Master YHWH." Ezekiel 11:14-21.

Notice that these promises were made to the House of Yisrael. We read again in Ezekiel the following promise:

"*16* Moreover the Word of YHWH came to me, saying: *17* Son of man, when the House of Yisrael dwelt in their own land, they defiled it by their own ways and deeds; to Me their way was like the uncleanness of a woman in her customary impurity. *18* Therefore I poured out My fury on them for the blood they had shed on the Land, and for their idols with which they had defiled it. *19* So I scattered them among the nations, and they were dispersed throughout the countries; I judged them according to their ways and their deeds. *20* When they came to the nations, wherever they went, they profaned My set apart Name - when they said of them, These are the people of YHWH, and yet they have gone out of His Land. *21* But I had concern for My set apart Name, which the House of Yisrael had profaned among the nations wherever they went. *22* Therefore say to the House of Yisrael, Thus says the Master YHWH: I do not do this for your sake, O House of Yisrael, but for My set apart Name's sake, which you have profaned among the nations wherever you went. *23* And I will sanctify My great name, which has been profaned among the nations, which you have profaned in their midst; and the nations shall know that I am YHWH, says the Master YHWH, when I am set apart in you before their eyes. *24* For I will take you from among the nations, gather you out of all countries, and bring you into your own land. *25* Then I will sprinkle clean water on you, and you shall be clean; I will cleanse you from all your filthiness and from all your idols. ²⁶ I will give you a new heart and put a new spirit within you; I will take the heart of stone out of your flesh and give you a heart of flesh. ²⁷ I will put My Spirit within you and cause you to walk in My statutes, and you will keep My judgments and do them. ²⁸ Then you shall dwell in the land that I gave to your fathers; you shall be My people, and I will be your Elohim. ²⁹ I will deliver you from all your uncleanness. I will call for the grain and multiply it, and bring no famine upon you. ³⁰ And I will multiply the fruit of your trees and the increase of your fields, so that you need never again bear the reproach of famine among the nations. ³¹ Then you will remember your evil ways and your deeds that were not good; and you will loathe yourselves in your own sight, for your iniquities and your abominations. ³² Not for your sake do I do this, says the Master YHWH, let it be known to you. Be ashamed and confounded for your own ways, O House of Yisrael! ³³ Thus says the Master YHWH: On the day that I cleanse you from all your iniquities, I will also enable you to dwell in the cities, and the ruins shall be rebuilt. ³⁴ The desolate land shall be tilled instead of lying desolate in the sight of all who pass by. ³⁵ So they will say, This land that was desolate has become like the garden of Eden; and the wasted, desolate, and ruined cities are now fortified and inhabited. ³⁶ Then the nations which are left all

around you shall know that I, YHWH, have
rebuilt the ruined places and planted what was
desolate. I, YHWH, have spoken it, and I will
do it." Ezekiel 36:16-36.

So this is the context of the New Testament, and the texts must be read and understood within that context. The House of Yisrael was in exile and only now, at the time of the writing of this book, is their period of punishment scheduled to expire.[121]

The starting point of the New Testament texts properly detail the birth, life, teachings, death and resurrection of the Messiah. They then proceed to provide an account of the Assembly of Talmidim, and the spreading of the Good News around specific parts of the world. There are some selected letters followed by a prophecy concerning the Day of YHWH found in the Revelation.

Currently, most of the source texts for these writings are found in the Greek language, but that does not mean that they were all originally written in Greek. In fact, there is evidence that some of the earliest writings were in Hebrew and Aramaic – eastern Semitic languages. Indeed, the early Talmidim were, in large part, Yisraelites describing Hebrew individuals, speaking Hebrew and the setting was in a very Hebrew context.

It had long been held that Aramaic, which is a derivative of Hebrew, was the common language used by Yisraelites during the time of Messiah. We now know from the Dead Sea Scrolls that Hebrew was used as a written medium in first century times, a fact which was previously in question. Historians confirm the fact that Matthew wrote Scriptures in Hebrew. Papias (ca. 60-130 CE), bishop of Hierapolis, wrote that "Matthew collected the oracles in the Hebrew language, and each interpreted them as best he could."[122]

We can be confident that at some point there were some original New Testament writings in Hebrew and Aramaic. In fact, the early eastern assembly ultimately compiled 22 texts in Aramaic.[123] Again, this makes perfect sense since those who were native Hebrews and grew up with the Hebrew Scriptures fully understood the significance of the number 22 representing the alephbet, and of course, the Aleph Taw (𐤕𐤀).

To be fair, beyond Matthew and likely Hebrews, we do not know for certain whether the other New Testament texts were originally written in an eastern language. We simply do not have the original autographs, so we do not have direct proof of the language of any of the originals. While it is believed that Aramaic was the "lingua franca" of the Land of Yisrael prior to the coming of Yahushua, no doubt Greek was pervasive throughout the region from the previous Hellenization by Alexander the Great.

There can be no doubt that viewing the texts in their original language will result in the best understanding. We have seen the amazing complexity and depth of the Hebrew texts as well as the mysteries contained in the language. With that understanding, it is clearly desirous to view the New Testament texts in their original language.

Here is one insightful comment from a renowned Rabbi concerning the Hebrew language. "Our sacred literature does not use obscure language, but describes most things in words clearly indicating their meaning. Therefore, it is necessary at all times to delve into the

literal meaning of words to achieve complete understanding of what is actually meant."[124] Now mind you, he is referring to the Modern Hebrew Language that derives from the Ancient Hebrew.

According to the protestant reformer Martin Luther: "If I were younger I would want to learn this language [i.e. Hebrew], for without it one can never properly understand the Holy Scripture. For that reason they have said correctly: 'The Jews drink out of the original spring, The Greeks drink out of the stream flowing out of the stream, The Latins, however, out of the puddle.'"[125]

With the transmission of the eastern, Semitic Messiah into a western language, there were bound to be issues. It is not only the language, but the way of thinking. We have already discussed some of the differences between eastern and western thought, and languages. This causes some of the problems with translating and understanding the Scriptures in western languages such as English.

Recall that Hebrew is eastern, which is concrete and active. English is western which is abstract and passive. A good example of this difference can be seen in the translation of the Hebrew word "zakar" (𐤀𐤅𐤆𐤁).

This word is used all throughout the Scriptures, and is often translated into English as "remember." There are many passages which use this word. For instance: "Remember My Covenant." (Beresheet 9:15; 1 Chronicles 16:15). "Remember the Sabbath to keep it set apart." (Shemot 20:8). "Remember all the commandments of YHWH to do them." (Bemidbar 15:39). "Remember the former things." (Yeshayahu 46:9).

Now someone reading these passages in English

may believe that you are simply supposed to think about these things. In English, the act of remembering is primarily a mental exercise. Sadly, this is not the full intention of the passages. In Hebrew, the word "zakar" is an action word. It certainly means: "remember" or "recall." It also means: "to recall in such a way that it affects present feeling, thought or action."[126] In other words, we remember, and as a result of remembering – we act.

When we remember the Covenant, we keep it in our minds, and we walk according to the Covenant. That is why we are commanded to wear tzitzit, so we can remember the commandments and do them. (Bemidbar 15:39). When we remember the Sabbath, we rest and observe the Sabbath, we don't just think about it. Therefore, remembering in the Hebrew sense is not just about thoughts and recollection, it involves action.

Another good example of this difference is demonstrated through the word "shamar" (ꓤꓬW). This

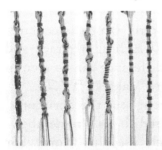

word is often translated into English as "hear," but once again, it means more than just listening. The word can be translated as "guard" or "watch over." In a more complete sense it means "hear and obey." So while the English translation is passive and infers the mere act of listening, the Hebrew active language infers listening coupled with the requisite action.

This gives a much better understanding to the statement made by Yahushua in Mark 12 when asked by the scribes which was the first of all the commandments.

Yahushua answered: "²⁹ . . . *The first of all the commandments is, Hear, O Yisrael YHWH our Elohim, YHWH is one (echad):* ³⁰ *And you shall love YHWH your Elohim with all your heart, and with all your soul, and with all your mind, and with all your strength: this is the first commandment.*"

Yahushua was stating that "The Shema" an important prayer and command found in Debarim 6, was the first of all commands. It begins with the word "Shema" and it is instructing the Covenant people to hear and obey YHWH. So Yahushua was telling people not simply to listen, but to obey.

This command also contains an amazing mystery. Debarim 6:4 is seen as follows in the Hebrew Script:

◁ ᕼᐊ ᐃYᐊᒿ YᎩᒿᐃᏓ∤ᐊ ᐃYᐊᒿ ∤ᐊᐊWᒿ ☉ᎩW

Here is another example of enlarged letters which are meant to draw out attention to the text. Indeed, the enlarged ayin (☉) and the enlarged dalet (◁) literally mean: "see the door." So through the Shema, we see the door to the Kingdom, the door to the Garden, and Yahushua said that He is that door. (John 10:7, 9).

These are two simple examples of words and their meanings not being fully expressed through translations from eastern to western languages. Often times the translated words simply do not adequately transmit the full meaning of the Hebrew text. Now there is no one to blame for this, it is simply a reality that needs to be examined and resolved. Failure to do so results in much being lost in translation.

So language and thought are factors in certain concepts and ideas being lost in translation. We will now examine some other translation problems that range from simple scribal errors, to expansions in the text, to true variances within texts. These issues exist and a person should not fear an open and honest exploration of these matters as they can help us get closer to the truth.

There are many who adhere to a certain version of the Bible, as if it is the sole authority of Elohim. They must recognize that their particular version is simply a translation, and an attempt to grasp the full meaning of the original text. Some translations are better than others, and I hope that it has been made clear by now the importance of reading and studying the Scriptures in the original Hebrew.

The best attempts of men to translate languages are never the same as the original. This is true when translating from an eastern language like Hebrew into a western language like Greek. It is a whole other problem when we do not have the original texts to translate. This is the case with the Greek manuscripts that make up the New Testament.

Now the same can be said about the Tanak. We do not have any original documents found in the Tanak. We understand that Mosheh transcribed the Torah in the presence of YHWH. So we have a strong recognition of authorship and the source of those writings – YHWH. We also have a fair degree of certainty that the Torah we have today is incredibly consistent with the original transmitted through Mosheh.

We can discern the accuracy of the Torah by comparing the texts previously considered to be the oldest copies of the Tanak with those found in the Dead

Sea Scrolls. Despite the difference of nearly 1,000 years, the differences were minor. There was incredible consistency between the texts, which is largely due to the meticulous practices used by scribes to avoid making mistakes.

Typically, a scribe would bath, or immerse, before beginning his work. There were various methods of counting the letters to insure that the copies contained the same content as the original. The painstaking traditions of Scriptural Scribes, sometimes known as soferim, are well documented, and quite effective at insuring accuracy.[127] This is not to imply that they were perfect. In fact, there are some who believe that the Tanak still needs corrections. Interestingly, most of those criticisms and revisions are outside of the texts of the Torah.[128]

This is very different from the way New Testament texts were originally copied. There was initially no standardized method of copying these texts, because many were likely not considered to be "Scriptures." Only after the passage of time did people understand the importance of preserving and accurately copying those texts. Currently, most New Testaments are translated from copies of Greek Manuscripts that have gone through numerous layers of copying.

"Manuscripts of the Greek New Testament fall into two major divisions: uncials and cursives or minuscule. The uncials are those penned in large, capital letters, while the minuscule are those in small letters which often were written cursively. Most of our manuscripts are minuscule, dating from the ninth century. The vellum uncials, some of which date back to the fourth century, are of inestimable worth as witnesses to the New Testament. The 'big three' of the uncials are the Vatican, the Sinaitic, and the Alexandrian Manuscripts."[129]

Some calculate the number of manuscripts to be in the area of 5,000. Some of the manuscripts are simply fragments as small as the size of a credit card. Because we have copies of copies, and due to the fact that there was originally no uniform method of transcribing and copying the texts, we have mistakes and differences between the various manuscripts, called variances. Some calculate these variances to range between 200,000 and 300,000.[130]

Now it is important to point out that these numbers can be very misleading. Most of these so-called variances are simple spelling differences and inadvertent omissions. These are typically easy to determine and correct. There are instances when there are some significant differences that can determine doctrine. In those cases it is important to discern which variance is the original understanding. Because we have no originals we are not always able to make an affirmative decision, and that is when translators make their best judgments. This is one of the reasons why we have different translations of the Bible.

A good example of finding the oldest and therefore the most accurate version can be found in 1 John 5:7-8. Here is what it says in a modern translation: *"⁷ For there are three that bear witness in heaven: the Father, the Word, and the Holy Spirit; and these three are one. ⁸ And there are three that bear witness on earth: the Spirit, the water, and the blood; and these three agree as one."*

This passage is often used to support the doctrine of the Trinity in Christianity which, as we have seen, is

a pagan concept derived from Babylon. Interestingly, the text of 1 John 5:7-8 was not found in any Greek manuscript until the invention of the printing press in the 15th Century. It was clearly not an original passage, but it was still included in the King James Version. Because of this fact, it has been removed from most modern translations.[131]

A problem does arise when we have two competing passages, and it is not so obvious which text accurately describes the autograph – the original text. A good example of this type of problem can be found in Mark 1:41, which describes Yahushua being approached by a leper.

Here is what a common translation provides, not including the name corrections: "*41 Then Yahushua, moved with compassion, stretched out his hand and touched him, and said to him, I am willing; be cleansed. 42 As soon as he had spoken, immediately the leprosy left him, and he was cleansed. 43 And He strictly warned him and sent him away at once, 44 and said to him, See that you say nothing to anyone; but go your way, show yourself to the priest, and offer for your cleansing those things which Mosheh commanded, as a testimony to them.*" Mark 1:41-44.

Notice that in this passage Yahushua healed the man, then He "*strictly warned him and sent him away.*" There are some translations that indicate Yahushua "*rebuked the man.*" This has been a puzzling passage for many because Yahushua first has "compassion" and then "rebukes" the man.

Here is an example of the oldest manuscript not necessarily being the accepted text. The surviving manuscripts of Mark preserve verse 41 in two different forms. The most common and accepted version, which is found in many modern translations, has Yahushua "moved with compassion" and later rebuking the man.

The Greek word for feeling compassion is "splangnistheis" and this is found in most of the existing manuscripts. Another manuscript, called Codex Bezae, includes the word "orgistheis" instead of "splangnistheis." Codex Bezae is one of the oldest witnesses,

and it is actually supported by three Latin manuscripts.

Orgistheis means: "becoming angry." Because of the agreement between Greek and Latin witnesses, "orgistheis" is generally conceded by textual specialists to go back at least to the second century CE, thus making it the oldest witness of this text. While Yahushua becoming angry does not fit within our accepted understanding, it certainly fits the context. First, it should be pointed out that Mark, on other occasions, describes Yahushua as becoming angry. So it would not be unusual for him to describe an angry Yahushua. (see Mark 3:5 and 11:15).

It is also important to remember that this man, being a leper, was in a place where he was not supposed to be. The passage clearly states that Yahushua was in a certain city. This is an important fact, because lepers were not supposed to be in cities. They were considered to be "tame" (𐤊𐤔𐤈) or "unclean." In fact, a leper was required to tear their clothing, shave their head and cry out "Unclean! Unclean!" so that people would not go

near them. (Vayiqra 13:45-46). This is what we call being quarantined.

Yahushua was what we might classify as "orthodox." He was strictly Torah observant, He had to be in order to be deemed "without sin." Therefore, it is very likely that Yahushua did, in fact, become angry at the man who was blatantly disobeying the commandments. It is consistent with the fact that after Yahushua healed the man, he sharply rebuked him and told him to go and obey the commandments.[132]

While Yahushua was clearly willing to heal the man, He may have been angered by the circumstances. He came, after all, teaching the fullness of the Torah.

So somewhere in the process of picking and choosing competing texts, the "compassionate" text won out, but it is likely wrong. This is why it is important for every reader to examine the texts, and become their own "textual critic." It is a very enriching experience because it forces us to examine the context of the life and ministry of Yahushua. Sometimes, this shatters our inherited paradigms, which is essential if we are to fully appreciate the work of the Messiah.

There are other reasons why translations fall short, due to mistakes made in the copying process. When examining copies of copies of copies . . . we know that there were individuals who were responsible for making those copies. They may have been professional scribes, or just a layperson desirous of making a copy of an important writing.

Today we have copy machines that make exact copies of originals. Hundreds and thousands of years ago it was a tedious process to make a copy. Unless close attention was paid by the copyist mistakes were bound to occur, and indeed they did occur. That is why we have a field of study known as textual criticism. Again, the process is not meant to "criticize" or diminish the Scriptural texts, but rather to glean through the myriad of typos and inconsistencies that exist in the competing manuscripts.

Since most of the Scribal errors are inadvertent, it is often easy to spot and correct a misspelling. Sometimes a sentence is copied twice or a sentence is skipped. Sometimes a word is simply omitted. The context of a passage or the style of the author can make it easy to correct a missing word or a wrong word. Sometimes a change is unintentional.

We already discussed the insertion of Easter in the King James Version, which has reinforced serious doctrinal errors. Whether that insertion derived from ignorance or ill intent is not certain. Clearly though, the translators replaced a Scriptural Appointed Time with a pagan holiday. The ramifications of such an error are immeasurable. Such a translation error has been used as a justification for countless Christians participating in the pagan celebration of a fertility goddess originating in Babylonian sun worship.[133]

In a related matter, there is another very obvious mistranslation that leads people to this pagan day. Most Christians believe that "Jesus" was resurrected on Easter Sunday. This is primarily the result of the mistranslated phrase "mia ton shabbaton" in Mark 16:2 and Luke 24:1. Both of these texts deal with the resurrection of Yahushua, and most translations provide "on the first day of the week." This promotes the idea that Yahushua

was resurrected on Sunday, essentially affirming Sunday as the Christian Sabbath.

The only problem is that the Greek word "shabbaton" clearly means "sabbaths." There is no way it would be translated as "week." A more proper rendering is "the first of the Sabbaths." Anyone familiar with the Scriptural Appointed Times understands that from Day 16 of Month 1, after the resheet barley offering, we begin a count of seven sevens and seven Sabbaths. This count will involve 49 days (7x7) followed by Day 50 – Shabuot, also known as Pentecost. So Yahushua was crucified on Passover Day and resurrected after 3 days and 3 nights on the weekly Sabbath, which was also "the first of the Sabbaths."

This mistranslation has been used for centuries to condone Babylonian sun worship practices in the Christian religion. Amazingly, it is clear to see in the Greek text, just as "pascha" clearly referred to Passover and not Easter.

There are other instances of doctrinal influences that have permeated texts, added as scribal notes. Now these notes are often recognized as being notes, and they are usually surrounded by parenthesis. Sadly, many readers do not recognize the distinction and inadvertently afford them the weight of Scripture.

For instance, in the New International Version of Mark 7:18-19, we read: "*¹⁸ Are you so dull? he asked. "Don't you see that nothing that enters a person from the outside can defile them? ¹⁹ For it doesn't go into their heart but into their stomach, and then out of the body." (In saying this, Jesus declared all foods clean.)*"

Some people attempt to use this passage to prove that Yahushua somehow abolished the dietary instructions contained in the Torah. They are ignoring the fact that Yahushua specifically said He did not come to destroy the Torah or the Prophets. *"Think not that I am come to destroy the Torah, or the Prophets: I am not come to destroy, but to fulfill."* Matthew 5:17.

The words in parenthesis in Mark 7 completely misrepresent the teaching of the Messiah – yet they are words included in the Bible. If a person did not know any better they would think that Yahushua was declaring all things clean. This may not seem strange to a westerner who has little understanding of the distinctions between clean and unclean, but to any Torah observant Yisraelite, the idea is unthinkable.

The passage also makes no sense, because in order for something to be considered food, it must be clean. To say it another way, only things permitted to be eaten in the Scriptures are food. All foods must be clean, otherwise they are not food. The Torah provides a clear presentation of food that can be eaten. Yahushua was in no way changing the Torah, or declaring everything edible.

The simple truth is that Yahushua did not make the statement. The fact that the text is in parenthesis reveals that it is a scribal note. It is an ignorant statement and it is not the inspired Word of YHWH. Sadly, many have been confused and deceived because this passage was included in certain Bibles.

Some other examples of scribal notes included within certain Bibles can be found in the first chapter of the Gospel of John. In John 1:38 we read: *"Then Jesus turned, and saw them following, and saith unto them, What seek ye? They said unto him, Rabbi, (which is to say, being interpreted, Master,) where dwellest thou?"* KJV. The words

in parenthesis are a translator's note, they are not original inspired words, and it is an incorrect interpretation. While teachers were considered to be masters in Greek society, a Rabbi was a teacher in Hebrew culture, not a master.

In John 1:41 we read an account of Andrew speaking to his brother Shimon: *"we have found the Messiah (which is translated the Christ)."* Again, the portion in parenthesis is an addition from an unknown person who is attempting to clarify how they thought the text should read. It is not Scripture, and a Hebrew speaking Yisraelite would not refer to their Messiah as Christ. Christ was a Greek term used by most pagans to describe their "anointed" deities. This insertion appears to justify the use of the label "Christian."

Yet another example is found in the following verse. *"And he brought him to Jesus. Now when Jesus looked at him, He said, 'You are Simon the son of Jonah. You shall be called Cephas' (which is translated, A Stone)."* John 1:42. Here again, the information contained in the parenthesis were added by a scribe. They were not in the original text, but most people do not understand that because the words are in their Bible, so they assume that they are part of the inspired text.

These are some examples of scribal insertions that can cause confusion. Translators chose to keep them in the text and many readers inadvertently presume that they were original words. Sometimes translations simply insert words and place them in italics. Most readers do not recognize those italicized words as being added words and usually consider them to be "inspired."

Sometimes confusion occurs simply because there has been a bad translation from one language to another.

We can see an example of this in Yeshayahu 35:8. Here is the text according to the New King James Version: "A highway shall be there, and a road, and it shall be called the Highway of Holiness. The unclean shall not pass over it, but it shall be for others. Whoever walks the road, although a fool, shall not go astray."

This verse makes no sense. It seems to be saying that a fool can walk on the Highway of Holiness, and even though a person is a fool, they shall not go astray as long as they are on the path. This is wrong. The righteous are on the way of Holiness, not fools.

We read an equally problematic translation in the King James Version: "And an highway shall be there, and a way, and it shall be called The way of holiness; the unclean shall not pass over it; but it shall be for those: the wayfaring men, though fools, shall not err therein." This passage says that wayfarers will be on the path and even though they are fools, they will not err while they are on the path.

Some translations actually get it right as follows: "And there shall be a highway, and a way, and it shall be called 'The Way of Set Apartness' The unclean does not pass over it, but it is for those who walk the way, and no fools wander on it." Yeshayahu 35:8 The Scriptures

So the KJV and NKJV actually say the opposite of what the verse means, largely because they simply do not understand that a fool does not partake in what is holy. This is a similar distinction as was made between clean and unclean. Again, it is an obvious problem. This is a simple example, although there are far too many for us to mention in this brief discussion.

The purpose of pointing out these errors is not to question the authenticity or reliability of the Scriptures. Rather, it is to demonstrate the fallibility of the men who

copied texts, and men who translated those texts into other languages. Mistakes have been made in translations that are sometimes minor and at times critical. Therefore, it is imperative that we study and examine the Scriptures to insure that we are reading and learning the Truth.

The problem has become so pervasive that even the names of the books have been mistranslated. As previously mentioned, the book often called "Numbers" is actually "Bemidbar" in Hebrew. Bemidbar means "in the wilderness" not "numbers." The book often called "Exodus" is actually "Shemot" in Hebrew, which means: "names." By changing the names of the Scriptural texts, the focus is deflected.

Throughout the Bible, particularly the New Testament, names are not translated consistently. For instance, it has already been mentioned that the Name of the Messiah is Yahushua. It is the same name as the patriarch commonly called Joshua. While there is no "J" in Hebrew or Greek, English translations should have at least called the Messiah "Joshua" if they were to be consistent.

Instead, they use a derivative of the Greek name Iesus, which has no connection with the Hebrew Name Yahushua. Instead, the name Iesus is connected with the pagan sun god Zeus.[134] The Name of the Messiah has been "Hellenized." It has been replaced with another pagan derived name, so now much of the world believes that the Messiah was named a meaningless English/Greek hybrid name – Jesus, instead of the Hebrew word Yahushua which means "YHWH saves."

In a bizarre translational twist, the translators of the King James Version actually reverse translated the name of the Patriarch Joshua into the Hellenized name Jesus.

Here is one example from the King James text: "*⁴⁴ Our fathers had the tabernacle of witness in the wilderness, as he had appointed, speaking unto Moses, that he should make it according to the fashion that he had seen. ⁴⁵ Which also our fathers that came after brought in with Jesus into the possession of the Gentiles, whom God drave out before the face of our fathers, unto the days of David.*" Acts 7:44 KJV. This passage is clearly referring to the Hebrew patriarch Joshua. So why would the translators change his name?

Here is another example of the same error. "*⁷ Again, he limiteth a certain day, saying in David, To day, after so long a time; as it is said, To day if ye will hear his voice, harden not your hearts. ⁸ For if Jesus had given them rest, then would he not afterward have spoken of another day.*" Hebrews 4:7-8 KJV.

Again, the context reveals that the passage is referring to Joshua, the son on Nun and not the Messiah. So the translators have not only corrupted the Name of the Messiah, but also the name of the patriarch, Joshua (Yahushua) son of Nun.

We can find many examples of the Hellenization of names in the New Testament texts. For instance, in Greek manuscripts the name of the prophet Elijah (Eliyahu) is indicated as Helias. Anyone familiar with sun worship knows that Helios is the ancient Greek sun god. So the Greek manuscripts, which provide us with our English New Testaments, actually replaced the name of a prophet with the name of a pagan sun deity. This was an ignorant and brazen act by those who wrote and copied the Greek manuscripts. The name Eliyahu actually declares that "El is YHWH."

Lazarus in the New Testament is the same name as Eleazer in the Tanak, who was the third son of Aharon and represents the priesthood, which was dead at the time of Yahushua's ministry. The death and resurrection of Lazarus (Eleazer) show a beautiful picture of Yahushua resurrecting the priesthood with Himself as the High Priest, according to the order of Melchizedek.

The name James was inserted into the New Testament and replaced the name of the individual who was actually named Yaakob. Again, Yaakob has deep significance as the son of Yitshaq, whose name was changed to Yisrael. Tradition holds that the name James was inserted in honor of King James. Whatever the reason, the change hides an important connection with the Hebrew origins of the individual.

Telling a person that their Bible is not 100% accurate is like dropping a nuclear bomb on their lap. Responses may vary from running and hiding or going into shock. Most people get defensive and angry. If your faith is based upon a book that has been translated untold times, pieced together from numerous sources and canonized by unknown people then your faith has been seriously misplaced. It is important to step back and recognize that the English language is a fairly new language. It did not exist at the beginning of time, nor was it even one of the languages confused and created during the Tower of Babel incident.

The English language has only been in existence around 500 years.[135] The Word of Elohim clearly existed prior to the development of English so to idolize a particular English translation is both egotistical and foolish. My faith is in a living and powerful Creator Whose Word is much more than ink on a page. Every person needs to get this straight so that they do not fall into idolatry over a codex. With this understanding let us now address some more critical problems with modern translations of the Bible.

One major loss from the Hebrew to English is the issue of the Names. We already discussed the fact that Names are to be transliterated - not translated. We know that the Name of the Creator was first revealed in Hebrew because that was the language of creation. Sadly, the Name of the Creator – 𐤉𐤄𐤅𐤄 has been replaced and hidden in most English translations of the Bible. Instead of reading the Hebrew Script (𐤉𐤄𐤅𐤄) or the English equivalent of the Hebrew consonants (YHWH), we read The LORD. Thus most English Bibles replace the Name with a title. You will also not find the plural Elohim, but rather the title God, which is a title given to every deity in history. So in the English translations the identity, name and very character of the Creator is hidden and suppressed. This is a great disservice to those attempting to know and enter into relationship with YHWH.

This is the problem with using titles rather than names. As previously mentioned, the Gideons have actually inserted the name of another god – Allah in some of their Bibles. In those texts, everywhere the English Bibles have the word God, they have used the name Allah. Allah is the name of the god of Islam which derives from moon god worship. Allah does not mean god. Allah is the name of a god, and in this instance the Gideons are essentially deflecting the truth of YHWH to Allah. For Christians to read about Allah and worship Allah is a grave mistake which is perpetrated by a horrible translation.[136]

Another major problem with many English

translations involves missing information that can only be found in the Hebrew language. I know of no better example than the Aleph Taw (𐤗𐤊) which can be found 7,363 times in the Hebrew Tanak, and 2,622 times in the Hebrew Torah.[137] Sadly, it is never found in a translation from Hebrew in popular English versions of the Bible. As a result, this signature of the Messiah, a mystery recognized by the Sages, is literally lost in translation. The significance of the Aleph Taw (𐤗𐤊) will be seen as we continue to examine and identify The Word of Elohim.

The same holds true with the various "jots and tittles" referred to by Messiah. (Matthew 5:18). There are numerous items in the Hebrew text that are included to draw our attention, like the enlarged bet (𐤁) of Beresheet 1:1, or the enlarged ayin (𐤏) and dalet (𐤃) in the Shema. (Debarim 6:4). There are inverted nuns that essentially bracket the text of Bemidbar 10:35-36. These jots and tittles, as well as many others, do not translate into the English, so they too are lost in translation.

All of this unseen information in English translations hinders our understanding of the written texts. As we study Scriptures the Spirit can reveal things over time that are not initially discerned. This is why participating in the "Torah Cycle" is so important.[138]

As we walk in the Covenant path, and synchronize our lives with the ways of YHWH, we receive continuously fresh revelation from the Torah. Even though we are reading the same texts over again, through the process we discern things that were not previously understood. There is a traditional concept known as PaRDeS, which is an acronym for 1) Peshat, 2) Remez, 3) Derash, and 4) Sod. These four categories describe the 4 different levels of understanding in the Scriptures from the plain meaning (peshat) to the secret meaning (sod).[139]

Whether you agree that there are 4 levels, more or less is not the point here. The important thing to remember is that there is a depth in the text that is completely hidden or missed by English translations. If you only want the "peshat" go ahead and stick with the English. If you want to go deeper then you should start looking at the Hebrew.

When dealing with the Greek, in order to get to the deeper levels, we need to make sure that the text actually makes sense on the surface. We also must make certain that those texts are properly translated within a Hebrew framework and understanding. Otherwise, the teachings of Yahushua end up getting distorted. An example of a commonly mistranslated Greek passage involved the teaching about the rich man. According to most Bible passages Yahushua teaches the following: "*I tell you, it is easier for a camel to go through the eye of a needle than for a rich man to enter the kingdom of Elohim.*" Matthew 19:24; Mark 10:25; Luke 18:25.

A camel could never fit through the eye of a needle. It is not "very hard" or "nearly impossible" - It is impossible. Therefore, Yahushua would be saying that it is easier for something impossible to occur than for a rich man to get into heaven, in other words: that too would be impossible. He then proceeds and says, with Elohim all things are possible. Therefore, most modern translations have Yahushua speaking in circles.

Now there are some who believe that He was not actually speaking about a sewing needle, but rather the "eye of a needle" as a small door on a city gate.

Another solution is found in the language itself. In the Greek we read the word "kamilos" (καμλοσ) which means "a cable" in these texts, not camel. This is confirmed by the Hebrew and Aramaic of Matthew 19:24 which provide "gamala" (ꓘ𝘭𝘺𝟙), which means a "thick or heavy rope." In other words, it is harder to put a rope through the eye of a needle, rather than a thread.

If you correct one word, then the passage makes much more sense. Yahushua was teaching that it easier for a cable to fit through the eye of a needle than for a rich man to get into heaven. In other words, it is easier to do something difficult, but possible, than it is for a rich man to get into heaven. Therefore, it is difficult, but with Elohim, all things are possible.

Other ways that the Scriptures are misinterpreted and people misunderstand YHWH is because they are simply taken out of context. Take for instance the story of Job. Many believe that a proper teaching from that story is "The Lord giveth and the Lord taketh away." This is quoted constantly as "The Word of God" to support the notion that YHWH gives and takes as He wishes. It leads to the belief that we are just buoys bobbing around in this sea called life. We simply get blown around by the storming winds and waves in some sort of game played between YHWH and satan. Not so! When read in context we see that Job made this statement in error. He made this statement when he did not understand what was happening to him.

Sometimes there is important information that is simply not recognized, because of the focus on the Greek instead of the Hebrew. For instance in John 21 we read an interesting account of Yahushua after His resurrection. He appeared on the shore of Lake Kinneret while some of

His Talmidim were fishing. They were not having much success so Yahushua provided them with some advice.

"*[7] He said to them, 'Cast the net on the right side of the boat, and you will find some.' So they cast, and now they were not able to draw it in because of the multitude of fish. [8] But the other disciples came in the little boat (for they were not far from land, but about two hundred cubits), dragging the net with fish. [9] Then, as soon as they had come to land, they saw a fire of coals there, and fish laid on it, and bread. [10] Yahushua said to them, 'Bring some of the fish which you have just caught.' [11] Simon Peter went up and dragged the net to land, full of large fish, one hundred and fifty-three; and although there were so many, the net was not broken.*" John 21:7-11.

Many have no idea why the number of fish was 153, but if you have gotten this far in the book, you can probably guess that there is meaning in the Hebrew. As it turns out, there is a very significant phrase in Hebrew that equals 153 – "the sons of Elohim." In Hebrew it is "beni ha'Elohim" (ᚥᛁᚻᛚᚴᚼ ᛁᚤᚤ). Here is the calculation: ᚤ = 2, ᚥ = 50, ᛁ = 10, ᚼ = 5, ᚴ = 1, ᛚ = 30, ᚼ = 5, ᛁ = 10, ᚥ = 40.

This is a profound revelation presented in typical Hebraic fashion. The Messiah was demonstrating that His Talmidim were supposed to be gathering the Lost Sheep of the House of Yisrael and bringing them back into the Covenant so that they could be called Sons of El in accordance with Hoshea 1. They were supposed to be fishing for men instead of fish in accordance with Yirmeyahu 16:16. This was the purpose of the Messiah's first coming which has been lost in time, tradition and translation. The plan of restoration involves reuniting the divided Kingdom of Yisrael with Messiah as the Head, not to start a new religion or a new assembly

called the church.

Christianity has lost this context, and that is one of the main reasons why the Christian Bibles have suffered. There are a number of ways that the texts in the Bible have been mistranslated and misunderstood. Much has been lost in translation, and there are many other instances beyond the examples provided above. The point of this chapter is not to pick apart every translation, but rather to make the reader aware of the fact that there are translation problems that exist.

We also need to be aware of the fact that those of us raised in a western culture may not have the same frame of reference as one raised in an eastern culture. Since all of the texts were written by persons with an eastern mindset we need to be careful to take that into consideration when we read, study and translate those texts.

What we see in Christianity is that a selected group of writings have been compiled by men we do not know. Through time, it was decided that certain writings would be canonized, while others would not be canonized. There is no evidence that YHWH gave any directions in this regard, or that the men who made these decisions were supernaturally inspired. Many think that is the case, but we do not know for certain.

For instance, there is nothing in Paul's letters stating the Word of YHWH appeared to him and told him to write certain words. Again, he professes to have had an encounter on the road to Damascus, and I do not doubt that he did. Even so, that does not mean that everything he wrote would then become Scriptures, given equal or greater weight than YHWH, Messiah or Mosheh. If that were the case, then why were not all of

Paul's letters included in the New Testament.

If I asked most Christians how the writings in their "Bible" were selected and compiled, most would not have a clue. Regardless, they would likely continue to profess the "infallibility" of their particular version and entrust their doctrinal beliefs on some translator from the past. I must confess that I used to do the same thing. Life was much simpler and less complicated in those days; living in a state of selfimposed ignorance always is. This is too important of an issue to ignore any longer.

Even though I could not explain some of the inconsistencies that I perceived, it was easier to believe some of the patchwork explanations that I was given rather than to lay bare all of my preconceived doctrines and reexamine all of my inherited beliefs. Thankfully, I was faced with undeniable evidence regarding certain translation errors which opened wide the floodgates.

This is the best thing that ever could have happened to me, because it forced me to dig deeper into my understanding and look at the roots of my faith and core beliefs. It allowed me to seek out the roots of paganism that have been incorporated into the system of Christianity which I was born into and from which I received my original faith. Since that time I have been on a continuing journey to purify my life and my faith.

My relationship with my Creator has been strengthened, because as I willingly shed the traces of paganism and false doctrines that I had inherited. It allowed me to receive a more thorough washing from the Living Water of the Torah, and from the shed blood of the Messiah, which brought me closer to YHWH. I yearn for a greater cleansing and we all must pursue purity, which is ultimately our quest.

Before proceeding further it should be confirmed that the Word of YHWH is infallible. It is the fallibility of the men who have copied and translated certain versions of Scriptural texts over the centuries that has resulted in undeniable errors.

I am now aware that there are clearly errors in various manuscripts, copies and translations. My reaction to this truth is not for my faith to wither up like a plant that receives no nourishment because its roots have been cut off. On the contrary, my eyes have been opened to the delusion that I was under most of my life while I endeavored to find out the truth. I had to step out of the religious matrix that I found myself in.

I existed within a religion that claimed to hold the truth, but it practiced and promoted pagan doctrines that were far from the ways of the Creator. I needed restoration and we have many examples of restoration in the Scriptures. Restoration always requires "shuwb" – repentance and a "return" to YHWH.

I found in the writings a very significant example of restoration in the Kingdom of Yahudah. There came a time when a boy named Josiah became King after his father Amon was assassinated. His name in Hebrew is Yoshiyahu (𐤉𐤄𐤆𐤅𐤊𐤆), which literally means: "YHWH my foundation." Interestingly, the first time we read about Yoshiyahu we read: 𐤉𐤄𐤆𐤅𐤊𐤆-𐤊𐤕. (2 Chronicles 33:25). So the Aleph Taw (𐤊𐤕) was attached to "YHWH my Foundation." We can deduce that the Aleph Taw (𐤊𐤕) is "YHWH my Foundation."

Yoshiyahu was eight years old when he became king. The text explains that: *"in the eighth year of his reign, while he was still young, he began to seek Elohim of his father David."* We already saw the connection between the number 8 and the Covenant, which is evident in the life of Yoshiyahu. In fact, we are told: "*And he did what was right in the sight of YHWH, and walked in the ways of his father David; he did not turn aside to the right hand or to the left.*" 2 Chronicles 34:2.

Interestingly, the text says that he sought "*the Elohim of his father David*" and he "*walked in the ways of his father David.*" We already read that his father was Amon, so why now does the text refer to his father David. Only when we recognize that this is not the first time that Yoshiyahu is mentioned in the writings does this make sense. In fact, this boy king was prophesied at Bethel many years prior to his birth.

After the division of the Kingdom of Yisrael, the House of Yisrael under Yereboam set up a false religion and a false altar at Bethel – the House of YHWH. In a very profound event, prefaced by the word "behold" we read about a man of Elohim who came from Yahudah to Bethel by the Word of YHWH. Here is the account: "*2 . . . he cried out against the altar by the Word of YHWH, and said, O altar, altar! Thus says YHWH: 'Behold, a child, Yoshiyahu by name, shall be born to the house of David; and on you he shall sacrifice the priests of the high places who burn incense on you, and men's bones shall be burned on you. 3 And he gave a sign the same day, saying, This is the sign which YHWH has spoken: Surely the altar shall split apart, and the ashes on it shall be poured out.*" 1 Kings 13:2-3.

There is an amazing prophetic meaning in this text, and we saw the fulfillment in the young King Yoshiyahu. He first purged Yahudah and Jerusalem of the pagan idolatry that infested the Land. He also extended that purging to the Lands of the Northern Kingdom – the House of Yisrael. He cleansed all the

Land of Yisrael, and then returned to Jerusalem. As they began to repair the House of YHWH during this time of restoration, an incredible event happened – they discovered the Torah in the House of YHWH.

They did not simply find the Torah, they read it and they acted upon it. They renewed their Covenant relationship and an important part of that was the Appointed Times. The observed the Passover, which is the Covenant meal. *"Yoshiyahu kept a Passover to YHWH in Jerusalem, and they slaughtered the Passover lambs on the fourteenth day of the first month."* Here is a summary of his reign: *"Thus Yoshiyahu removed all the abominations from all the country that belonged to the children of Yisrael, and made all who were present in Yisrael diligently serve YHWH their Elohim. All his days they did not depart from following YHWH Elohim of their fathers."*

He was not perfect. In fact, he died an early death because he strayed from the will of YHWH, but his actions brought the people back into the Covenant of YHWH. It is his response to the truth and the Torah that provide an excellent pattern for today. Yisrael remains divided and fractured, filled with pagan practices and doctrines. We need to purge those abominations from our lives and rediscover the Torah – the Scroll of the Covenant.

This is the process that many are undergoing and it is intimately connected with our understanding of the Scriptures. As we begin to examine the Scriptures we also examine our beliefs and our faith. Hopefully, this results in the revelation that the Torah provides the Covenant path. When we understand the Covenant, and its' renewal, we begin to build on the proper foundation – YHWH.

This pattern of cleansing and rediscovering the Torah, followed by a renewal of the Covenant and the Passover, was exactly the path that occurred in my life. I now have a better understanding of how to approach the Scriptures, which has resulted in the process of restoring proper balance in my life. I have gained a greater appreciation for the Tanak, and in particular the Torah. It was this restoration to the Torah that has brought me into a better understanding of the Messiah. I now see and understand the Living Torah, the Hebrew Messiah Yahushua, as opposed to the Hellenized lawless christ named Jesus presented by Christianity.

The idea of examining and correcting mechanical and translational errors in the writings is not so daunting when we truly understand the perfect Aleph Taw (𐤗𐤀) manifested in Yahushua - the Word of Elohim.

14

The Word

After all of these examples of mistakes, mistranslations and errors, how can we be certain what is the true Word of Elohim. To answer that, it is important to examine just exactly what is "the Word."

The first mention of "the Word" in the Scriptures is found in Beresheet 15:1. *"After these things the Word of YHWH came unto Abram in a vision, saying, Fear not, Abram: I am your shield, and your exceeding great reward."*

What should alert everyone's attention is the fact that the Word of YHWH came to Abram in a vision. He saw the Word, which was a visual manifestation of the sound spoken by YHWH. There is more information beyond what has been translated, and it is helpful to examine a more precise rendering of the Hebrew text.

A literal reading of Beresheet 15:1 is as follows: *"After these words the Word of YHWH existed for Abram in the vision saying 'Abram, you will not fear I am your shield your wages will be made to increase greatly.'"*[140]

The word that we read referencing the Word of YHWH is "debar." It consists of a dalet (◁), a bet (𝟃), and a resh (𝟃) – Door, House, Head. So the Word is the door to the house, and it is the head of that house.

Debar is found earlier in the text, but it is

translated as "speak" or "spoke." In either sense, the emphasis is sound, but with Abram, that sound becomes visible. In fact, the Gematria value of "debar" is 206, which is the same as the word "ra'ah" (ᴚ𐤊ᴚ), which means: "see."

Amazingly, when we "see" (ᴚ𐤊ᴚ) the "word" (ᴚ𐤏ᐃ) we have the numerical value of 412, which is the same as "house" (𐤗ᴢ𐤏). It is also the value of "the ark" (ᴚ𐤏𐤗ᴚ). This is just another example of the amazing complexity and unity of the ancient Hebrew language. The messages built into the language are incredible.

In the Hebrew passage cited above we also see "the word" (ᴚ𐤏ᐃ) and "YHWH" (ᴚ𐤙ᴚᴢ) connected to one another as: ᴚ𐤙ᴚᴢ-ᴚ𐤏ᐃ. So we can see a direct relationship between the Word and YHWH, the Word of YHWH was spoken, yet visible. This brings us back to the untranslated Word - the Aleph Taw (𐤗𐤊).

When we begin to see the connection between the Aleph Taw (𐤗𐤊), the Word and the Messiah things start to become clearer. Just as YHWH had communicated with mankind in various ways throughout history, His Word in the flesh, the Messiah, was His ultimate expression. What began as a message in the heavens came down to the earth in the flesh.

Instead of merely telling mankind about truth, He also lived out that truth before their eyes. One of the great debates from the time of Yahushua was the belief in the resurrection. It was hotly disputed between certain sects of Yisraelites. Yahushua did not simply teach about the resurrection, he was actually resurrected. Therefore, His life and ministry were a demonstration of the truth of YHWH. He was the living Word.

With that understanding, we can then see the

Messiah, as the Word, all throughout history. For instance, at the beginning of the Scroll of Yirmeyahu we read: *"¹¹ Moreover the Word of YHWH came unto me, saying, Yirmeyahu, what do you see? And I said, I see a rod of an almond tree. ¹² Then said YHWH unto me, Thou hast well seen: for I will hasten My word to perform it."* Yirmeyahu 1:11-12.

Once again, in the Hebrew we see "the Word" connected to "YHWH" - ᐊᎩᘈᘔ-ᕦᎩᐊ. This is the same Word that appeared to Abram, and the Word of YHWH "came" which is ᘔᎩᘔ. Remember that this was the first word (ᘔᎩᘔ) spoken by Elohim, and it means: "be or exist." So the text reads: "exist the Word of YHWH." The Word of YHWH "existed" before Yirmeyahu. The word was personified in the presence of the prophet. So when YHWH manifests Himself in the physical realm He does so through His Word.

As if there was any question that this Word of YHWH was the Messiah, the writer of a popular New Testament text actually provides the answer to this great mystery of the ages – the mystery of the Aleph Taw (✗𝋊), the Word that existed from the beginning.

Remember how the first sentence of the Torah proclaimed: *"In the beginning created Elohim* ✗𝋊 *the heavens and* ✗𝋊 *the earth."* The Good News according to John provides: *"In the beginning was the Word, and the Word was with Elohim, and the Word was Elohim."* John 1:1. So the Aleph Taw (✗𝋊) was the Word, and the Word was Elohim. This text is essentially a Midrash, or exegesis, of Beresheet 1. It describes what happened in the beginning and places the Messiah into proper context.

Let us continue and see what else the text

provides: "² *He was in the beginning with Elohim.* ³ *All things were made through Him, and without Him nothing was made that was made.* ⁴ *In Him was life, and the life was the light of men.* ⁵ *And the light shines in the darkness, and the darkness did not comprehend it.* ⁶ *There was a man sent from Elohim, whose name was John.* ⁷ *This man came for a witness, to bear witness of the Light, that all through him might believe.* ⁸ *He was not that Light, but was sent to bear witness of that Light.* ⁹ *That was the true Light which gives light to every man coming into the world.* ¹⁰ *He was in the world, and the world was made through Him, and the world did not know Him.* ¹¹ *He came to His own, and His own did not receive Him.* ¹² *But as many as received Him, to them He gave the right to become children of Elohim, to those who believe in His name:* ¹³ *who were born, not of blood, nor of the will of the flesh, nor of the will of man, but of Elohim.*" John 1:2-13.

So the Word was associated with a person, the Messiah, and He was also called "Light." This is the "light," the "owr" (אור), that was from the beginning - before the sun, the moon and the stars were created. This light is "life," and it is placed in men. Interesting, the Scriptures record that "the life is in the blood" (Vayiqra 17:11), so we see this connection with the blood and the life.

The Word was connected with the Light, and we see no greater picture of this than inside the House of YHWH. Remember how the Tabernacle was constructed to symbolize a body, with YHWH enthroned within. The menorah provides the light of life within the house – the body.

This becomes even more profound when we examine the scene in Yirmeyahu. The Word of YHWH came to Yirmeyahu and asked him what he saw. In other

words, what did the Word look like? Yirmeyahu responded that he saw "maqel shaqed" (◁𝖕W 𝟆𝖕𝓨), literally "almond rod" or "branch of an almond tree." So Yirmeyahu saw an almond branch.

The word for "almond" is "shaqed" (◁𝖕W), and it also means: "awake or watchman." That is why YHWH told Yirmeyahu that he saw well, because He "watches" (◁𝖕W) over His "Word" (𝟆𝖸◁) to accomplish it. So Yirmeyahu saw the Word - an almond branch. This is highly significant as the Word was manifested as an almond branch. The gematria for shaqed (◁𝖕W) is 404, and it is the same as "qadosh" (W◁𝖕), which means: "set apart" or "holy." Interestingly, it is also the same as the word used to describe the "anointing" (𝖸日W𝖸𝖹𝖄) of the furnishings in the tabernacle, which included the menorah, representing an almond tree. (see Bemidbar 7:1).

The gematria for both "see" (𝖸𝖪𝖰) and "word" (𝟆𝖸◁) is 206, so again, we see the connection between seeing the word, which is also heard. This was revealing a mystery that had occurred hundreds of years earlier when YHWH confirmed His chosen one - the High Priest Aaron (Aharon).

After the rebellion of Korah and the congregation, it was time to make clear once and for all who was His Anointed. You see, YHWH alone decides who gets to enter into His House and minister before Him. Korah and his clan were popular, and apparently there were many who thought they were a better choice. After Korah was consumed by the earth, and Aharon stopped a plague with his censor, YHWH had the leaders bring their rods to the Tabernacle. He chose the rod of Aharon and made it blossom with almonds as a sign.

Here is the text that describes the event

"¹ And YHWH spoke to Mosheh, saying: ² Speak to the children of Yisrael, and get from them a rod from each father's house, all their leaders according to their fathers' houses - twelve rods. Write each man's name on his rod. ³ And you shall write Aharon's name on the rod of Levi. For there shall be one rod for the head

of each father's house. ⁴ Then you shall place them in the Tabernacle of meeting before the Testimony, where I meet with you. ⁵ And it shall be that the rod of the man whom I choose will blossom; thus I will rid Myself of the complaints of the children of Yisrael, which they make against you. ⁶ So Mosheh spoke to the children of Yisrael, and each of their leaders gave him a rod apiece, for each leader according to their fathers' houses, twelve rods; and the rod of Aharon was among their rods. ⁷ And Mosheh placed the rods before YHWH in the Tabernacle of witness. ⁸ Now it came to pass on the next day that Mosheh went into the Tabernacle of witness, and behold, the rod of Aharon, of the house of Levi, had sprouted and put forth buds, had produced blossoms and yielded ripe almonds. ⁹ Then Mosheh brought out all the rods from before YHWH to all the children of Yisrael; and they looked, and each man took his rod. ¹⁰ And YHWH said to Mosheh, <u>Bring Aharon's X𐤊- rod back</u> before the Testimony, to be kept as a sign against the rebels, that you may put their complaints away from Me, lest they die. ¹¹ Thus did Mosheh; just as YHWH had commanded him, so he did." Bemidbar 17:1-11.

Verse 10 is of particular note because the rod was described as "et-metah Aharon" (𐤰𐤉𐤀 𐤄𐤈𐤅-𐤕𐤀). The Aleph Taw (𐤕𐤀) was attached to that rod, which was thereafter placed in the Tabernacle before the testimony *"as a sign."*

Also, in the Hebrew, instead of simply "bring" Aharon's rod "back", we read "shuwb shuwb" Aharon's rod "shuwb." Remember that "shuwb" (𐤁𐤅𐤅) is all about returning to YHWH. So in the midst of the rebellion YHWH was emphasizing a return through the Almond Branch. That is why this event is classified as a sign. We are to look for the Rod of YHWH, the Word of YHWH, for He is the Chosen High Priest Who can stand before the Testimony. He is the One Who will lead the way back to the House. Any other way is rebellion.

The Testimony is "adot" (𐤕𐤅𐤃𐤏) in Hebrew. From the Ancient Hebrew characters we understand it to mean: "see the door that connects to the Covenant." This was a prophetic event pointing to the Messiah. It was the Word later manifested to Yirmeyahu. This branch was once alive and attached to an almond tree. It was later broken and dead, but brought back to life.

The rod is also a symbol of authority, and it was a title given to the Messiah. (Isaiah 11:1). Indeed the Prophet Isaiah (Yeshayahu) reveals another mystery about this rod: *"¹ There shall come forth a Rod from the stem of Jesse, and a Branch (natzar) shall grow out of his roots. ² The Spirit of YHWH shall rest upon Him, The Spirit of wisdom and understanding, The Spirit of counsel and might, The Spirit of knowledge and of the fear of YHWH."* Yeshayahu 11:1-2.

Notice the Prophet is mentioning four categories

of Spirits, which amount to seven total: 1) The Spirit of YHWH; 2) The Spirit of Wisdom; 3) The Spirit of Understanding; 4) The Spirit of Counsel; 5) The Spirit of Might; 6) The Spirit of Knowledge of YHWH; and 7) The Spirit of the Fear of YHWH. So he is describing seven spirits branching out from this rod. What we have is a menorah – the seven branched almond tree that provides light in the Tabernacle.

"*31 And you shall make menorot (𐤗𐤒𐤉𐤌) of pure gold: of beaten work shall the menorah (𐤀𐤒𐤉𐤌𐤌) be made: his shaft, and his branches, his bowls, his knobs, and his flowers, shall be of the same. 32 And six branches shall come out of the sides of it; three branches of the menorah (𐤀𐤒𐤉𐤌) out of the one side, and three branches of the menorah (𐤀𐤒𐤉𐤌) out of the other side: 33 Three bowls made like unto almonds, with a knob and a flower in one branch; and three bowls made like almonds in the other branch, with a knob and a flower: so in the six branches that come out of the menorah (𐤀𐤒𐤉𐤌-𐤉𐤌). 34 And in the menorah (𐤗𐤒𐤉𐤌) shall be four bowls made like unto almonds, with their knobs and their flowers. 35 And there shall be a knob under two branches of the same, and a knob under two branches of the same, and a knob under two branches of the same, according to the six branches that proceed out of the menorah (𐤀𐤒𐤉𐤌-𐤉𐤌). 36 Their knobs and their branches shall be of the same: all it shall be one beaten work of pure gold. 37 And thou shalt make the seven lamps thereof: and they shall light the lamps thereof, that they may give light over against it.*" Shemot 25:31-37.

The menorah is spelled various ways in the passage, clearly pointing to certain hidden truths. Notice

that the first reference is plural – menorot. The second reference includes a vav (Y) in the middle. The first revelation of the vav (Y) is found in Beresheet 1:1. It is in the sixth word in the Scriptures, "v'et" (XᏔY), and precedes the Aleph Taw (XᏔ).

In Beresheet 1:1, the v'et (XᏔY) was in between the heavens (ᏎWᎩᏐᎩ) and the earth (ᏒᏐᏔᎩ). So the Aleph Taw (XᏔ) connects the heavens and the earth. It is the revelation of YHWH in physical creation. This should make us think of the "ladder" that Yaakob saw at Luz. Remember that Luz means: "almond tree." That ladder connected the heavens and the earth. Yaakob later called Luz, Beit El (Bethel), which means: House of Elohim. So here we have the menorah, representing an almond tree being placed in the House of Elohim. The pattern was being fulfilled.

As if this could not be any clearer, Yahushua specifically identified Himself with Bethel (Luz) when He proclaimed: "*Verily, verily, I say unto you, Hereafter you shall see heaven open, and the angels of Elohim ascending and descending upon the Son of man.*" John 1:51. This was the vision that Yaakob saw when he slept at Bethel. The ladder connected the heavens and the earth, just as does the Aleph Taw (XᏔ) in Beresheet 1:1.

So inserting the vav (Y) in the midst of the menorah is a clue that this menorah is a prophetic symbol of the Aleph Taw (XᏔ). In that word the vav (Y) stands between "mem nun" (ᎩᎩ) and "resh hey" (ᏐᏐ). The gematria for vav (Y) is 6, and it is associated with "man" since man was created on Day 6 of Creation week. By placing the vav (Y) at the center of the menorah we see an immediate connection with the "shamash," or servant light, which is the middle light in a menorah. This correlates with the Aleph Taw (X𐤊) being the "suffering servant" prophesied by Yeshayahu.

By adding the vav (Y) to menorah (𐤀𐤒𐤍𐤅) it changes the gematria value from 295 to 301. Amazingly, the word "esh" (W𐤊) has the value of 301. Esh (W𐤊) means: "fire." The first time we see "esh" (W𐤊) in the Scriptures is within the first word – be<u>resh</u>eet (X𐤆W𐤊𐤒𐤉). The esh (W𐤊) is at the center of the beginning, and is surrounded by the word "covenant" – brit (X𐤉𐤒𐤉). So the fire is, once again, at the center of the Covenant as the vav (Y) is at the center of the menorah.

To emphasize this point, the first time we see the esh (W𐤊) by itself in the Scriptures is during the Covenant with Abram. The esh (W𐤊) is the fire that passed through the pieces in the Covenant. It passed through the blood meaning that the esh (W𐤊) was the only party responsible for the penalty when the Covenant was broken. (Beresheet 15:17). The fire is essential to the relationship with YHWH. The "set apart fire" (esh qodesh) is the fire on the altar. The fire is the place where YHWH deals with men, and the fire on that altar consumes the offerings presented by men.

The word "qara" (𐤊𐤒𐤐) also equals 301. Qara (𐤊𐤒𐤐) means "call," and it was the word used to describe the beginning of creation when Elohim "called" the light day. (Beresheet 1:5). We already discussed the relationship between the Light and the Aleph Taw (X𐤊).

Another word that shares the gematria value of 301 is "the rock" or "ha'tzor" (𐤒𐤅𐤑𐤄). We read about "the rock" at Horeb. It is the rock that Mosheh struck in the wilderness. From "the Rock" Yisrael was provided

water to drink in the wilderness. They were also provided with manna (𐤉𐤌) to eat. Interestingly, the "mem nun" (𐤉𐤌) in menorah preceding the vav (𐤉) is the same word used for "manna." The "mem nun" (𐤉𐤌) or manna is the first two letters in every spelling of menorah.

This leads us directly to another profound revelation in the passage in Shemot 25 describing the menorah. Amazingly, the word for "manna" (𐤉𐤌) is actually affixed to the word "menorah" (𐤀𐤓𐤅𐤉𐤌). On two occasions in Shemot 25 we literally see manna-menorah (𐤀𐤓𐤅𐤉𐤌-𐤉𐤌). Now often the word "min" (𐤉𐤌) precedes another word, and means "from," but there can be no doubt that a mystery was being revealed by the very fact that it is the same word used for manna.

In fact, this is essentially answering the question of the Children of Yisrael concerning the manna when they asked: "What is it?" (Shemot 16:15). Of course the answer was already provided in the passage where the manna was named. There we read: "*And the House of Yisrael called its* X𐤊*-name Manna* (𐤉𐤌)." Shemot 16:31.

The Aleph Taw (X𐤊) was joined to the manna. Also, in Shemot 16:35 on two occasions when it describes how the children of Yisrael ate the manna we read et-ha'manna (𐤉𐤌𐤀-𐤄X) or X𐤊-the manna. Incredibly we see that the Aleph Taw (X𐤊) was the water, and the manna in the wilderness. The children of Yisrael literally ate and drank the Aleph Taw (X𐤊). The Aleph Taw (X𐤊) was their source of life. It provided living water and bread from heaven.

The Aleph Taw (X𐤊), the Manna and the Menorah are all tied together. So there can be no mistaking this connection, in a later text the Aleph Taw

(X◁) is directly connected to the menorah. We read X◁-menorah (ᖶᕾᕿ𝍢-X◁) and manna-menorah (ᖶᕾᕿ𝍢-𝍢𝍢) in Shemot 37.

The menorah clearly represents an almond tree, and it is made from one piece of fine gold. There is incredible symbolism in the menorah as the number of branches equals the number of Spirits that will rest upon the prophesied "Branch" - v'natzar (ᕿᕾᕿ𝍢). (Yeshayahu 11:1). Also in the prophecy of Yeshayahu we see the vav (𝍢) attached to the natzar (ᕿᕾᕿ). Because of this obvious Messianic connection, those who believed that Yahushua was the Messiah called themselves Natzrim.

Notice also the number of bowls made like almonds - 22. The bowls contain the pure olive oil, and the oil represents the Spirit. The source of that oil was described in a vision to the Prophet Zechariah. (see Zechariah 4). The number 22 is associated with the Menorah, which lights the Tabernacle, and those seven branches give light by the Seven Spirits. The number 22 is clearly associated with the 22 letters of the alephbet. Once again we see light connected with the Word.

Through the menorah we see the 22 letters being associated with the light, and the Word of YHWH. This is confirmed by other texts. "*Your Word is a lamp to my feet and a Light to my path.*" Psalm 119:105. "*For the commandment is a lamp, and the Torah a light, reproofs of instruction are the way of life.*" Proverbs 6:23.

So when we read about the Word, it is the language expressed by the Creator in the Hebrew Script, but it goes beyond simply letters written on a scroll. We must recognize that it is much more than a text written by the hand of man, and placed into a collection of

documents called the Bible. While those writings are an expression of the essence, work and teachings of "The Word" they are not the Word.

In fact, in Psalm 119:130 we read "*The 'entrance' of Your words gives light; It gives understanding to the simple.*" NKJV. The word translated as "entrance" is "pittuach" (ⴄ✕𝌏) in the Hebrew. It actually means: "sculpture" and derives from "patach" (ⴄ✕𝌏) which means: "to open wide, to loosen, to carve, to appear, to break forth, to draw, let go free." So from the Hebrew we see that it is the picture presented by the words that gives light. The words reveal and show us the light, but the writings themselves are not the actual light.

Bibles get old, tattered and their bindings fall apart. Scrolls get worn, torn, brittle and fragmented. All of these texts are works of the hands of men. Many are translations and writings in various languages, again, attempting to relate things to people of different languages and cultures. They are susceptible to fire and water – the writings are all temporal.

The author of the Book of Hebrews said it well. "*[12] For the Word of Elohim is living and powerful, and sharper than any two-edged sword, piercing even to the division of soul and spirit, and of joints and marrow, and is a discerner of the thoughts and intents of the heart. [13] And there is no creature hidden from His sight, but all things are naked and open to the eyes of Him to whom we must give account.*" Hebrews 4:12-13.

So the Word of Elohim is alive and powerful. He discerns, and to Him we must give an account. We are told by the Prophet Amos that there would be a famine of the Word. "*[11] Behold, the days come, saith Adonai YHWH, that I will send a famine in the land, not a famine of bread, nor a thirst for water, but of hearing* ✕𝌀 *word (debar)* of YHWH: [12] *And they shall wander from sea to sea, and from the north even to the east, they shall run to and fro to seek* ✗✗-*debar-YHWH, and shall not find.*" Amos 8:11-12.

Interestingly, we have no shortage of Bibles, Tanaks or Torah Scrolls, so when the passage refers to "the Word" it must be speaking of something different. Something other than written texts.

Actually, in the Hebrew, the meaning is evident. The Aleph Taw (✗✗) is attached to "debar" - the Word, and at the end "the Word" is surrounded by the Aleph Taw (✗✗) and YHWH. The point could not be any clearer, "the Word" in this passage is clearly speaking of the Messiah, Who is the Son of Elohim. Some translations provide that people will not find "it," as if the Word is a thing. There is no "it" in the text, actually they will be looking for the Word, the Messiah, and will not find Him.

This is by no means an exhaustive review of the Aleph Taw (✗✗) in the Scriptures. It simply is meant to demonstrate the importance of studying the Hebrew texts, and I hope that the point is abundantly clear.

The Christian faith spends much time examining their Greek manuscripts of the New Testament which are describing a fulfillment of the Scriptures, originally provided in the Hebrew. As a result, when they read John 1:1 they miss the depth of the statement "In the Beginning was the Word and the Word was with Elohim and the Word was Elohim." They focus on the Greek word "logos" and the connection with the Aleph Taw (✗✗) is lost. The Aleph Taw (✗✗) was present all throughout time, and worked intimately with men to restore creation through the Covenant.

Ultimately, the Aleph Taw (✗✗) manifested in

the flesh as Yahushua the Messiah. Yahushua Himself rebuked the religious people of His day for esteeming the written texts and completely missing the point. Here is what He said: "*37 And the Father Himself, who sent Me, has testified of Me. You have neither heard His voice at any time, nor seen His form. 38 But you do not have His word abiding in you, because whom He sent, Him you do not believe. 39 You search the Scriptures, for in them you think you have eternal life; and these are they which testify of Me. 40 But you are not willing to come to Me that you may have life.*" John 5:37-40.

The Scriptures that Yahushua was referring to did not include the New Testament. The Scriptures were the Torah, the Prophets and the Writings. Even though the writings testified concerning Yahushua, it is imperative to have the Word "abiding in you." This Word is the Aleph Taw (✕✦) essentially repairing our DNA and transforming us into the image of Elohim so that we can be sons and daughters.

We saw the Aleph Taw (✕✦) at the beginning creating all that we know. Just as the Word was spoken in the beginning, the Word must again intervene and repair that which was corrupted. This is the work described in the Scriptures and it will be completed in the end.

15

In the End

The existence of the Bible with such a vast collection of intact ancient documents is nothing short of a miracle. While the journey has been difficult and tenuous, the result is incredible. The fact that there is such a volume of copies is without equal when compared to other ancient documents.

We have discussed some of the problems with copies and translations, all of which are outweighed by the incredible truths contained in the texts. As we endeavor to "*study to show ourselves approved . . . rightly dividing the word of truth*" the rewards are plentiful. (2 Timothy 2:15). That, after all, is the way YHWH operates.

One thing is certain, YHWH does not leave His treasures out in the open for fools to stumble upon. He hides His treasures where only the diligent can find them. So while we can discern problems that have occurred with the ancient texts, they are not insurmountable. Those who diligently search out the truth can find it.

Likely the most significant and easiest errors to detect and correct in the English translations concern the Names of YHWH and Yahushua. You must know the Name of the Elohim Who you claim to serve, as well as

the name of His Son.

To emphasize this point an ancient Proverb actually asked this poignant question: "*Who has ascended up into heaven, or descended? Who has gathered the wind in his fists? Who has bound the waters in a garment? Who has established all the ends of the earth? What is His Name, and what is His Son's Name, if you know?*" Proverbs 30:4.

Sadly, people have not known the Name of the Father or the Son, because the Bibles they have been reading altered and hid them. This error traces back to the so-called "original Greek" texts. Thankfully, there are currently versions that are restoring the Names, even displaying them in the ancient Hebrew script.[141]

Beyond the issue concerning names, the other types of problems involving copyist errors, missing information, misspellings and mistranslations can all be worked out. The point in examining and revealing these errors is not to diminish those texts, but realign the focus and priority from translations of texts to the perfect living Word Yahushua.

Yahushua said: "*Heaven and Earth shall pass away, but My words shall not pass away.*" Matthew 24:35; Mark 13:31; Luke 21:33. When we understand that He is "the Word of YHWH" Who appeared throughout history and guided His Covenant people in the Way, His words take on an entirely new dimension.

In the Revelation of Yahushua as written by John, Yahushua appears in the representation of a Menorah. "*[12] And I turned to see the voice that spoke with me. And being turned, I saw seven golden lampstands; [13] And in the midst of the seven lampstands one like unto the Son of man, clothed with a garment down to the foot, and girded about the chest with a golden band. [14] His head and his hairs were white* like wool, as white as snow; and his eyes were as a flame of fire; [15] And His feet like unto fine brass, as if they burned in a furnace; and His voice as the sound of many waters. [16] And He had in His right hand seven stars: and out of His mouth went a sharp two-edged sword: and His countenance was as the sun shineth in His strength." Revelation 1:12-16.

Here we see Yahushua "in the midst of the seven lampstands" – The Menorah. Some English translations have "candlesticks." This really distracts from the menorah which is fueled by oil, not candles. We have already examined the connection between the Messiah and the light. The Menorah stands in the House of Elohim and provides light. It represents the Tree of Life in the Garden of Eden, the almond tree (Luz) in the House of Elohim (Bethel).

Yahushua then proceeds to reveal a great mystery. In the English we read: "I am Alpha and Omega, the beginning and the ending, saith the Lord, which is, and which was, and which is to come, the Almighty." Revelation 1:8 see also Revelation 21:6 and 22:13. This English translation was clearly taken from a Greek manuscript, because it actually refers to two Greek letters.

It is important to remember that this was a Hebrew Messiah, appearing in the midst of a Menorah, speaking to His Hebrew Talmid. Chances are pretty good that He did not choose to give this revelation in the Greek language. The Alpha (A) is the first letter in the Greek alphabet, and the Omega (Ω) is the last letter in the Greek alphabet. So if we place this passage in its proper Hebrew context we have Yahushua saying that He is the Aleph Taw (✕𐤊).

Now this revelation at the end brings us back to the beginning. This is why Yahushua indicated that He

was the beginning and the end. By making this connection we see that He was "The Word" at creation. He spoke the Words that created, and His Words will never pass away.

In fact, the Book of Revelation makes this very plain when describing the Messiah. "*[12] His eyes were like a flame of fire, and on His head were many crowns. He had a Name written that no one knew except Himself. [13] He was clothed with a robe dipped in blood, and His Name is called The Word of Elohim.*" Revelation 19:12-13.

Therefore, our focus should be on the Word that was at the Beginning, the Word that manifested in the flesh, died and rose again. While that Word is described in written texts, those texts are not to be confused with the Word. Remember that the menorah represents the 7 Spirits of YHWH (Yeshayahu 11:1). The Messiah, represented by the Menorah, was filled with all 7 Spirits.

After His death and resurrection, He then sent His Spirit on the Day of Shabuot, the same day that YHWH spoke from Sinai. This was not a coincidence. It revealed the pattern of the Spirit and Truth. You must have the Spirit to follow the Truth.

Much of the information contained in this book revealed the importance of studying the Hebrew language. There truly are great mysteries contained in the Hebrew Scriptures, and there is much knowledge to be gained. We are clearly supposed to diligently study, but the acquisition of knowledge alone is futile without the Spirit. In fact, it is the Spirit of Knowledge that we should desire. (Yeshayahu 11:2).

Many people read and memorize the words on the pages, but their spiritual eyes and ears remain closed to the truth. The acquisition of knowledge can be deceptive as a person can become deluded and self absorbed, believing that their knowledge will somehow save them.

We need to be transformed by the Word, and the only way that happens is by the Spirit. We are created to be in an intimate, loving relationship with YHWH. He is more concerned with our hearts than with our brains. Only when we read the words and then manifest the Word through our lives does that Word come alive within us and through us.

Paul actually said it well in his first letter to the Corinthians: "*And though I have the gift of prophecy, and understand all mysteries and all knowledge, and though I have all faith, so that I could remove mountains, but have not love, I am nothing.*" 1 Corinthians 13:1.

This is why Yahushua indicated that the Shema was the first commandment. "*⁴ Hear, O Yisrael: YHWH our Elohim, YHWH is one! ⁵ You shall love YHWH your Elohim with all your heart, with all your soul, and with all your strength. ⁶ And these words which I command you today shall be in your heart. ⁷ You shall teach them diligently to your children, and shall talk of them when you sit in your house, when you walk by the way, when you lie down, and when you rise up. ⁸ You shall bind them as a sign on your hand, and they shall be as frontlets between your eyes. ⁹ You shall write them on the doorposts of your house and on your gates.*" Debarim 6:4-9.

Love has always been at the center of the Covenant. It is, after all, a Marriage Covenant. YHWH does not want a relationship with robots or drones. He desires those who know Him and willingly love Him. In other words, those who are obedient out of love. This is why we bind the words as signs on our hands, and between our eyes. We have the words in our minds, but

they must translate through our actions – represented by our hands.

Marriage is the pattern established through creation that reveals the desire of YHWH. He wants to become one with us in love. Again, the message is clear in the language. The word for "love" in Hebrew is "ahabah" (ﬡﬣﬠﬡ). It has a gematria value of 13. The word for "one (unified)" is "echad" (ﬡﬣﬢ). It also has a gematria value of 13. So unified love equals 26. Amazingly, the gematria value of YHWH (ﬡﬗﬡﬕ) is 26. Notice the parallels between "love" (ﬡﬠﬡﬗ) and YHWH (ﬡﬗﬡﬕ). The "arm" (ﬕ) that "connects" (ﬗ) is the father – ab (ﬠﬡ). He performs this through His Spirit – hey (ﬡ).

We can see this truth manifested through the Messiah, the Arm of YHWH. Messiah Yahushua, the Aleph Taw (ﬢﬡ), joins us in love. He circumcises our hearts so that we can truly love Him. We see that the outward circumcision occurs on the male sexual organ that joins a man and woman together. This intimate physical act involving that circumcised organ is exclusive between the husband and his bride. Likewise, the circumcision of the heart is required for us to have an intimate spiritual relationship with YHWH. Only when our hearts are circumcised can we obey Him with all our heart, with all our soul (nephesh) and all our strength. (Debarim 6:5; Mark 12:30).

The essence of the Renewed Covenant is that we have the Torah in our hearts, not just our minds. (see Yirmeyahu 31). We must have the Word in our hearts so that we walk according to those words. This is why Yahushua so often rebuked the religious leaders, they had knowledge, but they lacked understanding. They had an outward appearance of righteousness, but their hearts were corrupted. They did not have love. He called them white washed sepulchers filled with dead men's bones. (Matthew 23:27). In other words, they looked great on the outside, but they were unclean on the inside.

Their problem was that their hearts had not been circumcised. That circumcision was promised by Mosheh. *"And YHWH your Elohim will circumcise your heart and the heart of your descendants, to love YHWH your Elohim with all your heart and with all your soul, that you may live."* Debarim 30:6 (see also Yirmeyahu 4:4).

The circumcision of the heart cannot be performed by the hands of any mortal man, only by the Spirit can our hearts be circumcised. This is the essence of the Renewed Covenant. Just as Joshua (Yahushua) circumcised the flesh of the Children of Yisrael after they crossed over, so Yahushua the Messiah will circumcise our hearts.

No one uncircumcised will be permitted into the House of YHWH. (see Ezekiel 44:6-9). Since the House of Yisrael was divorced because of her adultery, she needs to be cleansed, and renewed. As the exile comes to a close, and as YHWH prepares to restore that relationship, those within the House of Yisrael must receive a renewed spirit and a renewed heart. (Ezekiel 11:19; 18:31; 36:26).[142] They must be circumcised. Through the Renewed Covenant made with the House of Yisrael, YHWH will put the Torah in their minds <u>and</u> write the Torah on their hearts. (Yirmeyahu 31:33).

Thus we need the Spirit and Truth. Yahushua specifically addressed this point. *"[23] But the hour is coming, and now is, when the true worshipers will worship the Father in spirit and truth; for the Father is seeking such to worship*

Him. ²⁴ *Elohim is Spirit, and those who worship Him must worship in spirit and truth." John 4:23-24.*

We must all undergo the spiritual transformation that was revealed through the Torah and the Prophets. The Scriptures contain truth, but without the Spirit, they are simply words on a page. The Spirit is the life, and the power of the Word. There are many evil people throughout history who have memorized, quoted and twisted the written Scriptures. In fact, we even read in the New Testament how satan quoted Scriptures as he tempted Yahushua in the wilderness. (Matthew 4).

The Word of Elohim is perfect and cannot be manipulated or twisted. We can see through the Scriptures that the Word has always been acting and operating throughout history. The Word was spoken and that resulted in Creation. That Word, the Aleph Taw (✗𝋇), consisted of the alephbet. Each of the 22 characters in the alephbet has significance and meaning. YHWH actually revealed His truth through that alephbet, and the Messiah directly identified with the entire alephbet.

In the beginning was the Word, and all things were created by the Word. Through that Word, the truth of YHWH was spoken into creation. It was built into man from the beginning. It exists in the very fabric of creation. The Garden, which was located in Eden, revealed the ways of YHWH, and as man obeyed the Commandments of YHWH he was blessed in paradise.

Adam was made in the Image of Elohim. His DNA was encoded with the language of the Creator. Adam dwelled in the Garden, and was connected to YHWH and to life as he continued to partake of the Tree of Life. He did not need any written Scriptures, the

Word was built into his very being, and he literally consumed it as he partook of the Tree of Life. This is why we were shown the connection between the manna and the menorah, which represents the almond tree – The Tree of Life.

Adam was able to share intimate communion with Elohim in the Garden through the Messiah, as long as he obeyed. You see, obedience to the commandments is not a burden or some narcissistic requirement imposed by YHWH upon mankind. To the contrary, obedience to the commandments is intended to set men free on the path to life in paradise. We know that the man and the woman both participated in disobedience involving the serpent or rather "the shining one" – the nachash. This disobedience disrupted the order and essentially corrupted man's DNA.

Even though man was expelled for his disobedience, he understood the need to live that truth until a solution was provided. Traces of those truths were still in his DNA. Our modern scientific advances have enabled us to peer into the microscopic universe and see the signs of the Creator within us. Through these advances we have been given a glimpse into the language of the Creator.

Adam also carried with him the truths obtained in the Garden. That knowledge was insufficient to give him access back into the Garden. Regardless, he continued to live that truth and transmit it to Creation through the language of Creation – the Hebrew language.[143]

The truth was also displayed in the heavens for all to see. Those signs in the heavens were understood by the ancients, but have been hidden and disguised in time. They are mysteries waiting to be rediscovered. These

signs were important in revealing the birth of the Messiah.[144] They will be important in discerning the times in the end and will actually reveal His return.

When discussing the signs of the end Yahushua stated: *"And there will be signs in the sun, in the moon, and in the stars . . ."* When discussing His return He said: *"Then the sign of the Son of Man will appear in heaven, and then all the tribes of the earth will mourn, and they will see the Son of Man coming on the clouds of heaven with power and great glory."*[145] Therefore, the heavens continue to reveal truth and the signs that they provide will be important through the end of the age.

So it should be clear that YHWH has communicated with mankind in various ways from the beginning, and His Word was involved in all of these forms of communication. When He spoke this present existence into being, He used a form of communication that was audible and resonant.

He filled Creation with life, and He revealed His character and nature through Creation. He showed through man, made in His image, how He would divide and reunite in order to procreate and populate His Creation. As man and woman join together and become one, new life comes into existence from the seed of the man when it enters into the woman.

This is a pattern that needed no writing to communicate. This principle of the seed is imbedded into all of creation. Since man was made in the image of Elohim, we can see through man how YHWH would take part of Himself, His Seed, and propagate a family to fill His House.

He revealed that life comes from death. As a seed is buried in the ground and dies, from that death comes renewed life. It is a picture of resurrection built into the fabric of creation.

We now have writings that reveal how YHWH worked with a righteous line to establish His Covenant. That line, beginning with Adam, told a story through 10 generations that led to Noah. We see Noah then entering into a Covenant with YHWH as a Mediator for all of Creation. The rainbow was given as a sign of that Covenant. It is a sign that has continued throughout history. It consists of seven colors of light, which is clearly related to the menorah.

After another 10 generations we see that Covenant process leading to a man named Abram, later renamed Abraham. The life of Abraham reveals the Covenant journey - the way back to the Garden. As a result of that Covenant, the Bride of YHWH (Yisrael) was given a written set of instructions. The Torah was the Ketubah – the Marriage Contract. It was a wedding gift directly from YHWH to Yisrael, through Mosheh. As a result, it is unique and stands apart from all other writings on the planet.

YHWH also spoke through signs, which were visible reminders of the Covenant promises. We already mentioned the rainbow. Abraham was given the sign of circumcision, which involved shedding blood of the Covenant participant. It also created a perpetuity as the seed of the man passes through the cutting of the Covenant into the woman. The resulting male offspring are then circumcised on the eighth day.

The eighth day is a prophetic event revealed

through the Appointed Times.[146] The eighth letter in the alephbet, represented on a two dimensional medium is ℏ. The het (ℏ) is commonly thought to represent a fence. It also clearly looks like a ladder, and one should immediately think of the ladder that connects heaven and earth, seen by Yaakob at Bethel. All those in the Covenant marked on the eighth day want to ascend on that ladder.

This leads to another aspect of the het (ℏ). If you twist the het (ℏ) into another dimension you have the double helix which represents DNA. The shedding of blood on the eighth day reveals the need to have our DNA repaired. The Passover and Unleavened Bread are also a sign, involving the redemption of the firstborn. From this event we see the blood of the Lamb of Elohim, the firstborn of YHWH, as the needed sacrifice to fulfill the Covenant. The blood of the Lamb is spread on the doorposts of the house as a Threshold Covenant.[147]

All those in the Covenant are then supposed to actually become a sign as they observe the Sabbath. By resting on Day 7, they become a visible reminder, and a sign of the Covenant between YHWH (the Husband) and Yisrael (the Bride). (Shemot 31:13).

YHWH also spoke through His prophets. Sometimes those words were written and sometimes the messages were acted out or lived by the prophet. We have some written prophecies in the Prophets (Nebiim). We also have a history of Yisrael along with selected Psalms and Proverbs in the Writings (Kethubim). The Marriage Covenant with Yisrael was the beginning of the collection of writings that we refer to as the Scriptures – the Tanak.

The Writings (Kethubim) provide an incomplete

history, according to the Prophets (Nebiim). While we can see the need and promise of a Messiah embedded all throughout the Tanak, those texts do not describe the actual coming of the Messiah.

The Tanak was incomplete and cried out for more. There were promises to be fulfilled concerning the restoration and renewal of the Covenant with Yisrael. While there were writings known as the Maccabees, which provided additional historical data, they still did not complete the story and reveal the Messiah. This is why the New Testament was compiled, to provide a completion to the Writings.

It is here that we must reinforce the fact that all of the writings contained in most present day Bibles are not what were originally considered to be Scriptures. The compilation of the Bible was a process that occurred after the existence of the Scriptures and was largely the product of Christianity. Bibles include the original Scriptures followed by various writings intended to complete the unfinished story of the Tanak.

When we use the term "Scriptures" we are talking about writings that speak to Truth and reflect the Word of YHWH. That is why most people now refer to the entire Bible as "Scriptures." Regardless of your definition of Scriptures, it is important to distinguish between the written texts and the Word of YHWH. While writings often recount His Words spoken and transmitted through men, those Writings are not exclusively the Word. The Messiah is the Word. The Scriptures provide instruction in a written language, and point us to the Word, Who is manifest throughout the entire universe. He is not limited to ink strokes on paper or papyrus.

The texts found within The Bible, while spoken or inspired by YHWH, were compiled by men. Each individual text must be accorded the weight appropriate to it. Again, it is imperative to understand that the Torah is distinct from all others. It is the foundation for the Covenant process that will restore Creation with the Creator. It contains the very terms of the Marriage Covenant.

The Torah provides the rules for life. It provides a definition for sin (chatta'ah) and righteousness (tzadeek), holy (qadosh) and profane (chalal), clean (tahor) and unclean (tame). These are all distinctions that a Covenant people must know and learn. The Covenant path is the path to a Wedding and a House. The Bride must learn the conduct befitting of a Bride who will marry and dwell in the House of the Creator of the Universe.

The Prophets and the Writings further detail that process and point us to the need for Messiah – the Word made flesh. After the coming of Messiah to fulfill the needed atonement for the Covenant people, the exclusive Scriptures used by people remained the same – the Torah, the Prophets and the Writings. Those who had seen and heard the Messiah needed nothing more.

As time passed and witnesses died, there was a need to pass on their testimony and a history of what had occurred. This resulted in a variety of writings being circulated, many of which did not always agree. As a result, many years after the death and resurrection of Yahushua men felt compelled to consolidate those writings, and select texts to add to the original Scriptures.

This process was ultimately accomplished by and

through the Christian religion. Ironically, Christianity rejected the Marriage Covenant with Yisrael, and promoted a new and different covenant with an entity called The Church. In fact, those with any sense of the Hebrew roots of the faith were essentially excluded from the Christian religion, and had little influence in that process of compiling the Biblical texts.

So we now have 27 texts contained in most New Testaments. The question is whether these are the exclusive texts that YHWH intended to be used by people to read and learn about His only begotten Son the Messiah. No one can say for certain. It should simply be understood that none of those texts can ever be used to justify or promote a change in the foundation laid by the Torah, the Prophets and the Writings.

To do so would collapse the entire house, and this is why Christianity has developed so many fractures and divisions – they have eroded the foundation of truth that the Messiah clearly came to affirm and reveal. (see Matthew 5:17). This has opened the door for critics who point out the inconsistencies between Christian doctrine and the Tanak.

What many Christians do not realize is that the Plan of YHWH is revealed through the Torah. He did not wait until the New Testament was written to reveal His Covenant Plan. As a result, the Talmidim of Yahushua used their testimony and the Tanak to demonstrate that Yahushua was the Messiah.

They did not have the New Testament nor did they need the New Testament. This may sound revolutionary, but it is true. Philip was able to convince the eunuch from Ethiopia that Yahushua was the Messiah using only his testimony and a Scroll of Isaiah

(Yeshayahu) (Acts 8:26-40). I would dare say that most Christians could not use the Torah or the Prophets to lead people to faith as did the early Talmidim. In fact, most Christians are unable to test the teachings of the Apostles against the Torah as did the Bereans. (Acts 17:11).

The Gospels now provide us with an important testimony concerning the Messiah. They also reveal the implementation of the Renewed Covenant promised in the Tanak. These accounts are very important because they show us how Yahushua fulfilled prophecy. They too must always be read in the light of the Torah, and with an understanding that they do not contradict or change the Torah in the least bit.

While I believe that all writings in the collection of texts called The Bible have value, I do not necessarily believe that they all carry the same weight. For instance, the words *In the beginning Elohim created the heavens and the earth* (Beresheet 1:1) clearly eclipse passages such as *"Greet Prisca and Aqulas, and the house of Onesiphoros"* (2 Timothy 4:19). In fact, there is really no comparison.

The distinction gets even greater when we examine the languages of the texts. The first sentence of the Torah in Hebrew has profound meaning and messages built into the text. This is actually the case with every sentence, even every letter and space in the Hebrew Torah. This emphasizes the importance of studying the texts in the Hebrew language, and not limiting yourself to a particular translation. The differences between east and west are significant and profound. This also plays a role in determining which texts should actually be classified as Scriptures.

Now to be fair, I doubt Paul ever intended his

letters to be treated equally with the Torah. But, by doing so, Christianity has diminished the uniqueness, the import and the significance of the Torah. They seem to forget that Yahushua even made a distinction between the commandments by referring to the *weightier matters of the Torah.*" (Matthew 23:23).

Now I believe that Paul's letters contain valuable information, but they were typically addressed to particular individuals or assemblies. They often dealt with cultural issues and specific problems that the recipient was experiencing at the time. They are too often taken out of their historical context, and used to support doctrines that are diametrically opposed to the Torah. You cannot simply take a sentence from a letter and then create a new doctrine from it. Everything must be read consistent with the Tanak.

By canonizing the letters of Paul and some of the other Apostles, Christians have actually transformed letters and teachings into Scriptures. It is this blurring which causes confusion in Christian circles. They quote these letters from men with the same or greater weight than Mosheh or the Messiah – even YHWH. This has caused incredible problems, confusion and even false doctrines concerning the rapture.[148]

Let me provide a simple example. Did not YHWH command us to rest on the Seventh Day – the Sabbath? It was one of the Ten Words spoken by the very voice of YHWH from Mount Sinai. It was later written on the Tablets by the very finger of YHWH. It was also spoken by Mosheh to the people, and then written in the Torah by Mosheh.

Amazingly, Christians do not feel the need to obey this command, and have numerous excuses to

justify their rebellion and lawlessness. In fact, most believe that this day set apart from the beginning of creation was somehow changed, even though there was nothing in their Bibles that would indicate such a change.[149] Regardless, since they believe Paul abrogated the annulment of the Torah through his letters, they follow Paul over YHWH.

This is a prime example of the Christian religion failing to properly prioritize the Scriptures. The religion has often minimized the most important texts, and relegated them to the status of "old." As a result, their religious doctrines and tradition often trump the clear and express commandments found within the Torah.

Since the Sabbath was designated as a sign for the Bride, a sign of the Covenant, you must participate in this prophetic Covenant sign if you want to be in the Covenant. (Shemot 31:17). The Christian Church currently finds itself outside of the Covenant Assembly. Christianity has rejected the sign of the Seventh Day – the Sabbath. Instead, Christians choose to observe a Sunday Sabbath, specifically established by the Roman Catholic Church in contravention to the Commandments of YHWH.

It is imperative that those seeking truth in the Bible understand how to prioritize those texts. To emphasize this fact, it may be helpful to look at how those in Judaism deal with their Scriptures – the Tanak. After all their Scriptures are the same Scriptures that were used by the Natzrim. Today, most Synagogues have a Torah Scroll which is kept in an Ark. They do this because Mosheh was instructed to place the Torah by the side of the Ark of the Covenant as a witness. (Debarim 31:26). Since the Torah is at the heart of the Covenant, the Scroll is treated with the utmost honor and respect. It is read every Shabbat since Shabbat is the sign of the Marriage Covenant.

There may also be Haftarah readings that come from the Prophets. These texts are secondary to the Torah. While still considered anointed Scriptures, they do not rise to the level of the Torah. So on the surface, the Jews appear to have a proper understanding of the priority given to the various contents of the Tanak.

Sadly, despite understanding the priority of the texts, most have not recognized Yahushua the Messiah – the Living Word of Elohim. The traditions surrounding their texts have often clouded the revelation of the Messiah found within those texts. That is why Yahushua specifically rebuked their predecessors, the Pharisees, for elevating their traditions above the commandments. Those traditions prohibited many Yahudim from recognizing Him as the Messiah.[150]

Throughout the centuries, the religion of Judaism has since compiled those traditions into extensive writings and commentaries on the Torah, the Prophets and the Writings. These teachings have been collected in the Talmud and the Mishnah. While those writings are only men's opinions and teachings, many in Judaism have turned them into a law in and of themselves.

This is due, in large part, to the belief that aside from the written Torah, there was also an oral Torah given to Mosheh that was handed down and eventually put into writing. I do not subscribe to this belief because

it is the same sin that the Pharisees committed. It empowers men to make and alter the Torah of YHWH. It is nothing more than a tradition used to justify changing the Torah, just as Christians hold to their tradition of a Sunday Sabbath.

The very Scriptures that they esteem clearly refute the notion of an oral Torah. "*³ And Mosheh came and related to the people all the Words of YHWH and all the right-rulings. And all the people answered with one voice and said, 'All the Words which YHWH has spoken we shall do.' ⁴ And Mosheh wrote down all the Words of YHWH . . .*" Shemot 24:3-4. This passage is quite clear that Mosheh wrote down all of the Words, thus eliminating the possibility that there were more Words that were not written down.

So the notion of another Torah, beyond what was written down is not possible. Clearly there are aspects of Torah observance that require instruction and guidance. Once we understand that we must obey a commandment, there are often questions concerning how to obey. This does not mean that there is another Torah, it simply means that we must ask YHWH how to obey. It also reveals the need for our hearts to be circumcised and for the Torah to be written on our hearts and in our minds. By establishing the oral Torah, the Jewish religion has essentially elevated the opinions of Rabbis to the level of, and sometimes beyond, the Commandments of YHWH. This is similar to what Christianity has done with the Epistles.

So my advice is to avoid the commentary until you have actually read and studied the Scriptures. Every individual on this planet would do well to open their Bible to the Torah and start reading and rereading the words found therein from the beginning. They should do this before they spend too much time getting confused reading about a Torah based solution or teaching to a select assembly of people in a particular geographic location. That can come later, once a proper foundation of Torah has been established.

The problem that I have observed is that most Christians focus on the New Testament as their primary text. As a result, most lack a proper foundation of the Tanak. It is like skipping the meal, and going straight for the dessert. If you keep doing that you will end up being malnourished. That, of course, is what Christianity is suffering from: spiritual malnourishment. While you might acknowledge that the Messiah came, if you do not understand why He came, and what He taught, your belief is incomplete.

If you start developing doctrine based upon a sentence from an Epistle, believing that the Tanak is old or irrelevant to your life, you are bound to end up in doctrinal trouble. You are out of order and need to restore a proper understanding of the texts. Once you begin to examine the contents of the Bible in their proper order, you would then do well to examine the substance of those texts.

If you believe that your faith and eternal destiny rely upon understanding the Covenant and the promises of YHWH, then it is critical to insure the accuracy of your translation of the Scriptures. In fact, you must understand the Covenant before you can fully understand the renewed Covenant.

The information concerning the Covenant and its renewal is found in the Tanak. The fulfillment is found in the New Testament. I therefore desire an accurate

translation of all of these texts so that I can properly understand their application to my life. It is not wrong or sinful to question the authenticity or accuracy of your translated Bible, and I would invite every person to conduct their own research regarding the Scriptures that they decide to read and study.

This is a righteous act as long as your desire is to discern the truth, and to know your Creator and His will. You will not be struck by lightening or condemned to hell if you prayerfully and humbly research your Bible to discern its accuracy. Nor will you be chastised for researching the original Hebrew texts.

There is no doubt that when we read translations we often lose some of the content that is found in the Hebrew. For instance, in the Hebrew language, the gematria of the word father – "ab" (𐤀𐤁) is 3. The gematria of mother – "em" (𐤀𐤌) is 41. The gematria of the word child – "yeled" (𐤉𐤋𐤃) is 44. Thus, in the Hebrew, the union of father and mother equals child. This is just a simple example of countless teachings and lessons that can be found in an examination of words in Hebrew. It also reveals that the Hebrew language is intimately tied with Creation.

Anyone can examine the Scriptures in this fashion with some basic knowledge and skills. There is a perfection in the numbers that shows a uniqueness of the Hebrew language. There is significant evidence that Hebrew was the source language from which all others sprang.[151] By studying the Scriptures in the original Hebrew we are able to derive an incredible wealth of information. You will, without a doubt, find more than a translation, which is not always accurate, and certainly does not contain the depth that you will find in the

Hebrew.

There will actually come a day when YHWH will restore a pure language and unity. *"For then I will restore to the peoples a pure language, that they all may call on the name of YHWH, to serve Him with one accord."* Zephaniah 3:9. Until then, we continue our search for the truth in the texts that we have.

If you choose to continue to research this subject you will find out for yourself what thousands of years of translations and interpretations have done to the New Testament translated texts. This may seem like a daunting task, but in reality there are many study aids available that allow a beginner to start dissecting and examining the Scriptures.

Does this mean that we throw out our English Bibles? Absolutely not. They are essential starting points for those who speak English. I suggest that you obtain a Hebrew – English Interlinear Bible and a concordance. You can purchase these tools as books or computer programs or apps. This allows you to see a word for word translation of the Scriptures, and if you have a question regarding the translation of a particular word, you can then look it up.

You do not have to know any Hebrew to start your studies, although I highly recommend that you learn the Hebrew alephbet. You can then start to pronounce, and eventually memorize those letters and then words. There are many good Hebrew language software programs available or better yet, see if you can find someone who teaches Hebrew personally.

Now you must understand that most of the tools you will find involve the modern Hebrew script, not the ancient Hebrew. You will want to understand the

differences in the character sets between the modern Hebrew and the ancient Hebrew. There are tools to assist you in understanding the ancient Hebrew language.[152]

The fact that the ancient Hebrew language is a pictographic language makes it very interesting to learn the meanings of words based upon those pictures. Studying the ancient language adds an entirely new dimension to understanding the texts. Rather than simply memorizing definitions of words, you start to see how those ancient words are constructed. You can then enhance your studies by examining the numerical values of the letters and words to find further information.

The point of this emphasis on the original language is not meant to complicate matters or imply that you must become a Hebrew scholar in order to understand YHWH and His plan. Indeed, YHWH has made His truth so simple that a child can understand it. Yahushua specifically stated: "*Assuredly, I say to you, whoever does not receive the Kingdom of Elohim as a little child will by no means enter it.*" Mark 10:15.

Despite the fact that we have revealed transmittal errors, the purpose of this book is to extol the written Scriptures by revealing the incredible complexities and mysteries in the Hebrew texts. As translations have not always transmitted those truths, we all do well to examine the ancient Hebrew language through which creation and truth were revealed.

While your first response to this subject may be to reel back and throw up a wall of defense, you owe it to yourself and your faith to insure that your Scriptures are leading you in the proper direction. Critics have, in some instances, correctly picked at inconsistencies in an attempt to invalidate or diminish the Christian faith. More often than not, Christians have chosen to remain ignorant regarding textual problems rather than addressing them openly and honestly.

The wonderful part of this exercise is that it will not hurt, but rather enhance your faith. It will show you that indeed, as the Scriptures prophesied, we have inherited some lies.[153]

The study will help you identify those lies and rid them from you life. As a result, you will become a more confident, effective and productive servant of YHWH. It will help you better defend those Scriptures, understand the Covenant and walk the Covenant path. This will, in turn, allow YHWH to pour out incredible blessings upon your life as you walk in obedience to His ways.

It is my hope that I have demystified the subject of the Bible, and the Scriptures contained therein. My desire was to put things into a proper perspective, and give the reader a new appreciation for the Tanak, and particularly the Torah. My hope is that the reader develops a hunger to dig deeper into the ancient texts that are full of life, relevant instruction and spiritual food.

If more Christians would learn to focus on the Torah, the Prophets and the Writings we would see a powerful restoration occur throughout the Earth. It would put an end to many of the false doctrine that have been perpetrated throughout the centuries. It would bring unity to the Assembly of Believers rather than the disunity and division that has resulted from the formation of religions and denominations which all lay claim to their interpretation of the Bible. This is needed

to prepare the Redeemed for the return of the Messiah.

"*²¹ YHWH is well pleased for His righteousness' sake; He will exalt the Torah and make it honorable. ²² But this is a people robbed and plundered; all of them are snared in holes, and they are hidden in prison houses; they are for prey, and no one delivers; for plunder, and no one says, Restore!*" Yeshayahu 42:21-22.

I believe in the inerrancy of the Word, but I do not believe in the inerrancy of men's translations of the written Word. Finally, I believe that we must carefully define what constitutes the Word and for certain, all of the Scriptures rest upon the Torah, which is the foundation of the true faith presented by the Creator of the Universe.

The Torah was not changed by Yahushua, nor was it changed by Paul. The Scriptures clearly reveal that YHWH does not change (Malachi 3:6). Accordingly, if He did intend to create a new religion, wouldn't it have been more appropriate for Him to do it. Since He was present in the flesh, and reinforced the Torah, why would anyone in their right mind think that a mere mortal (i.e. Paul) had the intent, ability or authority to change the Torah or start a new religion. The answer is obvious: he did not.

Therefore, if you are involved in a religion that subscribes to the false belief that Paul contradicted or changed the Torah, then you are in a false, anti-Elohim, anti-Messiah religion. You are following a lie rather than the clear, unadulterated dictates of YHWH. Thankfully Paul likely did not contradict the Torah. It appears that if his letters are properly translated, he taught the Torah and supported the Torah.

The main problem is that people often attempt to

understand the teachings of Paul without a proper understanding of the Tanak. So many times I have seen, heard and read Christians teach the Good News of salvation and then encourage new converts to get a hold of a copy of the New Testament. They might even encourage the new convert to read the Psalms and Proverbs, but often the Torah, the Prophets and other writings of the Tanak are given secondary treatment. This may not be their intention, but the message is loud and clear. The Tanak is considered old – essentially replaced by the New Testament.

The Tanak is about much more than Yisrael, it is about the redemption of all creation. It is all about the Messiah, and Yahushua even testified to that fact. *"Then He said to them, 'These are the words which I spoke to you while I was still with you, that all things must be fulfilled which were written in the Torah of Mosheh and the Prophets and the Psalms concerning Me."* Luke 24:44. Yahushua also declared: *"For if you believed Mosheh, you would believe Me; for he wrote about Me."* John 5:46.

Unless and until you see the significance of these much neglected texts, you will never see, or enter into the fullness of that which YHWH has for you. You may think that you know the Messiah, but if you cannot see the Messiah in the Torah, the Prophets and the Writings then you may not really know Him. You may have been taught a false Messiah.

This will actually result in a dreadful fate for many as told by Yahushua: *"²¹ Not everyone who says to Me, 'Lord, Lord,' shall enter the kingdom of heaven, but he who does the will of My Father in heaven. ²² Many will say to Me in that day, Lord, Lord, have we not prophesied in Your name, cast out demons in Your name, and done many wonders*

in Your name? [23] *And then I will declare to them, I never knew you; depart from Me, you who practice lawlessness!"* Matthew 7:21-23.

When you do something in someone's name, you are exercising their authority. There are many people who do amazing things in the authority of the Name, but that does not mean that they are walking according to the Torah. Yahushua states that He never knew those people because they were "lawless." The word "lawless" actually means "without the Torah." So Yahushua clearly means that He does not know lawless people and He casts them out.

It is time to restore the Torah to its rightful place as the foundation upon which all of the other texts, including the New Testament, rest. Once this occurs, then true restoration will begin to occur.

The Torah, after all, was the Ketubah – the Marriage Covenant with the Bride of YHWH. Only when viewed as the terms of the Marriage Covenant with the Creator does the text transform from the "Old Testament" to the Torah - from irrelevant to critical.

Christians have falsely claimed that "The Church" is the Bride. Sadly, Christianity clearly rejects and ignores the Covenant. If you desire to join the Bride, the Wedding invitation was clearly provided by the Messiah Yahushua. He shed His blood as the Passover Lamb of Elohim. All who desire may come under that blood and join the Covenant – the Covenant mediated by Yahushua and renewed with the House of Yisrael and the House of Yahudah. (Yirmeyahu 31:31). Someday soon, the Messiah will regather and reunify His Kingdom and His Bride, and all will be done according to the patterns and prophecies provided in the Tanak.

(Ezekiel 37; Hoshea 1).

As we approach the end of the age, we need the patterns in the Torah, and the words of the Prophets to guide us. Those Scriptures are consistent, and what has been labeled "old" is by no means old. Take for instance the prophecies of Yeshayahu. They have much to say about the future and are very important to understand the days and years to come. For instance read how an "Old Testament" prophecy describes a future event. *"All the stars of the heavens will be dissolved and the sky rolled up like a scroll; all the starry host will fall like withered leaves from the vine, like shriveled figs from the fig tree."* Yeshayahu 34:4.

Now read what happens at the sixth seal in the New Testament text of Revelation. *"13 the stars in the sky fell to earth, as late figs drop from a fig tree when shaken by a strong wind. 14 The sky receded like a scroll, rolling up, and every mountain and island was removed from its place."* Revelation 6:13-14 NIV. Both of these prophecies are describing the same event, and both are relevant to the future.

It is, therefore, imperative to look at the truth of Elohim as one unified (echad) truth. There is no New Testament that replaces the Old Testament. The notion that YHWH changes or replaces His Covenant is a lie that has deceived many and leaves them unprepared to face the future. His ways in the beginning are the same as His ways in the end. (see Malachi 3:3-7). That is why YHWH instructs us to *"ask for the ancient paths (the path of the ages) where the good way is and walk in it; then you will find rest for your souls."* Yirmeyahu 6:16.

This is the same thing that the Aleph Taw (✗✗), the Messiah was instructing men: *"28 Come to Me, all you who labor and are heavy laden, and I will give you rest.* [29] *Take My yoke upon you and learn from Me, for I am gentle and lowly in heart, and you will find rest for your souls."* Matthew 11:28-29. The Aleph Taw (𐤕𐤀) was the beginning and the end, the first and the last. (Revelation 1:11; 22:13). The Aleph Taw (𐤕𐤀) was the path of the ages from the Aleph (𐤀) in the beginning through the Taw (𐤕), the culmination of the Covenant.

So in the beginning YHWH created through sound. All the letters of the Aleph Bet, found within the span of the Aleph Taw (𐤕𐤀) brought the physical universe into existence. The path of YHWH and the truth contained within the Aleph Taw (𐤕𐤀) was transmitted orally through Adam and his progeny.

The truth transmitted by YHWH is known as the Torah – the instructions of YHWH. Those instructions were known by Adam in the Garden. They tell us how to live in the Garden, and also reveal the path back to the Garden. The Torah provided the path, and the path was paved with the blood of the Aleph Taw (𐤕𐤀). When that truth was transcribed directly from YHWH through Mosheh, it showed how the Aleph Taw (𐤕𐤀) would be revealed, and then be written on the hearts and minds of men.

Since the time when the Words were written, we have seen Yisrael divided and expelled from the Land. The prophets have revealed how the Aleph Taw (𐤕𐤀) would come as the Messiah and restore the Covenant people – Yisrael. Essentially, the written Scriptures culminated in the physical manifestation of the Aleph Taw (𐤕𐤀) as the Messiah.

Now, nearly 2,000 years later we understand the distinction between the Word and the Scriptures. While we treasure the writings we recognize the fulfillment in the Aleph Taw (✕✗) – the Messiah. We have some of the history of that physical manifestation, along with an account of some of the words spoken by the Messiah. We also have various Epistles, as well as a variety of other texts describing this important time and event.

Some of those texts are contained in the New Testament, while others were excluded – often for good reason. In any event, all of these writings describe a very limited time in history during the life of Yahushua, and for a brief time following His resurrection. Since that time we see religions take over and attempt to control and even manipulate history through writings.

We know that the followers of Yahushua later separated from those who formalized the religion of Judaism at Yavneh. The religion of Judaism was, in large part, a reaction to the Messiah and the destruction of the Temple in Jerusalem. Those in Judaism rejected Yahushua as the Messiah, and did all in their power to distance themselves from the followers of Yahushua.

They codified their traditions, and they placed their emphasis on the Scroll of the Torah, rather than the living Torah sent by YHWH. While Judaism has, at least superficially, esteemed the Torah above all other texts, they have hidden the Torah behind their man made traditions and customs. This is the same thing that Yahushua rebuked their predecessors, the Pharisees, for doing. It is why they continually fail to see the Messiah as many of their ancestors did. They were blinded by their traditions, and they need to have their eyes opened to the Aleph Taw (✕✗).

Christianity has since done something similar with the Bible and their christ. They have esteemed the

texts in the Bible, but often their traditions and customs violate the very words contained in the Bible. There are denominations and divisions based upon particular translations, and the doctrines which they ultimately espouse. Christians make arguments about inerrancy, as if a particular version is perfect, opposed to other versions. Many have resorted to idolizing an English translation of the Bible while neglecting the chosen language.

There is no question that scribal errors have been transmitted over the centuries, but even more profound than that, the various translations from Aramaic and Hebrew to Greek and to English provide some very different meanings all together. They have also ignored or simply missed significant information.

By engaging in such polemics concerning English translations, people are missing the point. It is YHWH and His Word that are perfect, not a particular book written with words that did not even exist at the time of creation. As a result of these language issues, many Christians have failed to see the Aleph Taw (𐤕𐤀) and His righteous path.

YHWH originally wrote His perfect words on Tablets that He prepared for His Bride. Those tablets were broken, and later a man presented another set, a replacement set of tablets. YHWH, once again, wrote His perfect Words on that second set of tablets. That pattern of His perfect Word written on stone was a fulfillment of the pattern presented through the aben that was anointed (moshiach) at Luz - in the House of El. (see Beresheet 28:18 then Beresheet 39:14).

This is why it is so helpful to look back to the beginning in order to understand the end. When we examine the original language and creation we get a clear view, and a confirmation, regarding the path of YHWH. With that basic understanding we are then able to understand the absolute relevance of the Torah – the instructions of YHWH. Those instructions are intended to show a Covenant people how to walk in His Ways so that they can be restored. Only then, when we view subsequent texts through the lens of the Torah, can we have confidence in our understanding of those texts.

We are now incredibly blessed to have selected writings that we can read, study and speak. These texts are critical to those who desire to walk the Covenant path that leads us back to the Garden. Some of these texts are Words spoken by YHWH directly to men, while others are Words transmitted from YHWH through men. Still others are instructions and historical accounts. All are intended to direct men to the living Word – Yahushua the Messiah.

We must understand that in the beginning YHWH spoke His alephbet into creation. He revealed His truth and expressed Himself through the Aleph Taw (𐤀𐤕). It is the Aleph Taw (𐤀𐤕), the Word that manifested in flesh, that is the Living Word. He sent His Spirit to circumcise our hearts and inscribe His Word on our hearts and on our minds. We must allow that Word to work within us as we walk the Covenant journey, and become children of the Light. Only then will we truly understand the Way of YHWH provided in the Scriptures.

Endnotes

[1] The notion that we are only around 6,000 years in this cycle of time appears to fly in the face of modern science, which places the age of the universe at over 13 billion years. The issue in Genesis is not necessarily the age of the universe, but rather the beginning of this present Age, or physical existence. One problem with science is that it primarily rejects the notion of a Creator, and the creation of man. As a result, science needs a lot of time to explain and justify the notion of evolution. The simple fact is that if we calculate time from the Hebrew texts we are approximately 6,000 years in the cycles of the ages since mankind was created. Just exactly what occurred before Genesis 1:1 and 1:2 is a mystery, but we are able to calculate time from Creation Day 1, which was Day 1 of Month 7 3,986 BCE or October 7, 3986 BCE. (see www.torahcalendar.com).

[2] The term "god" is a generic term which can be attached to any number of powerful beings described in mythology and worshipped in pagan religions. Some use a capital "G" to refer to "the God of the Bible" but I find it a disservice to apply this label to the Creator of the Universe when the Hebrew Scriptures clearly refer to Him as Elohim. The pagan origins of the word "god" are discussed in the Walk in the Light series book entitled "Names." Elohim (𐤉𐤆𐤄𐤋𐤀) is technically plural, but that does not designate more than one Creator. The singular form is El (𐤋𐤀) and could refer to any "mighty one," but because the plural is used to describe the Creator, it means that Elohim is qualitatively stronger or more powerful than any singular El (𐤋𐤀). In Hebrew, the plural form can mean that something or someone is qualitatively greater not just quantitatively greater. We see in the first sentence of the Scriptures that "In the Beginning Elohim created" the Hebrew for "created" is bara (𐤀𐤓𐤁) which literally is "He created." It is masculine singular showing that while Elohim is plural He is masculine singular. For an excellent discussion of the Hebrew Etymology of the Name of

Elohim I recommend *His Name is One* written by Jeff A. Benner, Virtualbookworm.com Publishing 2002. The Hebrew language currently in use, often called modern Hebrew, is not the language used when the Scriptures were first spoken and written. The original Hebrew language is often called "ancient" or "paleo" Hebrew.

[3] See also Deuteronomy 19:15 *"One witness shall not rise against a man concerning any iniquity or any sin that he commits; by the mouth of two or three witnesses the matter shall be established."* This is why the Ten Commandments were written on 2 Tablets of Stone.

[4] The current modern Hebrew character set is sometimes referred to as Chaldean flame letters. This language was brought with the Yahudim (exiles from the House of Yahudah) after their Babylonian exile. It is important to understand a bit of history involving the Kingdom of Israel (Yisrael). After the death of King Solomon (Shlomo), the Kingdom was divided in two. The Northern Tribes were referred to as the House of Yisrael and the Southern Tribes were referred to as the House of Yahudah. The House of Yisrael was conquered and exiled by the Assyrians in the North. The House of Yahudah was conquered and exiled by the Babylonians in the South. There is a great deal of mystery associated with this language which is really a modern language. One thing is certain, it is not the original language of Yisrael. In fact, it is really a language that exclusively belongs to the Yahudim. Those from the House of Yisrael who desire to truly learn about their Hebrew Roots should be looking at the original Hebrew Language often referred to as Ancient Hebrew or Paleo Hebrew. This would have been the language used by Abraham, Yitshaq, Yaakob, Mosheh and the Assembly of Yisrael.

[5] While the notion that the Hebrew Language is the "mother tongue" of the planet is not a popular notion with secular scholars, there is evidence pointing to that fact. See *The Origin of Speeches Intelligent Design in Language*, Isaac E. Mozeson, Lightcatcher Books, 2006.

[6] There are many different Ancient Hebrew scripts discovered through archaeology. Since they were all written by different individuals there are stylistic variances

between them. The modern Hebrew used today is not the same language as the Ancient or Paleo Hebrew used by Ancient Yisrael. Therefore, throughout this text we will attempt to provide examples of words and phrases in their Ancient Script in order to glean the depth of their meaning. The Paleo Hebrew font primarily used in this book is an adaptation and interpretation of the various examples of Paleo Hebrew found throughout archaeology. Since there are a variety of scripts found in academia, this one script font developed by the author is being used for consistency and clarity in an attempt to represent the Creator's meaning in the "original" language. The author has developed a Font intended to represent the ancient language as might have been written by an individual person thousands of years ago.

7 It is important to recognize that there was a spiritual universe before "the beginning" of the physical universe. "The *time* between the *foundation of the world* in the *spiritual universe*, and Day One of the *physical universe* is referred to as Olam She'avar or The World that Was in Hebraic thought . . . Everything in the *spiritual universe*, including the angels and the *souls* of all people, were created *before the time of the ages* according to 2 Timothy 1:8-11, Titus 1:1-3 and Jude 1:6. This time in history is referred to as Olam She'avar or The World that Was in Hebraic thought. This was when the *foundation* of the earth was laid according to Job 38:4, Psalms 102:25, Isaiah 48:13, Zechariah 12:1 and Hebrews 1:10. Olam She'avar is referred to as the time *before the disruption of the world* in John 17:24 and 1 Peter 1:17-21. The children of Elohim were chosen during Olam She'avar *before the disruption of the world* according to Ephesians 1:3-6." *The 7000 Year Plan*, www.torahcalendar.com.

8 The Hebrew Scriptures contain numerous instances of what are commonly called jots and tittles. These typically include enlarged, diminished or reversed characters intended to draw the readers attention to something. No one knows exactly how they came into existence, although the popular opinion is that Mosheh included them in the original Torah. One thing is certain, they are not considered to be scribal errors and they have been maintained in all copies of the

Hebrew texts, although you will not see them in a translation.

9   The word "shi" ($\textbf{ZW}$) is used only three times in the Scriptures - Isaiah 18:7 and Psalms 68:29 and 76:11. In each case it has profound prophetic significance.

10   It is important to recognize that there is no such thing as a Hebrew numeral set, separate and apart from the Hebrew letters. As a result, each Hebrew character has a corresponding numeric value. This adds an interesting dimension to the study of Scriptures. Commonly called gematria, the study of the numeric values of characters and words can be quite revealing. There are various ways to count and study the numbers and the Chart in the Appendix merely provides the ordinal numbering and the primary gematria.

11   The numerical value of "beresheet" ($\textbf{XZWK49Y}$) is 913, calculated as follows: $\textbf{Y}$ = 2, $\textbf{4}$ = 200, $\textbf{K}$ = 1, $\textbf{W}$ = 300, $\textbf{Z}$ = 10, $\textbf{X}$ = 400. The numerical value of "beit" ($\textbf{XZY}$) is and has a 412, calculated as follows: $\textbf{Y}$ = 2, $\textbf{Z}$ = 10, $\textbf{X}$ = 400. The numerical value of "rosh" ($\textbf{WK4}$) is 501, calculated as follows: $\textbf{4}$ = 200, $\textbf{K}$ = 1, $\textbf{W}$ = 300.

12   While the most common form of son is "ben" ($\textbf{YY}$) in the Hebrew Script, the word "bar" ($\textbf{4Y}$) can also mean son. While there are some who advocate that bar is strictly Aramaic, there is evidence that bar was used in the Hebrew. (see Psalm 2:12).

13   The word et ($\textbf{XK}$), otherwise known as the Aleph Taw, consists of two Hebrew characters - the aleph ($\textbf{K}$) which is the first character in the Hebrew alphabet, and the taw ($\textbf{X}$) which is the last letter in the Hebrew alphabet. "This word $\textbf{XK}$ is used over 11,000 times (and never translated into English as there is no equivalent) to point to the direct object of the verb." (from Benner, Jeff A., *Learn to Read Biblical Hebrew*, Virtualbookworm.com 2004 Page 41.). It is embedded throughout the Hebrew Scriptures and while it has a known grammatical function, the Sages have long understood that it has a much deeper and mysterious function – many believe that it is a direct reference to the Messiah. As such, it plays an important part in understanding the Scriptural Covenants so we will, at

times, examine its existence and relevance throughout this text.

14 Memra actually means "word" in Aramaic. The notion of the Memra comes from the root mem resh (𐤓𐤌) which was the root used through Creation when Elohim "said" (𐤓𐤌𐤀𐤉), and the material world came into existence. The Memra became known as the Divine Mediator in Ancient thought. The Memra would mediate between the unapproachable Creator Elohim and created man. The Memra appears hundreds of times in the Aramaic Targums. Targum means: "translation" or "explanation." In the Aramaic Peshitta John 1:1 refers to that "Word" as the "Miltha."

15 Since the Aleph Taw (𐤕𐤀) represents the entire Aleph Bet, all of the characters contained between the aleph (𐤀) and the taw (𐤕), this is why the Messiah would be called the Word, or the Memra. Messiah is the utterance of the Creation within the physical universe. The Word, which came from and through the Creator in the spiritual realm then manifested in the physical.

16 Time is often described as a physical dimension. Just as height, length and width constitute the dimensions of our three dimensional physical world, so time is another dimension in the world as we know it.

17 There are many who have demonstrated through mathematics, the statistical impossibility of evolution. It does not take a mathematical genius to imagine the difficulty of such incredible complexity occurring from a random explosion. When we look at all of the marvelously complex systems that all must have been put in place at the same time to make a functioning mammal for example, it really must have resulted from intelligent design. For instance, you would need blood, a fully functioning circulatory system with a heart that beats on its own and a fully integrated respiratory system that also operates on "autopilot" otherwise the mammal could never sleep. The respiratory must immediately integrate with the circulatory system, feeding oxygen throughout the body which also must contain a skeletal and muscular system, as well as a reproductive system with both male and female species all

appearing at the same time and same location. This is just scratching the surface regarding the systems that all must be in place at the same time in order for the being to exist. There is no time for evolution, and the idea that all of these necessary systems occurred by chance at just the right time, for each species, is simply absurd. Instead of billions of years of progressive evolution, you need complex systems to occur at the same moment in time – this is the opposite of evolution and supports creation. Indeed, the Cambrian explosion clearly reveals that complex life came into existence suddenly, and the fossil record does not support the gradual progression espoused by evolution. Charles Darwin even admitted that without the support from the fossil record of the lengthy and gradual evolution his notions would fall flat, and they have. It is time for people to actually use their common sense and consider this complex universe rather than simply swallowing the ignorance of so-called "scientists" whose primary agenda is to disprove the existence of a creator. When provided with these statistics there are those who will doggedly attempt to dispel them, but the bottom line is that those who honestly and objectively examine this issue in light of the continual advances in science must surely acknowledge that the hypothesis called evolution has crumbled. See *Evolution: A Theory in Crisis* by Michael Denton, Burnett Books 1985. For interesting video presentations on evolution see *Unlocking the Mystery of Life* and *Darwin's Dilemma*, Illustra Media 2009.

[18] There is no doubt that we live in a finite "digital" universe. Our physical universe is controlled by mathematical laws. That is why the language of creation, Hebrew, is a mathematical language. For a purely scientific examination of this subject see *Cosmic Numbers* by James D. Stein and *The Mathematics of Life* by Ian Stewart.

[19] Numbers and letters are actually the same in Hebrew, they simply describe creation in a different way For instance the word for "water" is "mayim" (𐤌𐤉𐤌). Now the letter mem (𐤌) actually means: "water" and we can see it in the pictograph. The word "mayim" also clearly represents the motion as two mems (𐤌) surround a yud (𐤉).

Interestingly, modern science also attributes this same ration to water - H2O. The scientific formula of water consists of 2 Hydrogen atoms and 1 oxygen atom. So the essential elements are the same, just described differently. For a further discussion of this subject see *Letters of Fire*, Mattityahu Glazerson, The Kest-Lebovits JHRL, Jerusalem 1991 (English).

[20] It is important to recognize that because Hebrew is an eastern language, which tends to be more concrete than the abstract western languages, a direct translation would be quite choppy. One of the tasks of a translator is to smooth out that choppiness. In doing so they may actually change a concept or miss something important. Sometimes it is helpful to examine the rough "mechanical translation" to discern the original meaning of the text. Jeff Benner has developed some wonderful tools through examining the Ancient Language and providing mechanical translations of the Hebrew texts. The portion of text in the main body of the book was taken from Jeff Benner's, *Mechanical Translation of Genesis*.

[21] Some might argue that the word "bar" (𐤓𐤁) is actually an Aramaic derivative, and that the only Hebrew word for "son" is "ben" (𐤍𐤁). Interestingly, in the Ancient Hebrew "bar" (𐤓𐤁) literally means "head of house." The firstborn son was always considered the head of the house after the father. He would be the one who would step into the role of the father. So "bar" (𐤓𐤁) could actually be more specific than "ben" (𐤍𐤁) by referring to the firstborn son. Further, if you examine the Hebrew at Psalms 2:12 when we are told to "Kiss the Son," in an obvious Messianic reference, the "son" is "bar" (𐤓𐤁). This would be consistent that the Messiah is the firstborn of YHWH.

[22] *The American Heritage Dictionary of the English Language*, Fourth Edition, Houghton Mifflin Company, 2000, archived from the original on June 25, 2008, retrieved May 20, 2010 quoted from Wikipedia.

[23] http://www.livescience.com/5045-scientists-sound.html.

[24] The description of Creation is not what many would expect if it were describing perfection at the very beginning. We read: *"The earth was without form, and void; and darkness was*

on the face of the deep. And the Spirit of Elohim was hovering over the face of the waters." Beresheet 1:2. It appears to be a dark and ominous event, and many speculate why creation was in such a state. When we read about the time "before the foundation of the world" - "katabole" (καταβολῆς), we see something very interesting. The Greek word "katabole" (καταβολῆς) actually means: "destruction, a casting down, break down or disintegration." So it appears that there was a spiritual existence that occurred before the "casting down or destruction." This explains the New Testament text of 1 Peter 1:20 which indicates that the Messiah "was foreordained before the "foundation of the world" (καταβολῆς), but was manifest in these last times for you." It also explains the idea of predestination as described in the text of Ephesians 1:4. "Just as He chose us in Him before the "foundation of the world" (καταβολῆς), that we should be set apart and without blame before Him in love." So things happened, decisions were made, and destinies were determined before the destruction which leads us to understand that there was a destruction prior to the creation that we read about in Beresheet, which means that there was a creation before the destruction. For a more detailed discussion of the Greek word "katabole" see *Did God Know? A Study of the Nature of God* by Howard R. Elseth, Chapter 16, Calvary United Church, Inc. (1977). See also Endnote 7. This word is found ten times in the New Testament texts and is translated as "foundation." (see Matthew 13:35, Matthew 25:34, Luke 11:50, John 17:24, Ephesians 1:4, Hebrews 4:3, Hebrews 9:26, 1 Peter 1:20, Revelation 13:8 & Revelation 17:8). Interestingly, there is one verse where it is translated as "conceive." In Hebrews 11:11 we read: "*Through faith also Sara herself received strength to "conceive" (καταβολῆς) seed, and was delivered of a child when she was past age, because she judged him faithful who had promised.*" KJV. How amazing that the birth of the promised son, the son of the covenant, is connected with the word "katabole" (καταβολῆς).

25   YHWH is an English representation of יהוה in Modern Hebrew and ᛉᛉᛉᛉ in Paleo Hebrew. It is the four letter Name of the Elohim described in the Scriptures. This four letter Name has commonly been called the

"Tetragrammaton" and traditionally has been considered to be ineffable or unpronounceable. As a result, despite the fact that it is found nearly 7,000 times in the Hebrew Scriptures, it has been replaced with such titles as "The Lord," "Adonai" and "HaShem." I believe that this practice is in direct violation of the First and Third Commandments. Some commonly accepted pronunciations are: Yahweh, Yahuwah and Yahowah. Since there is debate over which pronunciation is correct, I simply use the Name as it is found in the Scriptures, although I spell it in English from left to right, rather than in Hebrew from right to left. For the person who truly desires to know the nature of the Elohim described in the Scriptures, a good place to start is the Name by which He revealed Himself to all mankind. A more detailed discussion of this very important issue can be found in the Walk in the Light series entitled *Names*.

[26] The ancient alephbet is the code from which all of existence was made and exists. As we examine the combinations of these characters on multiple dimensions and examine the numerical relationships with words we can gain amazing insight into the Creator and Creation. Of course this examination must be conducted in the Ancient Language.

[27] *Letters of Fire, Mystical Insights into the Hebrew Language*, Matityahu Glazerson, The Kest-Lebovits Jewish Heritage and Roots Library, 1984 quoting Sefer Ha-Yetzirah.

[28] We will see through this discussion that the religions of Christianity and Judaism essentially derive from the same source, they both have developed erroneous doctrines and traditions. Christianity is a derivative of the Natzerene sect of Yisrael. While Christianity claims to believe in a Hebrew Messiah Who came, died and was resurrected, they essentially reject the Instructions of Elohim. Judaism, on the other hand, is a derivative of the Pharisaic sect of Yisrael. While Judaism believes in the idea of a messiah, they do not subscribe to the Christian Messiah. In fact, they generally reject the Christian Messiah, and have created numerous man made doctrines and traditions beyond the Instructions of Elohim. For more information on these religions and how each has strayed from the Covenant path see the Walk in the Light series books entitled *Restoration*,

Covenants and *The Redeemed*.

29 It is well established that YHWH has a 7,000 year plan for creation patterned upon the first seven words of the Hebrew Scriptures and the seven day weekly cycle. There are six days for man, or flesh, and the seventh is the Sabbath of YHWH. This time is divided into 50 year Jubilee cycles so the time allotted to man is 120 Jubilee Cycles, which is 6,000 years. (see Beresheet 6:3). For a detailed discussion of the Sabbath see the Walk in the Light series book entitled *The Sabbath*.

30 Exodus (Shemot) 23:22 provides: *"But if you indeed obey His voice and do all that I speak (ᕴᎩᐊᛕ), then I will be an enemy to your enemies and an adversary to your adversaries."* The word for speak (ᕴᎩᐊᛕ) is essentially aleph (ᛕ) preceding "word" (ᕴᎩᐊ). The Gematria for "speak" is 207. It is the same as "light" and "see" so it appears that the Word of YHWH is something that we are supposed to see, not just hear.

31 Beresheet 28:10-22. See also Beresheet 35:14.

32 As discussed, time was a dimension created at the beginning of the physical universe. As such, it can be measured. The Creator set the sun and the moon for markers and we can measure days, weeks, months and years using these markers. Just as the Creator established the seven count of days from the beginning, He does the same for years. Years are counted in sevens, often referred to as Shemitah cycles. After seven Shemitah cycles (49 years) the 50th year is known as a Jubilee year. The Jubilee is when a restoration occurs. (Vayiqra 25) Many believe that the Messiah will restore all things in a Jubilee year.

33 The Creator is definitely concerned about what we put into our bodies. Since we were made in His Image it is important that we function with His Creation as intended. There are things in Creation that He made for food and things which were prohibited to be eaten. This began in the Garden and continues to this day. There is a reason for these instructions, but men continue to be "hell bent" to do as they please and make every excuse to profane themselves and disobey the commands. For a more detailed discussion regarding the dietary commandments see the Walk in the

Light series book entitled *Kosher*. Interestingly, the first time that green foods are mentioned in Beresheet 1:30 the Aleph Taw (𐤗𐤗) is affixed to "every green" (𐤐𐤒-𐤋𐤉-𐤗𐤗).

34   Beresheet 1:27; 2:7; 2:8; 2:15.

35   The events in the Scriptures often provide us with patterns that reveal mysteries. As was seen with Adam, we also saw Abram being placed in a "deep sleep." This was essentially connecting these to events which were both an important part of the Covenant process. For a more detailed description of these events and their connection see the Walk in the Light series book entitled *Covenants*.

36   If you have even a minimal understanding of the Torah, you will discern the connection that all of these share with "cleansing" including the Passover and the Red Heifer. (see Shemot 12; Vayiqra 14; Bemidbar 19). The notion of cleansing therefore ultimately involves our DNA. All of the sacrifices involve blood and they are all intimately connected with the Messiah. The Passover is interesting because the first instance occurred in Egypt and the blood was placed on the doorposts of the peoples homes. Thereafter, the sacrifice occurred at the House of YHWH and the sacrifice was thereafter eaten in the homes of those offering the lamb. The Red Heifer sacrifice is very unique and special as it is the one sacrifice always made outside the camp. This is significant because it relates to the first Passover and was necessary to transition a person from an unclean state to a clean state. There is a great mystery associated with this "red heifer" which is described as "para adamah" (𐤀𐤃𐤌𐤄 𐤐𐤓𐤄) in Hebrew. It literally means: "fruitful ground." Notice the word "adamah" which contains "adam" (man) and "dam" (blood). This subject is described in further detail in an article entitled *The Mystery of the Red Heifer* located at www.shemayisrael.net.

37   For an interesting discussion that focuses on the modern Hebrew language see video presentation entitled The Hebrew Language the DNA of Creation, Rabbi Mordechai Kraft www.youtube.com/watch?v=6_aFvmY8ZbI. While this video focuses on the modern Hebrew language it provides interesting insight and comments, some of which

can be applied to the Ancient Hebrew Language.

[38] See the text in Debarim 6:4. Undoubtedly, the most significant prayer in the Torah is known as The Shema found at Debarim 6:4. In fact, it was declared to be the first (resheet) of all the commandments by Yahushua. (see Mark 12:29). The Shema proclaims: "*4 Hear, O Yisrael: YHWH our Elohim, YHWH is one. (echad) 5 Love YHWH your Elohim with all your heart and with all your soul and with all your strength. 6 These commandments that I give you today are to be upon your hearts. 7 Impress them on your children. Talk about them when you sit at home and when you walk along the road, when you lie down and when you get up. 8 Tie them as symbols on your hands and bind them on your foreheads. 9 Write them on the doorframes of your houses and on your gates.*" Debarim 6:4-9. The Command to write the commands on our doorposts and our gates means that YHWH is in control of that space. His Commandments are the rule of that property, which represents His Kingdom on the Earth. So we are instructed to essentially establish the Kingdom of YHWH in every area of our lives. The text of the Shema in Hebrew is quite profound and contains an enlarged ayin (ﬠ) at the end of the word "shema" and an enlarged dalet (◁) at the end of the word "echad." The ayin dalet (◁ﬠ) is essentially announcing that we should "see" the "door." The Shema text is provided in Appendix D.

[39] The life of a creature is in its' blood. As a result, we are not to consume the blood. See Vayiqra 17:14; Debarim 12:16 and 15:23. Indeed, the texts actually state "the nephesh" is in the blood. Nephesh (ﬔﬗﬢ) is often translated as "soul," but it really means: "breath." So the life of a being is the breath of YHWH Elohim that was breathed into man. Man was initially formed from "dust" – aphar (ﬠﬡﬗ) in Hebrew. "*And YHWH Elohim formed man of the dust of the ground, and breathed into his nostrils the breath of life; and man became a living being.*" Beresheet 2:7. We must therefore recognize that our bodies are not just dust, or flesh. We actually contain the "breath of life" and only when Adam received that breath of life did he become a living being. We are actually the merging of the spirit and the physical, we are the image of YHWH – the representation of the Spiritual

Creator in the physical realm. Man is in a fallen state and deserves to die because of the sin that infects our bodies. We are all worthy of death because of that sin, and that is why YHWH established the concept of atonement. The blood of another can atone for our sins. The blood represents the life of a being, and this is why the blood is sprinkled on the altar. As we recognize that we should be placed on the altar, yet the blood of another will be sprinkled in our place, we see the Plan of Redemption orchestrated by and through YHWH.

[40] Some believe that blood is actually congealed light. We know that the life is in the blood (see Endnote 39). That life was the "breath of YHWH." It is important to understand that the life of YHWH was the first words spoken "exist light." (Beresheet 1:3). So that "light" was "life." As the dust of the ground was formed into flesh, the blood within coursed through his veins carrying that light of life. When that blood stops flowing, the light goes out and the "nephesh" departs from the flesh. The flesh then returns to the dust of the ground from which it came. Now some claim that this is a cultic doctrine originating from Love, The Law of the Angels by Gwen Shaw (Engeltal Press, 1979), but the concept traces right back from the beginning. Just how exactly the light of life is in the blood is a mystery, but it is clearly a spiritual truth that science has yet to explain.

[41] The light of life is the Messiah, and when we express belief in the Light we become Children of the Light. (John 12:36). See also Ephesians 5:8: "For you were once darkness, but now you are light in YHWH. Walk as children of light." See also 1 Thessalonians 5:5. Many of the Dead Sea Scrolls attributed to the Essenes describe the struggle between the children of the light and the children of the dark.

[42] The Persecution and Trial of Gaston Naessens by Christopher Bird at http://customers.hbci.com.

[43] According to Beresheet 3:15 "And I will put enmity between you and the woman, and between your seed and her Seed; He shall bruise your head, and you shall bruise His heel." This has long been held to be a prophecy concerning the Messiah. In between the phrase "He shall bruise your head" and "you

shall bruise His heel" is the word "etah" ($\mathfrak{A} \times \mathfrak{K}$).
Essentially it is the Aleph Taw ($\times \mathfrak{K}$) with a "hey" ($\mathfrak{A}$) at
the end. The "hey" ($\mathfrak{A}$) represents a man with upstretched
arms and means: "behold." So it appears that there is
something very significant occurring in this passage and an
examination in the Hebrew language reveals very
important information that is not seen in the English.

44 *"Elohim called the light Day, and the darkness He called Night.
So the evening and the morning were the first day."* Beresheet
1:5. So the darkness preceded the light. This was the pattern
of creation as light was introduced into creation. The day
pattern of dark preceding light is a pattern that we are
supposed to learn from.

45 See Psalm 136:9 and Psalm 89:37.

46 The Appointed Times are described in greater detail in the
Walk in the Light series entitled *Appointed Times*.

47 Scientists have examined the materials of the moon, and
they appear to have derived from the earth. If it is true, that
the moon was taken from the Earth, then it would parallel
the woman being birthed from the man.

48 This passage in the Psalms has great significance. Not only
do we learn how specific the Creator is concerning His
Creation, but we also see a connection between the stars and
"the exiles of Yisrael." This is a subject detailed in the
Walk in the Light series entitled *The Redeemed*.

49 *The Gospel in the Stars*, Joseph A. Seiss, Kregel Publications
p. 149 referencing *Miracle in Stone*.

50 Book of Enoch 108:7. Further information on this matter can
be read in *Witness in the Stars* by E. W. Bullinger 1893.

51 *Ibid The Gospel in the Stars* at p. 149.

52 See *The Nephilim and the Pyramid of the Apocalypse*, Patrick
Heron, Xulon Press 2005. See also *Genesis 6 Giants Master
Builders of Prehistoric and Ancient Civilizations* written by
Stephen Quayle, End Time Thunder Publishers, 2010.

53 *Genesis 6 Giants Master Builders of Prehistoric and Ancient
Civilizations, ibid.*

54 *The Dead Sea Scrolls - A New Translation*, Michael Wise,
Martin Abegg Jr., and Edward Cook, Harper Collins, 2005,
p. 94.

55 For further discussions concerning this issue, reference is

made to the Walk in the Light series books entitled *The Messiah*, *The Appointed Times*, and *The Final Shofar*.

⁵⁶ The instructions of YHWH are known as the Torah. In a very general sense, the word Torah is used to refer to the first five books of the Scriptures which some call the Pentateuch, or the five books of Moses. Torah may sound like a strange word to anyone who reads an English translation of the Scriptures, but it is found throughout the Hebrew text. The reason is because it is a Hebrew word which translators have chosen to replace with "the Law." Whenever the word "Torah" is found in the Hebrew, it has been translated as "the Law" in English Bibles. Therefore, if you grew up reading an English Bible then you would never have come across this word. On the other hand, if you read the Hebrew Scriptures the word Torah is found throughout the text. The word Torah (תורה) in Hebrew means: "*utterance, teaching, instruction or revelation from Elohim.*" It comes from horah (הורה) which means: "*to direct, to teach*," and derives from the stem yara (ירה) which means: "*to shoot or throw.*" Therefore there are two aspects to the word Torah: 1) aiming or pointing in the right direction, and 2) movement in that direction. The Torah (תורה) is the first five books of the Hebrew and Christian Scriptures. The Torah is more accurately defined as the "instruction" of YHWH for His set apart people. The Torah contains instruction for those who desire to live righteous, set apart lives in accordance with the will of YHWH. Contrary to popular belief, people can obey the Torah. (Debarim 30:11-14). It is the myriads of regulations, customs and traditions which men attach to the Torah that make it impossible and burdensome for people to obey. The Torah has been in existence as long as Creation and arguably forever because the instructions of YHWH are the ways of YHWH. The names of the five different "books" are transliterated from their proper Hebrew names as follows: Genesis – Beresheet, Exodus – Shemot, Leviticus – Vayiqra, Numbers – Bemidbar, Deuteronomy – Debarim. While it is generally considered that the Torah is contained exclusively within the 5 Books of Moses, in a broader sense one might argue

that they are included in the The Torah, The Nebiim (The Prophets) and the Ketubim (The Writings).

57   It is important to understand that YHWH has segmented time into Ages. Just as the Jubilee was previously mentioned as a segment of time, those Jubilees are also combined into Ages.

58   Yeshayahu (ישעיהו) is the proper transliteration for the Prophet commonly called Isaiah. His name in Hebrew means "YHWH saves."

59   Nechama Leibowitz, *New Studies in Bereshit*, p. 86.

60   Some believe a great planetary event may have occurred resulting in the breakup of the continents. This would have created diversity among the population on the planet. See *Worlds in Collision*, Immanuel Velikovsky, Paradigma Ltd. 2009. Seder Olam I says that Abram was 48 at the time of the dispersion. Midrash Yalkut Divrie HaYamim I says that construction on the Tower of Babel ended when Abram was 48.

61   For a further discussion of the prophetically important "eighth day" see the Walk in the Light series entitled *Appointed Times*.

62   Yirmeyahu (ירמיהו) is the proper transliteration for the Hebrew name of the prophet commonly called Jeremiah.

63   The Appointed Times are primarily detailed in Shemot 23 and 34; Vayiqra 16 and 23 Bemidbar 9, 28 and 29 and Debarim 16.

64   Yahudah is the proper transliteration of the name traditionally pronounced as Judah. It means "Yah be praised." (Beresheet 29:35). There is no "J" in the Hebrew language and Judah loses the Name of Yah which is intended to be a central part of the name. The name was first attributed to a child of Yaakob. Yahudah later became a Tribe and then it represented the Kingdom of the South after Yisrael was divided. The term also became known as the region the Tribe and Kingdom of Yahudah occupied. Ultimately, the word has transitioned into the word "Jew." The term originally referred to a member of the Tribe of Yahudah or a person that lived in the region of Yudea (Judea). After the different exiles of the House of Yisrael

and the House of Yahudah, it was the Yahudim that returned to the Land while the Northern Tribes, known as the House of Yisrael, were scattered to the ends of the earth (Yirmeyahu 9:16). The Yahudim retained their identity to their culture and the Land and thus came to represent all of Yisrael, despite the fact that the majority of Yisrael, the 10 tribes of the Northern Kingdom, remained "lost." As a result, the word "Jew" is erroneously used to describe a Yisraelite. While this label became common and customary, it is not accurate and is the cause of tremendous confusion. This subject is described in greater detail in The Walk in the Light Series book entitled *The Redeemed*.

[65] The number 70 has great significance in the Scriptures. One thing that it represents is all of the nations or people on the Earth. This derives from the fact that there were seventy nations who repopulated the earth after the flood. (Beresheet 10). 70 was also the number of beings, or souls, who went into Egypt with Yisrael. (Beresheet 46).

[66] The mixing and deliverance from Egypt was a precursor for another greater fulfillment of this Covenant that will occur through another cycle in the end. The Covenant people are currently mixed within the nations, and will some day be delivered from the Nations as Yisrael was once delivered from Egypt. This issue is discussed further in the Walk in the Light series books entitled *Covenants*, *The Redeemed* and *The Final Shofar*.

[67] See Shemot 33. The Aleph Taw (✕✗) is the Word made flesh – the manifestation of the bodily attributes of YHWH.

[68] For a more detailed discussion of Shabbat see the Walk in the Light series book entitled *The Sabbath*.

[69] Wikipedia http://en.wikipedia.org/wiki/Tanak. The Josephus quote from *Against Apion* can be found at 1.39-42.

[70] For a detailed discussion of the suffering servant, also known as Messiah ben Joseph, as well as the prophecies related thereto see the Walk in the Light series book entitled *The Messiah*.

[71] For a detailed discussion of the importance of Names in the Scriptures see the Walk in the Light series book entitled *Names*.

72 For a further discussion of the Appointed Time called Shabuot, see the Walk in the Light series book entitled *Appointed Times*.

73 For a further discussion of the Messiah and His fulfillment of the Appointed Times, see the Walk in the Light series books entitled *The Messiah* and *Appointed Times*.

74 www.matthewmcgee.org/paultime.html. Again, it was after the Jubilee and people understood that Yahushua would not be returning soon.

75 Ehrman, Bart, *The New Testament*, The Teaching Company.

76 Fr. Bellarmino Bagatti, *The Church from the Circumcision*, Franciscan Printing Press, Jerusalem p 13 (1971).

77 Eusebius, On the Theophania PG24, 623-8 from *The Church from the Circumcision, ibid*.

78 For a more detailed discussion of Scriptural prophecy and the end of days see the Walk in the Light book entitled *The Final Shofar*.

79 Wegner, Paul D., *The Journey from Texts to Translation*, BridgePoint Books, pp. 25-26 (1999).

80 Wegner, Paul D. ibid at p. 28.

81 http://phoenicia.org/pagan.html#ixzz2IQwxcNxG

82 www.iahushua.com Section 23 Bible.

83 W.H. Roscher, *Ausfiihrliches Lexicon der griechischen und romischen Mythologie* (Lexicon on Mythology).

84 Gilbert Meadows, *An Illustrated Dictionary of Classical Mythology*.

85 For a more detailed discussion of the Covenants described in the Scriptures see the Walk in the Light book entitled *Covenants*.

86 en.wikipedia.org/wiki/Biblical_canon#cite_note-1 citing McDonald, L. M. & Sanders, J. A., eds. (2002). *The Canon Debate. The Notion and Definition of Canon*, pp. 29, 34. Also references article written by Eugene Ulrich titled *The Notion and Definition of Canon*.

87 en.wikipedia.org/wiki/Biblical_canon#cite_note-2 citing McDonald & Sanders, editors of *The Canon Debate*, 2002, *The Notion and Definition of Canon* by Eugene Ulrich, page 28)

88 www.ccel.org

89 *The Church from the Circumcision, ibid* at p. 31.

90   E.H. Broadbent, *The Pilgrim Church*, Gospel Folio Press, 1999, p.90.

91   The Greek provides "ekklessia." The Hebrew Shem Tob version provides "House of Prayer." The Aramaic Peshitta translates as Assembly. In no case is there any mention of a newly created organization called "the Church."

92   see Encyclopedia Britannica 1911.

93   Codex Justinianus, lib. 3, tit. 12, 3; trans. in Philip Schaff, *History of the Christian Church*, Vol. 3 (5th ed.; New York: Scribner, 1902), p. 380, note 1.)

94   Eusebius, Vita Const., Lib. iii., 18-20.

95   Eusebius provides an account of Constantine's role in the Council. See Eusebius, *The Life of the Blessed Emperor Constantine*, Book 3, Chapter 10. The Council was arguably very anti-Semitic and it was instrumental in establishing the Roman Emperor as the Head of the newly established Roman Catholic Church. See www.newworldencyclopedia.org /entry/Constantine_I#cite_note-24. The Council was also an important step in transitioning the religion of Christianity from a sect rooted in Yisrael. The process of making the Emperor the head of the religion began with Constantine and culminated under Emperor Justinian. "When the Western world accepted Christianity, Caesar conquered; and the received text of Western theology was edited by his lawyers. The code of Justinian and the theology of Justinian are two volumes expressing one movement of the human spirit. The brief Galilean vision of humility flickered throughout the ages, uncertainly. In the official formulation of the religion it has assumed the trivial form of the mere attribution to the Jews that they cherished a misconception about their Messiah. But the deeper idolatry, of fashioning God in the image of the Egyptian, Persian, and Roman Imperial rulers, was retained. The Church gave unto God the attributes which belonged exclusively to Caesar." A.N. Whitehead, Process and Reality (Cambridge, 1929), p. 484f cited by *Eusebius: The History of the Church from Christ to Constantine*, Translated by G.A Williamson, Revised and Edited with a new introduction by Andrew Louth, Penguin Books (1989) pp.

[96] See Lactantius, a Christian author of the 3rd and 4th century who wrote in Latin, in his early 4th century *Divine Institutes*, book 4, chapter 20. He clearly demonstrates that the Christians had divided texts into two categories: 1) The Old Testament reserved for the Yahudim; and 2) The New Testament reserved for the Christians. So divisions were solidly entrenched by the 4th Century CE.

[97] *The Dead Sea Scrolls Bible*, Martin Abegg, Jr., Peter Flint & Eugene Ulrich, HarperCollins 1999, Introduction p. x.

[98] *The End of History, Messiah Conspiracy*, Philip N. Moore, Ramshead Press (1996) p. 393 quoting Reverend M. Abrahams, *Aquila's Greek Version of the Hebrew Bible*, London: Spottiswoode, Ballantyne & Co. Ltd., 1919, pp. 2-3.

[99] *Rabbi Akiba's Messiah: The Origins of Rabbinic Authority*, Daniel Gruber, Elijah Publishing 1999.

[100] www.britannica.com/EBchecked/topic/368081/ Masoretic-text

[101] The London Encyclopaedia, St. Justin the Philosopher, in his dialogue with Trypho the Jew in 150 CE, St. Ireneus of Lyons in his 'Against Heresies' in 180 CE.

[102] *The Dead Sea Scrolls Bible*, Martin Abegg, Jr., Peter Flint & Eugene Ulrich, Introduction p. xiv, Harper San Francisco 1999.

[103] Sidnie White Crawford, Lecture entitled *What Do the Scrolls Teach Us About The Bible?* The Scrolls, Scripture and Interpretation, Biblical Archaeology Review Lecture Series 2009.

[104] *The End of History, Messiah Conspiracy*, Philip N. Moore, Ramshead Press (1996) p. 220. This book provides a great deal of information concerning translation issues and attempts to remove the Messiah Yahushua from the religion of Judaism.

[105] *The Dead Sea Scrolls Bible*, Martin Abegg, Jr., Peter Flint & Eugene Ulrich, HarperCollins 1999.

[106] Information concerning Psalm 145 from Peter W. Flint, Lecture entitled *The Three Favorite Books at Qumran*, The Scrolls, Scripture and Interpretation, Biblical Archaeology Review Lecture Series (2009). Information concerning Beresheet 4:8 from article entitled *Cain and His Family*, A

Survey of the Scriptural and Legendary Traditions written by Jared L. Olar, published in Grace and Knowledge (2006).

[107] The Journey from Texts to Translations, Paul D. Wegner, Baker Books 1999 pp. 117.

[108] The Journey from Texts to Translations, ibid at pp. 125-127.

[109] Sources concerning the source texts found in the Dead Sea Scrolls and the Calendar of the Essene Community are as follows: The Dead Sea Scrolls - A New Translation, ibid. See also Jaubert, Annie, The Date of the Last Supper, translated by I. Rafferty, Alba House (1965); Pfeiffer, Charles F., The Dead Sea Scrolls and the Bible, Baker House (1969); Vanderkam, James C., Calendars in the Dead Sea Scrolls: Measuring Time, London: Routledge (1998); Finegan, Jack, Handbook of Biblical Chronology: Principles of Time Reckoning in the Ancient World and Problems of Chronology in the Bible, Revised Edition, Hendrickson Publishers, (1998); Flusser, David, The Spiritual History of the Dead Sea Sect, English Series edited by S. Himelstein and translated by C. Glucker, MOD Books (1989). Quote concerning the use of 1 Enoch in the Abyssinian Church in Ethiopia from The Interpretation of Genesis in 1 Enoch from The Bible at Qumran Vanderkam, James C., p. 130, William B. Eerdmans Publishing Company 2001.

[110] Lists and information regarding the non-canonized texts and canonical lists from Lost Scriptures Books that Did Not Make It into the New Testament, Bart D. Ehrman, Oxford University Press, 2003. Commentary concerning the esteem of those texts paraphrased from Lost Christianities The Battles for Scripture and the Faiths We Never Knew, Bart D. Ehrman, Oxford University Press, 2003

[111] The Indonesian Bible Society for The Gideons International publishes a translation of the New Testament called Perjanjian Baru. This text claims to be a translation of the King James Version 1986. In this translation, whenever the English word "God" is used, it is translated as Allah. For instance, in the Gospel of John 1:1-2 it provides the English texts as follows: "¹ In the beginning was the Word, and the Word was with God, and the Word was God. ² The same was in the beginning with God. ³ All things were made by him; and without him was not anything made that was made." In the

Indonesian text we read: "¹ Pada mulanya adelah Firman; Firman itu bersama-sama dengan Allah dan Firman itu adalah Allah. ² Ia pada mulanya bersama-sama dengan Allah. ³ Segala sesuatu dijadikan oleh Dia dan tanpa Dia tidak ada suatupun yang telah jadi dari segala yang telah dijadikan." So according to this Indonesian translation of the New Testament Allah was the Creator described in Beresheet 1, and the entire Tanak for that matter. That was not the intention of the author of the Gospel of John, but because of a translator, the entire meaning of the text has been changed.

¹¹² *Biblical Views: God Save the Queen: The Political Origins of Salvation*, By Henry W. Morisada Rietz, BAR 38:06, Nov/Dec 2012.

¹¹³ The life of Eusebius is not well known. Indeed the date of his birth is difficult to accurately discern. He "was born in the early 260s, probably in Caesarea . . . By the third century Caesarea had a population of 100,000. A pagan city under the protection of the goddess Tyche (Fortune), it had a cosmopolitan population with a large Jewish community, an almost equally large Samaritan community, and a growing Christian presence. Origen the Great Christian theologian had spent the last twenty years of his life there and had established a kind of Christian academy that had attracted Christian pupils from all over the East. This academy, with its library, was consolidated by Pamphilus . . . Eusebius became Pamphilus' pupil . . . he became bishop of Caesarea in about 313 and died on 30 May 339." *Eusebius: The History of the Church from Christ to Constantine*, Translated by G.A Williamson, Revised and Edited with a new introduction by Andrew Louth, Penguin Books (1989) pp. ix-xi. Eusebius ultimately became enamored with Roman Emperor Constantine. His writings must be viewed in the context of his theology, which was premised upon the idea that the Emperor was Elohim's representative on Earth. For more information concerning Eusebius' political theology, see Norman Bayne's essay, reprinted in Byzantine Studies and Other Essays (London, 1955), pp. 168-72.

¹¹⁴ Eusebius, *The History of the Church*, Book 1, Page 1.

¹¹⁵ Schaff, *History of the Christian Church*, VI, p.723, cited by D.

Cloud, *Rome & the Bible.*

[116] See video presentations *Lamp in the Dark* and *Tares Among The Wheat* for an informative history of the development of the Bible. Adullam Films 2012. See also *The Pilgrim Church*, E.H. Broadbent, Gospel Folio Press, 1999, p.90.

[117] *Paul and Jesus*, James D. Tabor, Simon & Schuster, 2012.

[118] http://en.wikipedia.org/wiki/Geneva_Bible.

[119] *The Bible of King James*, National Geographic, December 2011, p. 45.

[120] For a more detailed description of the Appointed Times see the Walk in the Light Series entitled *Appointed Times.*

[121] We know from the Prophet Ezekiel that the punishment for the House of Yisrael was originally established at 390 years. (See Ezekiel 4). Because they failed to repent, their punishment would be multiplied seven times (Vayiqra 26). As a result, the duration of the punishment for the House of Yisrael was 2,730 years. The House of Yisrael (Joseph) experienced 5 different exiles between 723 BCE and 714 BCE. Thus we would anticipate the punishment of Joseph to be concluded somewhere between 2007 and 2016 CE. As a result, the revelation of Joseph appears to be imminent.

[122] According to Papias: "Matthew composed his work in the Hebrew dialect, and each translated as best they could." Eusebius, Ecclesiastical History, 3.39.It was also mentioned by Origen, Epiphanus and Jerome. For further discussion on this subject see George Howard's translation of the Shem-Tob Gospel of Matthew (1995). According to Clement of Alexandria, the Epistle of Hebrews was written by Paul in the Hebrew tongue, and later translated into the Greek language by Luke. Clement of Alexandria, *Hypotyposes* referenced in *Ecclesiastical History*, Eusebius, 6.14.2.

[123] For an interesting examination on the Aramaic language and the validity of the Peshitta as a reliable New Testament source text see *Ruach Qadim*, Andrew Gabriel Roth, Tushiyah Press (2005).

[124] Rabbi Samson Raphael Hirsch (1808-1888).

[125] Martin Luther (1483-1546).

[126] Brown Driver Briggs, Hebrew Lexicon.

[127] For an interesting discussion regarding Scribes, with a specific focus on the Dead Sea Scrolls, see *Scribal Practices*

and Approaches Reflected in the Texts Found in the Judean Desert by Emanuel Tov.

[128] See the 21 Volume work of Professor Menachem Cohen of Bar-Ilan University. Prof. Cohen claims that there were 1,500 inaccuracies that needed to be corrected and using the Aleppo Codex. Many of the claimed inaccuracies involved vowel pointing which does not exist in the Torah.

[129] *How We Got the Bible*, Neil R. Lightfoot, Baker Books 2003 pp.41-42.

[130] A commonly held statistic is that there are over 5,000 known New Testament manuscripts containing over 200,000 variants. See *A General Introduction to the Bible*, Norman L. Geisler and William E. Nix, Moody Press (1968) p. 252.

[131] See the writings and teachings of Bart D. Ehrman, James A. Gray Distinguished Professor of Religious Studies at the University of North Carolina at Chapel Hill. While Professor Ehrman apparently lost his original faith due to his academic approach to studying the New Testament texts, he often provided interesting insight and studies regarding those texts. Sadly, the discovery of translation issues should in no way impact a person's faith in YHWH Elohim since His existence and authority are not based upon writings.

[132] *Misquoting Jesus, The Story Behind Who Changed the Bible and Why*, Bart D. Ehrman, HarperSanFrancisco, 2005 pp. 133-139.

[133] For a more complete discussion on this issue see the Walk in the Light series book entitled *Pagan Holidays*.

[134] For a more complete discussion on this issue see the Walk in the Light series book entitled *Names*.

[135] http://en.wikipedia.org/wiki/English_language#History

[136] The god Allah existed prior to the establishment of the religion of Islam. The *Encyclopedia of Religion* states: "'Allah' is a pre-Islamic name ... corresponding to the Babylonian Bel" (ed. James Hastings, Edinburgh, T. & T. Clark, 1908, I:326). There are numerous sources attesting to the fact that: "Allah was known to the pre-Islamic Arabs; he was one of the Meccan deities" (Encyclopedia *of Islam*, ed. Gibb, I:406). See http://www.shiloahbooks.com/download/Muslim%20Hist

ory.pdf. Therefore, while Allah is a god, he is not the Elohim of the Hebrew Scriptures. This demonstrates the problem with using the generic word "god."

[137]   *The Messianic אֵת Study Bible Translation of the Tanakh*, Sanford, William H. 2012.

[138]   The Torah Cycle is the tradition of reading through the Torah in the course of a year. During the Feast of Succot, the Cycle is completed and during a time known as Simchat Torah, the Scrolls are rolled back and the cycle is renewed. Some traditions use a 3 year cycle.

[139]   PaRDeS is a traditional form of Jewish exegesis which is helpful to demonstrate that there is great depth to the Scriptures. Translations are usually only able to provide a translation of the "peshat" or plain meaning of the text. As you go deeper into the levels of understanding, that is when translations really fall short. Peshat is the plain, simple or direct meaning of the text. Remez are the "hints" or the deep meaning beyond just the literal sense. Derash comes from the Hebrew "darash" which means: "inquire" or "seek." This is where we get the term "midrash." Sod means "secret" or "mystery" which is given through inspiration or revelation.

[140]   See Jeff Benner's *Mechanical Translation of the Book of Genesis*, Virtualbookworm.com Publishing (2007).

[141]   See the *Halleluyah Scriptures.*

[142]   In a very vivid method of illustrating a prophetic word, Ezekiel was told to lay on his left side to reveal the punishment upon the House of Yisrael and then to lie on his right side to illustrate the punishment upon the House of Yahudah. "*⁴ Then lie on your left side and put the sin of the House of Yisrael upon yourself. You are to bear their sin for the number of days you lie on your side. ⁵ I have assigned you the same number of days as the years of their sin. So for 390 days you will bear the sin of the House of Yisrael. ⁶ After you have finished this, lie down again, this time on your right side, and bear the sin of the House of Yahudah. I have assigned you 40 days, a day for each year.*" Ezekiel 4:4-6. So there would be 390 years for the House of Yisrael, and 40 years for the House of Yahudah. There is a mystery in the Torah about multiplying the term

of punishment that needs to be applied. Yisrael was told that they would be punished if they disobeyed and these punishments were clearly explained. They were then warned of the time of their punishment being multiplied if they continued to disobey. "²⁷ If in spite of this you still do not listen to Me but continue to be hostile toward Me, ²⁸ then in My anger I will be hostile toward you, and I Myself will punish you for your sins seven times over." Vayiqra 26:27-28. As a result, the punishment for the House of Yisrael would turn out to be 390 years times 7 for a total of 2,730 years. This seven-fold punishment of 2,730 years began in 723 - 714 BCE, and it will end between 2007 - 2016 CE. For a further discussion of this subject see the Walk in the Light series book entitled The Redeemed.

¹⁴³ While this author disagrees with the calendar concepts in the text there is useful information that can be gleaned from the Book of Jubilees. Here is a quote referencing the Hebrew tongue as the language of Creation. "²⁵ And YHWH Almighty said: 'Open his mouth and his ears, that he may hear and speak with his mouth, with the language which has been revealed' for it had ceased from the mouths of all the children of men from the day of the overthrow (of Babel). ²⁶ And I opened his mouth, and his ears and his lips, and I began to speak with him in Hebrew in the tongue of the creation. ²⁷ And he took the books of his fathers, and these were written in Hebrew, and he transcribed them, and he began from henceforth to study them, and I made known to him that which he could not (understand), and he studied them during the six rainy months." The Book of Jubilees Chapter 12:25-27.

¹⁴⁴ See Matthew 2 which describes how the Chaldean astronomers used a star to announce the Birth of the Messiah. The sign in the heavens that announced His Birth could be seen over Jerusalem on September 11, 3 BCE. That sign was described in Revelation 12:1.

¹⁴⁵ In the discourse presented in Matthew 24 Yahushua was asked: "What will be the sign of your coming, and of the end of the age?" (Matthew 24:3). After describing the conditions preceding His return, Yahushua stated: "Then the sign of the Son of Man will appear in heaven, and then all the tribes of the earth will mourn, and they will see the Son of Man coming on the

clouds of heaven with power and great glory." Matthew 24:30.
Also, in Luke 21, when asked about signs in the end,
Yahushua responded: "*And there will be signs in the sun, in the
moon, and in the stars . . .*" So just as there were signs in the
Heavens preceding His Birth and at the moment of His
Birth, there will also be signs in the heavens preceding His
return. For a further discussion of this subject see the Walk
in the Light series book entitled *The Final Shofar.*

[146] For a more detailed discussion of the Eighth Day Appointed
Time, commonly called Shemini Atzeret, see the Walk in
the Light series book entitled *Appointed Times.*

[147] The Passover and the Feast of Unleavened Bread, including
the redemption of the firstborn, are described as a sign in
Shemot 13 and it is directly related to the Shema. "*It shall be
as a sign to you on your hand and as a memorial between your
eyes, that YHWH's Torah may be in your mouth.*" Shemot 13:9,
16.

[148] The doctrine of a seven year tribulation period punctuated
by either a pre-trib, mid-trib or post-trib "rapture" is not
found anywhere within the Scriptures. In fact, the word
"rapture" is not found anywhere within the Scriptures. It is
completely inconsistent with the prophecies and patterns
provided in the Tanak. The entire point of the end times is
to prepare the Bride through refinement. We must look at
the pattern provided through the Passover from Egypt.
YHWH did not rapture His Bride from Egypt. He
protected His Bride from judgment and guided His Bride to
the place where they could enter into the Marriage
Covenant. This is the Covenant pattern that will be
repeated throughout the entire planet in the end. While
there will be a time when the Son of Man will come in the
clouds it will be after the tribulation when the messengers
will gather together His elect. (see Matthew 24:30-31). For a
further discussion concerning the end times and the
gathering of the elect see the Walk in the Light series book
entitled *The Final Shofar.*

[149] For a more detailed discussion of The Sabbath see the Walk
in the Light series book entitled *The Sabbath.*

[150] Matthew 15; Mark 7.

[151] *See The Word* written by Isaac E. Mozeson, S.P.I. Books

(2001).

¹⁵² Appendix B in this book provides a useful chart for examining the Hebrew characters and their gematria value. I also recommend the Ancient Hebrew research Center found at http://www.ancient-hebrew.org.

¹⁵³ Yirmeyahu 16:19 provides: "O YHWH, my strength and my fortress, My refuge in the day of affliction, the Gentiles shall come to You from the ends of the earth and say, "Surely our fathers have inherited lies, worthlessness and unprofitable things." The lies, worthless and unprofitable things are those traditions and doctrines not specifically founded upon the Word of Elohim.

Appendix A

Tanak Hebrew Names

Torah - Teaching

English Name	Modern Hebrew	Transliteration
Genesis	בראשית	Beresheet
Exodus	שמות	Shemot
Leviticus	ויקרא	Vayiqra
Numbers	במדבר	Bemidbar
Deuteronomy	דברים	Debarim

Nebi'im - Prophets

Joshua	יהושע	Yahushua
Judges	שופטים	Shoftim
Samuel	שמואל	Shemu'el
Kings	מלכים	Melakhim
Isaiah	ישעיהו	Yeshayahu
Jeremiah	ירמיהו	Yirmeyahu
Ezekiel	יחזקאל	Yehezqel
Daniel	דניאל	Daniel
Hosea	השוע	Hoshea
Joel	יואל	Yoel
Amos	עמוס	Amos
Obadiah	עבדיה	Obadyah

Jonah	יונה	Yonah
Micah	מיכה	Mikhah
Nahum	נחום	Nachum
Habakkuk	חבקוק	Habaquq
Zephaniah	צפניה	Zephaniyah
Haggai	חגי	Chaggai
Zechariah	זכריה	Zekaryah
Malachi	מלאכי	Malachi

Kethubim – Writings

Psalms	תהלים	Tehillim
Proverbs	משלי	Mishle
Job	איוב	Iyov
Song of Songs	שיר השירים	Shir ha-Shirim
Ruth	רות	Ruth
Lamentations	איכה	Eikhah
Ecclesiastes	קהלת	Qohelet
Esther	אסתר	Ester
Ezra	עזרא	Ezra
Nehemiah	נחמיה	Nehemyah
Chronicles	דברי הימים	Dibri ha-Yamim

Appendix B

Hebrew Language Study Chart

Gematria	Letter	Ancient	Modern	English	Picture/Meaning
1	Aleph		א	A	ox head
2	Bet		ב	B, Bh	tent floor plan
3	Gimel		ג	G	foot, camel
4	Dalet		ד	D	door
5	Hey		ה	H	man raised arms
6	Waw		ו	W, O, U	tent peg, hook
7	Zayin		ז	Z	weapon
8	Het		ח	Hh	fence, wall
9	Tet		ט	T, Th	basket, container
10	Yud		י	Y	closed hand
20	Kaph		כ	K, Kh	palm, open hand
30	Lamed		ל	L	shepherd staff
40	Mem		מ	M	water
50	Nun		נ	N	sprout, seed
60	Samech		ס	S	prop, support
70	Ayin		ע	A	eye
80	Pey		פ	P, Ph	open mouth
90	Tsade		צ	Ts	hook
100	Quph		ק	Q	back of the head
200	Resh		ר	R	head of a man
300	Shin		ש	Sh, S	teeth
400	Taw		ת	T	mark, covenant

Note: Gematria in a very simple sense is the study of the various numerical values of the Hebrew letters and words. Since there is no separate numerical system in the Hebrew language, all Hebrew letters have a numerical value so it is a very legitimate and valuable form of study. There are many different forms of Gematria. The Gematria system used in this chart is "mispar hechrachi," also known as Normative value. The Ancient font used is an attempt to blend the ancient variants into a uniform and recognizable font set that accurately depicts the original meaning of each character.

Appendix C

The Walk in the Light Series

Book 1   Restoration – A discussion of the pagan influences that have mixed with the true faith through the ages which has resulted in the need for restoration. This book also examines true Scriptural restoration.

Book 2   Names – Discusses the True Name of the Creator and the Messiah as well as the significance of names in the Scriptures.

Book 3   The Scriptures – Discusses the ways that the Creator has communicated with Creation. It also examines the origin of the written Scriptures as well as the various types of translation errors in Bibles that have led to false doctrines in some mainline religions.

Book 4   Covenants – Discusses the progressive covenants between the Creator and His Creation as described in the Scriptures which reveals His plan for mankind.

Book 5   The Messiah – Discusses the prophetic promises and fulfillments of the Messiah and the True identity of the Redeemer of Yisrael.

Book 6   The Redeemed – Discusses the relationship between Christianity and Judaism and reveals how the Scriptures identify True Believers. It reveals how the Christian doctrine of Replacement Theology has caused confusion as to how the Creator views the Children of Yisrael.

Book 7   The Law and Grace – Discusses in depth the false doctrine that Grace has done away with the Law and demonstrates the vital importance of obeying the commandments.

Book 8   The Sabbath – Discusses the importance of the Seventh Day Sabbath as well as the origins of the tradition concerning Sunday worship.

Book 9	Kosher – Discusses the importance of eating food prescribed by the Scriptures as an aspect of righteous living.
Book 10	Appointed Times – Discusses the appointed times established by the Creator, often erroneously considered to be "Jewish" holidays, and critical to the understanding of prophetic fulfillment of the Scriptural promises.
Book 11	Pagan Holidays – Discusses the pagan origins of some popular Christian holidays which have replaced the Appointed Times.
Book 12	The Final Shofar – Discusses the walk required by the Scriptures and prepares the Believer for the deceptions coming in the End of Days.

The series began as a simple Power point presentation which was intended to develop into a book with twelve different chapters but ended up being twelve different books. Each book is intended to stand alone although the series was originally intended to build from one section to another. Due to the urgency of certain topics, the books have not been published in sequential order.

For anticipated release dates, announcements and additional teachings go to:
www.shemayisrael.net

Appendix D

The Shema
Deuteronomy (Debarim) 6:4-5

Traditional English Translation

Hear, O Israel: The LORD our God, the LORD is one!
You shall love the LORD your God with all your heart, with all
your soul, and with all your strength.

Corrected English Translation

Hear, O Yisrael: YHWH our Elohim, YHWH is one (unified)!
You shall love YHWH your Elohim with all your heart, with
all your soul, and with all your strength.

Modern Hebrew Text

שמע ישראל יהוה אלהינו יהוה אחד
ואהבת את יהוה אלהיך בכל־ לבבך ובכל־ נפשך ובכל־ מאדך

Ancient Hebrew Text

Hebrew Text Transliterated

Shema, Yisra'el: YHWH Elohenu, YHWH echad!
V-ahavta et YHWH Elohecha b-chol l'bacha u-b-chol naf'sh'cha
u-b-chol m'odecha.

The Shema has traditionally been one of the most important prayers in
Judaism and has been declared the first (resheet) of all the Commandments.
(Mark 12:29-30).

Appendix E

Shema Yisrael

Shema Yisrael was originally established with two primary goals: 1) The production and distribution of sound, Scripturally based educational materials which would assist individuals to see the light of Truth and "Walk in the Light" of that Truth. This first objective was, and is, accomplished through Shema Yisrael Publications; and 2) The free distribution of those materials to the spiritually hungry throughout the world, along with Scriptures, food, clothing and money to the poor, the needy, the sick, the dying and those in prison. This second objective was accomplished through the Shema Yisrael Foundation and through the Foundation people were able to receive a tax deduction for their contributions.

Sadly, through the passage of the Pension Reform Act of 2006, the US Congress severely restricted the operation of donor advised funds which, in essence, crippled the Shema Yisrael Foundation by requiring that funds either be channeled through another Foundation or to a 501(c)(3) organization approved by the Internal Revenue Service. Since the Shema Yisrael Foundation was relatively small and operated very "hands on" by placing the funds and materials directly into the hands of the needy in Third World Countries, it was unable to effectively continue operating as a Foundation with the tax advantages associated therewith.

As a result, Shema Yisrael Publications has essentially functioned in a dual capacity to insure that both objectives continue to be promoted, although contributions are no longer tax deductible. To review some of the work being accomplished you can visit www.shemayisrael.net and go to the "Missions" section.

We gladly accept donations, although they will not be tax deductible. To donate, please make checks payable to "Shema Yisrael Publications" and mail to:

Shema Yisrael
123 Court Street • Herkimer, New York 13350

You may also visit our website or call (315) 939-7940 to make a donation or receive more information.

CPSIA information can be obtained at www.ICGtesting.com
Printed in the USA
LVOW01s2037220315

431520LV00018B/337/P